LIBERTIES LOST

Roger Nash Baldwin, autographed: "With regards. Roger Baldwin 1973."
—*Courtesy of Roger N. Baldwin Collection*

LIBERTIES LOST

The Endangered Legacy
of the ACLU

WOODY KLEIN

Foreword by Arthur M. Schlesinger Jr.

Introduction by Senator Robert C. Byrd

Afterword by Anthony Lewis

Westport, Connecticut
London

Library of Congress Cataloging-in-Publication Data

Liberties lost : the endangered legacy of the ACLU / [edited by]
Woody Klein ; foreword by Arthur M. Schlesinger, Jr. ; introduction by
Robert C. Byrd ; afterword by Anthony Lewis.
        p. cm.
    Includes bibliographical references and index.
    ISBN 0-275-98506-7 (alk. paper)
    1. American Civil Liberties Union.   2. Baldwin, Roger Nash,
1884–1981.   3. Civil rights—United States—History.   I. Klein, Woody,
1929– II. Baldwin, Roger Nash, 1884–1981.
    JC599.U5L47 2006
    323.06'073—dc22   2006001242

British Library Cataloguing-in-Publication Data is available.

Library of Congress Catalog Card Number: 2006001242
ISBN: 0-275-98506-7

First published in 2006

Praeger Publishers, 88 Post Road West, Westport, CT 06881
An imprint of Greenwood Publishing Group, Inc.
www.praeger.com

Printed in the United States of America

∞™

The paper used in this book complies with the
Permanent Paper Standard issued by the National
Information Standards Organization (Z39.48-1984).

10 9 8 7 6 5 4 3 2 1

Excerpts from the Roger Nash Baldwin Papers, Seely G. Mudd Manuscript
Library, Princeton University Library, are published with the permission of
Mary Ellen Baldwin and Princeton University Library.

Every reasonable effort has been made to trace the owners of copyrighted
materials in this book, but in some instances this has proven impossible.
The author and publisher will be glad to receive information leading to more
complete acknowledgments in subsequent printings of the book and in the
meantime extend their apologies for any omissions.

To my friend and mentor
Roger Nash Baldwin
and to the Baldwin family

CONTENTS

Photo essay appears following page 140

FOREWORD

Human Rights Must Prevail To the End

ARTHUR M. SCHLESINGER JR.

Roger Nash Baldwin was born in the administration of Chester A. Arthur and died in the administration of Ronald Reagan. This means that he was alive during the terms of almost half of our forty-four American presidents. At his birth the American Constitution was less than a century old. His death came half a dozen years after its bicentennial. His long life saw a steady strengthening in the constitutional protections of civil liberties for all Americans—a process to which no American made a greater contribution.

For the First Amendment is not self-executing. Indeed, that amendment forbade only the federal Congress to pass laws abridging the freedom of speech or the press or assembly or worship. State governments were not initially bound by the First Amendment, nor was private action. Thomas Jefferson, the stern critic of the alien and sedition laws, as president encouraged the governor of Pennsylvania to apply the law of seditious libel to an antiadministration newspaper. The number of First Amendment cases reaching the Supreme Court in the nineteenth century was negligible. Those that did generally received short shrift. "No group of Americans was more hostile to free speech claims before World War I than the judiciary," writes the First Amendment scholar David M. Rabban, "and no judges were more hostile than the Justices on the United States Supreme Court."

Roger Baldwin helped change all that. During the First World War, A. Mitchell Palmer, President Wilson's attorney general, organized the crackdown on free speech that led to the postwar Red Scare. Roger, after a year in prison for rejecting the draft, founded the American Civil Liberties Union in 1920. As head of the ACLU, he created a new sensitivity to and concern for the Bill of Rights. By 1925 the Supreme Court, led by Justices Holmes and Brandeis, extended First

Amendment protections to state governments through the doctrine of "incorporation."

Roger Baldwin cheerily and robustly propagated the gospel of human rights and civil liberties to the end of his life. He remained in many respects a nineteenth-century American—in his courtesy, his candor, his integrity, his magnanimity, and his largeness of vision. But even when he was in his nineties, he never seemed old. Hope, curiosity, passion, and, above all perhaps, humor kept him forever young. Human folly diverted, exasperated, but never finally depressed him. He joined the virtues of the past with a zest for the future. He had seen much tragedy in life, and he had no use for pollyannas. But he had an essential optimism. The instinct of freedom seemed to him so deeply rooted in the nature of man (and woman) that he was sure human rights must prevail in the end. This serene and unconquerable faith sustained his weaker brethren when he was alive, and his memory— and writings—will sustain us in the hard years to come.

—Arthur M. Schlesinger Jr.

New York City, December 6, 2004

PREFACE

Once in a lifetime—if we are fortunate—we come upon a fellow human being who has such a profoundly positive influence on our thinking that we almost naturally incorporate his or her philosophy into our own life's work and apply it as our own. Roger Nash Baldwin was such a man in my young life—in retrospect, an unforgettable mentor. As a teenager I came to know him as the father of a classmate in high school, Roger R. Baldwin, who—until this day—remains one of my closest friends. We were both students at the Fieldston High School, a progressive, private school in New York City and part of the Ethical Culture Schools. One of its early advocates, John Lovejoy Elliott, a protégé of its founder, Felix Adler, was a friend of the senior Baldwin. Elliott and Baldwin created the wartime Union Against Militarism just before World War I, an organization out of which evolved into the American Civil Liberties Union in 1920.

So my introduction to Roger Nash Baldwin as a youth would eventually have roots far deeper than I realized at the time. Many years later—after spending a great deal of time with the Baldwin family in New York City, at their weekend home in Oakland, New Jersey, and at their summer home in Chilmark on Martha's Vineyard—I came to realize I was often listening to the voice of the one man in American history who was then—and still is—considered this nation's number one shepherd of the Bill of Rights.

During my younger years as a newspaper reporter in New York, covering civil rights and civil liberties in the 1950s and 1960s, I often turned to the senior Baldwin for his extraordinary insight, advice, and historical perspective on the issues of the day—integration of the nation's public schools, voting rights, equal opportunity in education and in employment, equal justice under law, racial equality, rights of the poor, women's rights, and—perhaps most important—the right to speak out against our government's intrusion on individual privacy. I left the newspaper business in 1965 to serve as press secretary to New York Mayor John V. Lindsay. The mayor asked me to stand in for him on several ceremonial occasions when he could not be in two places at the same time.

Much to my great pleasure, on May 24, 1966, I was covering for Mayor Lindsay while he was in Albany, New York, meeting with Gov. Nelson A. Rockefeller. He asked me to take his place at a dinner for the Encampment for Citizenship honoring two great civil libertarians, Roger N. Baldwin and Norman Thomas, both in their eighties and both in the forefront of the battle for individual rights for more than half a century. I presented these men the highest honor that the City of New York can bestow on a citizen—the Gold Medal of the City of New York. I did so in the mayor's name, with this comment: "With the medals goes the Mayor's deepest affection and appreciation."[1] It was, to say the least, a moment that I have treasured ever since.

In this book I have compiled extracts of Baldwin's words that—if we did not know better—we might easily conclude were being spoken today. They reflect the most crucial national debate of our time. One of the most prescient messages delivered by Baldwin was in a speech in St. Louis, in October 1960, when he said the following: *"Neutralism has not been popular in American foreign policy. For a long time we proceeded on the theory that he who was not with us was against us, and frantic efforts were made to line up the uncommitted peoples. The United States should accept the principle of neutralism"* [italics mine].

Sound familiar? It should. Disregarding or perhaps unaware of this advice, here is what President George W. Bush said forty-one years later in his September 20, 2001, address to a joint session of Congress in the immediate aftermath of the terrorist attacks on the World Trade Center and the Pentagon on September 11: "Every nation, in every region, now has a decision to make. *Either you are with us, or you are with the terrorists* [italics mine]. From this day forward, any nation that continues to harbor or support terrorism will be regarded by the United States as a hostile regime."

In the intervening years since Baldwin's death twenty-five years ago, of course, others have carried on his battle to defend civil liberties. At the risk of being labeled "unpatriotic" or "un-American" or "giving aid and comfort to the enemy," there are many courageous Americans who are steadfastly keeping watch. I believe they are the true patriots of our times, the defenders of our liberties even when it is unpopular to be so identified.

Over the decades, as I came to know Roger Baldwin better, I came to appreciate his special blend of humor and wit. I was privileged to be on the list of people he sent handwritten postcards to when he was overseas, and each would, inevitably, be signed, "Your oldest friend, Bunkle." Bunkle is the name he was informally given by his two sons whom he adopted after marrying Evelyn Preston. It is derived from a condensation of "Baldwin" and "Uncle."

There was, I think, a dichotomy between Roger N. Baldwin, the man, and Roger N. Baldwin, the globetrotting civil libertarian who, at the invitation of Gen. Douglas A. MacArthur, set up a civil liberties agency in postwar Japan, and at the request of Gen. Lucius B. Clay, did the same in Germany. Baldwin was a paradox: He spent his early years as a conscientious objector who went to prison rather than compromise his principles opposing war; fighting for and working alongside working-men who clawed their way out of poverty to establish labor unions; recruiting the prestigious lawyer, Clarence Darrow, to represent the ACLU in the so-called Scopes "monkey trial" in Tennessee in the 1920s in support of evolution; opposing McCarthyism; taking on the Federal Bureau of Investigation; and helping create the Human Rights Commission at the United Nations. He mingled easily among the rich and powerful and yet, at the same time, preferred to live modestly as he had in the beginning of his career as a social worker in St. Louis, where he went on the advice of Louis Brandeis, then his father's lawyer, after he graduated from Harvard College with an M.A. in sociology in 1905.

I came to see him as a man, like any other, with flaws and peculiarities that few people knew about outside of his family. He was uncommonly frugal; he eschewed material comforts and the trappings of wealth while, at the same time, living extremely well after having married Evelyn Preston, an oil heiress. He nonetheless lived entirely on his modest salary at the ACLU and insisted on paying his way wherever he went. He was beyond temptation; he saved just about everything he could to be used for another, undetermined purpose at a later date. I could see during my visits with his family that he loved his two sons and his daughter—he had a wonderful laugh that made his eyes smile—but at the same time he could be self-centered, opinionated, judgmental, and had little patience with those around him who preferred leisure to work. Even in his own home he found it hard to communicate on personal matters—perhaps as a result of his upper-class "blueblood" upbringing in the wealthy suburbs of Boston as a member of an old Yankee family—"Boston Brahmins"—that traced its ancestors back to the *Mayflower*. He could also exhibit some impatience with small talk at times; after we had finished a brief telephone conversation and he had no more to say, he would simply hang up. Those of us who knew about this habit came to understand, indeed, wished we could do the same with others. But he was the only person I ever knew who could get away with it without causing irritation to his callers. One simply accepted that he had no more to say and did not want to waste words.

Baldwin compartmentalized his life. While thriving on being with people and enjoying the sophisticated urbane life of an upper-class gentleman, he also connected with plain people who had no such privileged background and were working men and women struggling with the daily necessities of life. All the while, Baldwin longed for places like Walden and was an adherent of Thoreau's philosophy of keeping life simple, penurious, and in harmony with nature.

He was once asked by a writer what he was most proud of in his years in civil liberties. He replied: "Pride isn't one of my attributes. Either pride or disappointment or failure doesn't seem to enter my calculations. I don't do something just because I think I'll win. It's the reformer instinct, I suppose. It has nothing to do with doing people good. I just try to put things to rights. I tackle the things that arouse me—injustice, cruelty, unfairness."[2]

Indeed, surrounded as he was by people of "old money" while having compassion for those less fortunate, Roger Baldwin was imbued with a desire to help others. He spent his life using his facile and ever-expanding mind, his wit, and his personal charm to cajole the American political establishment first, and then world leaders, into paying homage to his relentless campaign to bring freedom, equality, and justice to the people of all the nations of the world.

Through it all he remained an optimist. And he skillfully steered his life from the political left to become what one would today call a centrist with a chameleon-like ability to get along with practically anybody no matter what his or her political, religious, or cultural beliefs. After launching the American Civil Liberties Union in 1920 and serving as its executive director during the event-filled three decades that followed, he spent the remaining years of his long and productive life working as head of an international nongovernmental organization that played a key role in influencing the United Nations to stress human rights around the world.

However, Baldwin did make misjudgments along the way to becoming the symbol of civil liberties in America. One black mark on his record he himself admitted late in his life: the ACLU's failure to challenge President Franklin Delano Roosevelt's Executive Order 9066 on February 19, 1942, to evacuate some 120,000 Japanese-Americans from their homes in California and move them to detention camps elsewhere. Baldwin admitted that the ACLU—and he personally—had made a major error in judgment here, which he always regretted. The ACLU called the Japanese evacuation "the worst single violation of the civil rights of American citizens in our history," but this boldness came long after the issue had become academic.[3] Baldwin later said, in 1970: "It was a tragedy that took long to repair at the cost of one of the most grievous violations of citizens' civil rights in history."[4] And, in 1976, he remarked: "One of the few persistent criticisms of the ACLU record has been that we initially failed to challenge the government's wartime executive order to remove the entire Japanese population, aliens and citizens alike, from the West Coast states."[5]

Forty-five years ago he summed up his worldview with words that—all too sadly—apply to today's world more than ever: "I think most Americans would be surprised and hurt to know that among most peoples abroad we are regarded as a country so rich and self-righteous in our belief in the superiority of the 'American way of life' that we cannot sense the misery of the vast majority, or their insistent almost revolutionary demands for a decent life."[6]

Asked at age ninety-six what advice he had for the younger generation, he replied, simply, "Develop your interests. Grow. Enjoy more things. Because most of them get into a specialty, a rut of one thing only, and they don't live fully. They don't have many outlets for their capacity. Music. Art. Nature. Reading. The drama. I mean all these things should have attention. One should not live just in a small area of life. Cover it all. As much as you can."[7]

Despite all of his contradictory traits, he was consistent and completely dedicated to fighting for what he believed was right and just. "Our nation's security lies in our liberties," he wrote only months before he died in 1981. "If we sacrifice our liberties, then what do we have to fight for?" This question rings true today more than ever in America. Of all the tenets he believed in, I think that the one he felt most passionately about was the right of the individual citizen to go about his or her business without interference from the government. He also believed, beyond any doubt, that the most difficult task the ACLU faced was "to defend the thought we hate."[8]

This book, therefore, is an effort to put the issue of civil liberties in the framework of history, to offer some lessons from the past that are as applicable today as they were decades ago, and to awaken readers to the real and present danger of our government running roughshod over our basic rights in the name of national security. For me, the lessons that Roger Baldwin taught us have both personal and professional meaning. They resonate for this observer because they represent the core values for which America stands. One hopes that this volume will contribute in a small way to the ongoing dialogue in our nation on this subject and help awaken the conscience of all Americans to the gathering storm that threatens the very essence of our democracy.

Roger Baldwin covered it all—in his words and in his extraordinary actions. Perhaps his most salient observation of all is a simple reminder to all of us: "The fight for liberty never stays won. We will have to keep winning it over and over again, we will have to amass our forces and resist."[9] In this book I have highlighted in each chapter many of Baldwin's insightful truisms that make us realize we have not made a great deal of progress when it comes to protecting our civil liberties.

The historic struggle at the outset of the twenty-first century in America between the urgent need for national security to protect our citizens from terrorists and the equally important constitutional commitment to maintain our civil liberties is the subject of this book. Passage of the USA Patriot Act in 2001 in the immediate aftermath of the history-making attacks on the World Trade Center and the Pentagon was a milestone setback in the history of civil liberties. The USA Patriot Act enabled the federal government to launch invasive actions against Americans that invade our privacy and clearly infringe upon our civil liberties. While the Act has undergone changes, it still emphasizes national security over hard-won civil liberties.

We as Americans have already lost some of our liberties—not all at once, but gradually—as our government chips away at the constitutional rights of each of us as individuals. Certainly the revelation by *The New York Times* in December 2005 that President Bush had authorized the National Security Agency to secretly monitor the international telephone calls and e-mails of U.S. citizens without court-approved warrants to establish possible links with Al Qaeda terrorists abroad, is a glaring example.

Lending credibility and authenticity to the fact that our civil liberties are, indeed, endangered are commentaries in this book written about Baldwin's writings by some of the nation's most distinguished civil libertarians, public officials, academics, journalists, and other national leaders; their observations are not intended to serve simply as testimonials to Roger Baldwin, the man. Rather, they are included to support the validity of what Baldwin wrote and what he stood for. Baldwin's influence on the body politic in this new American century is palpable; his words are a stunning reminder that only when we learn from history will we fully understand how to cope with the present and the future. As Baldwin put it in 1967 in a memorandum to his personal file: "The lesson of history needs constant repetition for us in the United States in terms of our time."

—Woody Klein
Westport, Connecticut

NOTES

1. Woody Klein, *Lindsay's Promise: The Dream That Failed* (Macmillan, 1970), 168–69.

2. "Barely Winded at Eighty," interview with Willie Morris, *New Republic* (January 25, 1964): 8–10.

3. Roger N. Baldwin, "John Haynes Holmes: Preacher and Prophet, 1879–1964," speech at the Community Church of Boston Conservatory Auditorium, Sunday, May 3, 1964.

4. Draft of article for the *Civil Liberties Review* (January 1975); from Roger R. Baldwin Collection, Roger N. Baldwin, "The Meaning of Civil Liberties," introduction in Vol. 1, *American Civil Liberties Annual Reports* (New York, 1970).

5. Roger N. Baldwin, draft for *Civil Liberties Review* (1976); from Roger R. Baldwin Collection.

6. In a speech, "Prospects for Personal Freedom," made on May 12, 1961, at Wayne State University.

7. From the text of an interview in *Civil Liberties*, the ACLU newspaper (September 1980), 14.

8. Baldwin, "The Meaning of Civil Liberties," xxv–xxxi.

9. From "Traveling Hopefully," videotape produced by the ACLU for ninety-fifth birthday dinner for Roger N. Baldwin, July 13, 1979; courtesy of the American Civil Liberties Union.

ACKNOWLEDGMENTS

I am deeply indebted to my acquisitions editor at Greenwood Publishing Group, Hilary Claggett, for guiding this book from its initial proposal to the final product. Her expertise in the subject matter and her commitment to excellence was critical to helping me with the scope and content of the book.

I am grateful, too, to my close friend, Roger R. Baldwin, and his daughters, Lauren and Geraldine Baldwin, for making photographs and other vital materials available from the family archives. I also wish to express my profound appreciation to my close friend and Columbia Journalism School classmate, Albert Charles Lasher, for his thorough research at the very outset of this project that enabled me to get if off the ground. I am also indebted to my dear friend and researcher/copy editor, Thelma Shiboski, for the many long hours she spent working on this manuscript.

In the course of my research, I was consistently helped by a group of superb reference librarians at the Westport Public Library, led by Deborah Celia, who did an extraordinary amount of work. She deserves enormous credit, as do her colleagues, Westport reference librarians Margie Freilich-Den, Beth Dominianni, Susan Madeo, Interlibrary Loan; Elizabeth Paul, Janie Rhein, Joyce Vitali, and, above all, Marta Campbell, Head of Collection Management, and Maxine Bleiweis, library director.

My gratitude also to Anthony D. Romero, executive director of the American Civil Liberties Union, Emily Tynes, communications director of the ACLU, and the ACLU Los Angeles office. I am also thankful for the assistance of Michael O'Connor, Marcia Goldstein, Kathleen Knackal, Leanne Small, and Margaret Maybury at Greenwood Publishing Group; and Kim Hoag, of Bytheway Publishing Services.

I would also like to recognize the valuable work of Richard A. Comfort, Ph.D., who diligently compiled the index to this volume, thus making it easily useable to the layman.

Further, I am indebted to Daniel J. Linke, University Archivist and Curator of Public Policy Papers, Seeley G. Mudd Manuscript Library, Princeton University, and Matthew Reeder, Special Collections Assistant, Seeley G. Mudd Manuscript Library, Princeton University. I also wish to thank the staffs of the Oral History Research Office at Columbia University; the Harvard University Law Library; the Widener Library at Harvard; the Radcliffe Institute for Advanced Study, Arthur and Elizabeth Schlesinger Library on the History of Women in America; the Pusey Library at Harvard, the Andover Harvard Theological Library, the UCLA Charles E. Young Research Library, Department of Special Collections; and the UCLA Asian American Studies Center.

My thanks, too, to former Westport (CT) First Selectwoman Diane Goss Farrell, who helped me obtain a commentary from U.S. Senator Christopher Dodd (D-CT); and to Emanuel Margolis and John Simon, both personal friends and nationally known civil libertarians, for lending their encouragement.

Finally, I owe a deep debt of gratitude to my wife, Audrey, for her encouragement from the outset, her willingness to work alongside me on this complex project, and her ability to constantly lift my spirits and keep me organized and sane. And, this book would not be complete without my heartfelt thanks to my daughter, Wendy, for her enduring love, and for her appreciation of my journalistic efforts, imperfect as they may be, in the cause of civil liberties, civil rights, and equal justice.

INTRODUCTION

A Life Dedicated To Civil Liberties

SENATOR ROBERT C. BYRD

4,861 words. That's how many words it took to craft the Preamble to the Constitution of the United States, the Constitution itself, and the Bill of Rights. Simple words serve as the bedrock for this Republic and as the shield for the individual rights of all Americans.

Yet today, we see an almost constant effort to erode those individual rights.

With every day that has passed since the September 11 attacks, the White House has sought greater authority to fight the war on terror. And, with every power secured, with every precedent set, it encroaches that much further into the civil liberties of the American people.

Freedom of speech is threatened.

Freedom to dissent is ignored.

The rights of individual Americans, bought and paid for by the sacrifices of generations of Americans, are jeopardized.

At times of national distress, it is natural to want to come together and look for leadership from a single, clear voice. But America's song has never been expressed by a single note. It was never intended to be. America's music is not a solo, but rather a symphony made richer by the harmony of different views. Our Founders rejected a monarchy and sought, instead, a Republic. They chose a representative form of government that allowed the many voices of America to be heard.

The Constitution's Framers intended the government to ensure those promises set forth in the Preamble to the Constitution—not only to provide for the common defense, but also to establish justice, secure domestic tranquility, promote the general welfare, and secure the blessings of liberty to ourselves and our posterity.

That is not easy. Nor is it intended to be. Defending freedom and individual liberty requires knowledge, understanding, vigilance, and perseverance. I know that. Roger Baldwin knew that. And he dedicated his life to that effort, as is evident in his writings in this book.

I am reminded of the closing lines from Tennyson's "Ulysses":

> tho' We are not now that strength which in old days
> Moved earth and heaven, that which we are, we are,—
> One equal temper of heroic hearts,
> Made weak by time and fate, but strong in will,
> To strive, to seek, to find, and not to yield.

Those who believe in freedom and liberty, not just for some but for all, will continue to challenge, to question, and never to yield in defense of the Constitution and the American people.

———

Democrat Robert C. Byrd is the Senior Senator from West Virginia and a longtime, highly respected defender of the United States Constitution.

Introduction to Chapter 1

The ACLU, as it has expanded in numbers, funds, affiliates and influence, has become integrated throughout the country, bound by the Bill of Rights.

—Roger N. Baldwin, 1971

America, in its quest to form a "more perfect union," has had a great many social reformers. Roger Nash Baldwin, a social reformer, stood among them. In politics, of course, that boisterous little man, President Teddy Roosevelt, comes to mind with his booming voice and an even more dominating personality. One of his closest friends and most trusted advisers during the early period of his life in New York City when he was police commissioner was Jacob Riis (1849–1914), the Danish-born journalist and social reformer, who emigrated to the United States in 1870. He became a crusading police reporter for the *New York Herald Tribune* and later for the *New York Evening Sun*. His writings on slum dwellings festering in the Lower East Side and the abject poverty of urban life were vividly recorded in his first book, *How The Other Half Lives* (1890), and earned him the everlasting friendship of Theodore Roosevelt, then police commissioner of New York. Roosevelt called Riis "the most useful citizen of New York." Roosevelt, of course, would later become president in 1901 when President William McKinley was assassinated, and Roosevelt, who had been elected vice president a year earlier, succeeded him. Another crusading newspaper reformer who ranked with Riis was Lincoln Steffens, author of *The Shame of the Cities*, which exposed political corruption. "My special business," he declared in 1907, "is to write about graft, grafters, and American political injustice generally."[1]

This "exposé journalism" aroused the people to action. The impact of idealistic writers and an increasingly aroused public spurred political leaders to take practical measures. Many states enacted laws to improve the conditions under which people lived and worked. At the urging of such prominent social critics as social worker Jane Addams (1860–1935), child labor laws were strengthened and new ones were adopted, raising age limits, shortening work hours, restricting night work, and requiring school attendance. An active reformer throughout her career, Jane Addams was a leader in the women's suffrage and pacifist movements, for which she received the 1931 Nobel Peace Prize. Among some of the more notable women social reformers was Lillian D. Wald (1867–1940), American social worker and pioneer in public health nursing. In 1893 she organized the Visiting Nurse Service, which became the nucleus of the Henry Street Settlement in New York City. Emma Willard (1787–1870), American educator, pioneer in women's education, became famous for offering collegiate education to women and new opportunity to women teachers.

Susan B. Anthony organized the American Woman Suffrage Association, of which she was president. Helen Keller (1880–1968), American author and lecturer, blind and deaf from an undiagnosed illness at the age of two, lectured all over America and in Europe and Asia, raising funds for the training of the blind and promoting other social causes. Margaret Sanger (1883–1966) was an American leader in the birth control movement. She organized the first American (1921) and international (1925) birth conferences and formed in 1923 the National Committee on Federal Legislation for Birth Control, and she visited many countries abroad, lecturing and establishing clinics. Eleanor Roosevelt (1884–1962) was an active worker in social causes before she married (1905) Franklin Delano Roosevelt, a distant cousin. As wife of the governor of New York and then as wife of the U.S. president, she played a leading part in women's organizations and was active in encouraging youth movements, in promoting consumer welfare, in working for the civil rights of minorities, and in combating poor housing and unemployment. After her husband died in 1945, she was a U.S. delegate to the United Nations, and in 1946 she was made chair of the Commission on Human Rights, a subsidiary of the UN Economic and Social Council. In that capacity, she was a key figure in the creation of the groundbreaking Universal Declaration of Human Rights (1948).

Other political and journalism social reformers during Roger Baldwin's life included Eugene Debs (1855–1926), a strong proponent of unions for labor who forged his own version of American Socialism, which he used as a platform for his campaign for president in 1912; Woodrow Wilson (1856–1924), arguably the greatest politician of the Progress Era whose greatest accomplishment, ironically, did not come at home but in the international arena with the creation of the League of Nations; and, finally, Walter Lippmann, who wrote brilliantly of the liberal vision.

Not the least among all of these reformers—and many others not mentioned—was Roger Nash Baldwin (1884–1981). He first founded the American Union Against Militarism and then in 1920 the American Civil Liberties Union, whose legal eagles' first priority was defense of the First Amendment and antiwar dissenters and conscientious objectors, of which he was one. A friend and colleague of many of the above-named individuals, Baldwin's life story follows.

—W. K.

NOTE

1. Otis Pease, ed., *The Progressive Years: The Spirit and Achievement of American Reform* (New York: George Braziller, 1962), 131.

CHAPTER 1

THE MAKING OF
A REFORMER

The Roger Baldwin Story:
A Prejudiced Account by Himself

Despite armed power, I am sure the forces of law and freedom are growing, and I am grateful for the chances I have had to play a part in the struggle. I keep my faith in mankind's progress toward an ordered world of peace, law, and freedom. It will be that or nothing.

—Roger N. Baldwin, 1971

Author's Note: Following is the text of an unpublished autobiographical account of Roger Baldwin's life he provided to this author in 1971. The title is his own. Since Roger Baldwin's life has been part of the public record—there have been several books and numerous articles about him in magazines and periodicals—his own perception of how he lived, what he accomplished, and what he thought was important is especially enlightening. His own narration offers some insights into his otherwise complex, often paradoxical mind that was born into wealth and yet, at the same time, sought out the poorest, most downtrodden people in the nation to identify with. It is no accident that he married into wealth—that enabled him to be the low-salaried public servant that he was for so many decades. But it is to his credit that he put his vision for mankind ahead of any material goals, if any, that he may have had. Here is his story.

—W. K.

In Baldwin's Words

I call myself a political reformer, and it is about as near as I can come to describing the unclassified occupation that marks my whole life. I have been at various times social worker, teacher, executive, and organizer. But the field was always political, the relation of people to government. That might make me a political scientist, but I can't claim it as a teacher and I don't believe anyway in science in politics. Yet the American Political Science Association has been my trade union for many years, just as previously it was the National Conference on Social Welfare in social work and reformist years. I never did quite accept the pretensions of most social work to doing people good. I have tried to base reforms on what I figured people really wanted—based on the U.S. Constitution—not what I wanted for them. That got me into a lot of confusion because so many people have conflicting wants. But I have stuck pretty close to the under-dog and his wants on the principle that he should be given his chance.

I guess I was conditioned that way ever since I was a kid. I was born into a time, place and family where concern with social problems was inescapable. My parents were liberal Unitarians, and I a natural product of a suburban Boston community where Unitarians were among the best people, or we thought so. My paternal grandfather was a sort of lay preacher, president of the Boston Young Men's Christian Union and friend of nonconformist Brahmins, and he must have influenced me more than I knew. I caught the spirit of public service from Unitarian "lend a hand" concerns and the good people I looked up to. I started my infantile social work at about ten, went to church with unquestioning belief in man, if not God, and read history outside of school with a reformer's eye on the side of the under-dogs and the rebels. Not that I did not like our society; I did. I liked it so much that I was certain that democracy would perfect it, and that good people like us would prevail. Was I the natural liberal of my time, with Negroes at our dinner table along with Uncle William, a railroad president and reformer, trustee of Tuskegee, with my father's business associates, Jews, his intimate friends, and with my mother an agnostic and something of a feminist?

Harvard, the inescapable after my Wellesley public school years, did not change my interests in people outside. Through Philips Brooks House, the religious center, I took on adult education classes for working people, taught by students, and student entertainment groups for Boston social settlements. I had no social philosophy except to be helpful and enjoy it. Perhaps that's what has always moved me in all my social relations because I enjoy people of all sorts, curious about their problems, happy to share whatever I can. I guess that explains why, after a year of pure fun and adventure with my family in Europe,

I accepted the offer that came to me to go into social work and teaching in St. Louis. I had consulted my father's lawyer, Louis D. Brandeis, who advised me to take it as against a business offer from my father's partners. He saw that I was already committed and that St. Louis, where he had begun his career, would fit me better than Boston where I had too many ties to make my own way.

It was a good choice. To prepare I took a Harvard summer course in sociology which I was to teach at Washington University (1906 to 1910). For the job at a neighborhood slum settlement I went to New York, where my aunt, Ruth Baldwin, widow of my Uncle Bill, introduced me to all the up-lifters. From the perspective of the years, I could not have chosen better than the jobs with the Ethical Society and Washington University. Both have remained my closest contacts for over half a century on my numerous St. Louis visits. Washington University gave me an LLD after sixty years, and the Ethical Society heard my final "sermon" when I was eighty-five. My friends in St. Louis are the sons and daughters of my contemporaries, now almost all gone, who treat me like one of their peers because I still love to canoe, camp and keep up my acquaintance with birds, trees, plants, whatever moves and grows out-of-doors.

In recent years I have added to nature study a worried concern with conservation of the whole natural habitat for mankind. That interest was embedded years ago in my boyhood association with Bradford Torrey, a naturalist author that I read weekly in the *Boston Transcript*, Torrey is editor of Thoreau's journals, and also my neighbor. Birds became a major concern, and all my life I've been attracted to feathers and organizations of naturalists—the Nuttal Club in Cambridge, the American Ornithologists Union and much later the National Audubon Society in which I served as a director and vice-president. But of all associations, those Missouri rivers! I spent my happiest days in a canoe, there and elsewhere, alone or with a companion, in spiritual unity with the universe. Floating in silence in the wilderness I became just a point in time and space, part of the whole and the whole a part of me.

St. Louis lasted eleven years, 1906 to 1917, when the First World War uprooted me. I had been tempted to leave before by New York job offers—one rather ironically, as it turned out, the job Harry Hopkins later had in social work. Not that I would have followed his career, for I was by then a political reformer and had graduated from social work. I had been university teacher, chief probation officer of the juvenile court, head of a settlement in the slums and, the last seven years in

St. Louis, secretary of the Civic League, a crusading good-government agency of the city's leadership.

But in those years I had developed outside my occupations a curiosity about challenges to the social services in which I worked. I sought answers to poverty, injustice and inequality. I sought out the socialists and found them with a scheme of salvation but too doctrinaire, too German and too old. I worked with the militant labor leaders and found them too arrogant, too scornful of intellectuals and reformers. Then I found the anarchists—libertarians, they called themselves—through a visit to St. Louis by Emma Goldman. I studied the literature of protest, the utopias, the kind of nonconformist authors not taught at Harvard, particularly the Russian Peter Kropotkin, to whom I was most drawn, and some of whose works I later edited. Emma and I became close friends and so remained through the years until her death. Despite our many disagreements and my confusions, Emma never compromised; I often did. Compromise breeds confusion.

The International Workers came to St. Louis and claimed my attention by their demonstrations for unemployment aid. I found them members with vision and courage, and a simple working-class resistance to "capitalism." Years later, after I got out of prison as a conscientious objector, I joined the IW for a brief period to get a card as a passport when I worked all over the middle west as a manual laborer for a few experimental months. It was the only radical organization I ever joined. I found some precious friends among these working-class idealists, especially Ralph Chaplin, the sensitive poet who edited the IWW paper, who ended his life as a devout Catholic convert.

I left St. Louis for Washington and New York in 1917 when I was thirty-three. I was free to take on a wartime job just for expenses, because I had no family responsibilities. I had adopted by order of the Juvenile Court ten years before two little boys, orphans, and raised them as best a bachelor could in a boarding-house among helpful friends. They were by 1917 grown and off on jobs. One went to the war and died years later in an accident; the other went to prison, as I did, as a conscientious objector, and lived up to recent years.

My job in New York and Washington with the American Union Against Militarism was among my old friends in social work, headed by Lillian Wald of the Henry Street Settlement, New York. I had represented it in St. Louis. I knew at once when World War I broke that I could have no part in it; it was against both my then radical ideas and later the pacifism which quickly followed as I read the accounts of the British conscientious objectors, and remembered the impractical advice of the Sermon on the Mount. I rejected organized violence for any purpose, however good, and I have never faltered since in my refusal to take part in it.

But the war issues that faced us at once in 1917 were civil liberties—freedom of speech, press and assembly by critics and opponents of the war. So pressing and numerous were the issues that a separate bureau was formed in the Union under my direction. It soon outgrew its parent and became an independent agency in New York, headed by a Quaker lawyer, Hollingsworth Wood, Norman Thomas, my life-long colleague and friend in every cause that mattered to me, Dr. John Lovejoy Elliott—as near my minister as ever I had one, my Ethical Society mentor in St. Louis—and other old and new friends with a single purpose, to save what we could of the Bill of Rights from the passions of war. We did our self-imposed duty without fear or interference until toward the end of 1918 when our office was suddenly raided as suspect of encouraging the very conscientious objectors we were defending. We hired an influential pro-war Democratic lawyer who convinced the authorities that such good people were above suspicion.

Just at the time of the raid I was called for military service and refused. I was of course arrested, indicted, tried and convicted, with the then maximum sentence of a year, which I started serving on Armistice Day, going to a New Jersey prison through the confetti-filled streets of New York. I spent six months in this prison in Newark under an Irish warden who'd have none of "England's war," and four months in a country penitentiary to which I was moved as a trouble-maker. I had organized the prisoners to help one another. The penitentiary was under a fellow-member of the national social work organization, which dropped me from a committee over his strenuous opposition at the convention he attended.

I enjoyed the years in prison with the two months off for good behavior, because it was an adventure and I was doing what I believed. I liked many of the prisoners, no better and no worse than those outside, with few exceptions; they were just those who got caught. One of my great friendships grew out of prison, with Mrs. Caroline Bayard Colgate, a New Jersey woman active in helping prisoners. She developed quite a coterie of my young friends in jail she helped. She wrote up her experiences with the latter in a book, *Off the Straight and Narrow*. My friendship with her lasted until her death many years later.

When I left prison in 1918, I had only one major purpose, to marry the woman I had known in public work for some years, Madeleine Z. Doty, a well-known journalist and author, a lawyer who did not practice and a feminist who never took my name. After our honeymoon I followed another plan I had nurtured in jail, and with her enthusiastic approval. It was to spend a few months as a manual worker in basic industries dependent entirely on my earnings, to get the experience of working-class life first-hand in a turbulent period. Whatever I would do, the experience would be useful. It lasted four months, enough to learn even more than I expected, and enough to avoid ever repeating it. I always found a job all through the mid-west, and I even came home with a little money from the smelter, the steel mill, the railroad yard, and the brick kiln. I wound up in Pittsburgh during the great steel strike as a spy for the union at the request of William Z. Foster, its head.

I had toyed with the idea of getting a job with a union but my colleagues insisted on my getting back into civil liberties, then in as critical state as during the war. I was willing if nobody objected to a jailbird. None did. So out of my wartime bureau the American Civil Liberties Union was formed in 1920, with me as director, and new and enlarged national personnel—and more money as well.

> I was for the underdog, whoever he was, by training and instinct, and I had an endless capacity for indignation and injustice. Any challenge to freedom aroused me, and I was not satisfied until I had acted.

In 1970, the Union was fifty years old, and I have been with it all this time, not with intention, but because I never seemed able to quit for more than a brief leave of absence. Always there was some new challenge, some new task to intrigue me, for it is an endless but always hopeful struggle that was to be won over and over. For thirty years, from 1920 to 1950, I served as executive director, when at the age of sixty-five I retired of my own choice to serve as an adviser on international affairs. I have survived two successors as executive director but have never looked over their shoulders. In general I have agreed with the Union policies, controversial as they must be. We had our internal splits over Communist influences, which were healed by excluding them in a long and sometimes turbulent controversy over the method. Since then, in 1940, no political intrusion has troubled the Union, and the organization, as it has expanded in numbers, funds, affiliates and influence, has become integrated throughout the country, bound by the Bill of Rights.

The heart of the Union's efforts has always been its interventions in the courts; the protectors of constitutional rights, and its greatest victories have been the decisions of the U.S. Supreme Court. It was one of my deepest satisfactions to obtain the sponsorship of our fiftieth anniversary by Chief Justice Earl Warren, as our chairman.

—·—

The Union has not claimed all of my pubic interest. My commitment to freedom, equality and justice has led me into other more or less related movements. For twenty years I headed a small agency in New York of non-partisan liberals to help free political prisoners in foreign lands. We protested, pulled diplomatic wires, and visited European prisons— and helped free some. For twenty-five years I served on the board of the National Urban League for Negro social work. Issues of academic freedom enlisted me as a member of the Harvard Overseers' committee on the economics department for almost twenty years of interesting if somewhat futile effort, during which I was invited to give the 1934 Godkin Lecture on industrial conflict under the New Deal.

These were all very remarkable connections. One was the Fellowship of Reconciliation, uncompromisingly pacifist and anti-capitalist, on whose board I long served despite my objections to sectarianism. Three years later, in 1927, I took a leave of absence from the Civil Liberties Union, to spend a year in Europe in behalf of political prisoners, with three months in the Soviet Union, where I inquired into liberty and repression, later publishing a book, much too hopeful as I soon found out, on the forces of education and "proletarian freedom" to modify a tight party dictatorship. When fascism and Nazism threatened to triumph in 1934, I was disturbed enough to write some pro-Soviet and pro-Communist sentiments that really represented no retreat from my commitment to freedom; but they looked so, and have been embarrassing quotes for my opponents ever since.

—·—

The Nazi-Soviet Pact of 1939, a traumatic shock to me, ended any ambivalence I had about the Soviet Union, and all cooperation with Communists in united fronts. I know that peace and world order require the divided world to find a common base, but I am not trying, unlike many pacifist colleagues, to anticipate it. I was confirmed in my rejection in 1967 when I visited Moscow after forty years, to find even more conformity to the State's dictators. I was appalled, not frightened as Mrs. Roosevelt wrote she was.

With the Communists at home, I had many contacts ending in 1939, in defense efforts and in united fronts for good causes. I was in most of them, but three I really worked at: anti-imperialism, peace and de-mocracy, and the Loyalist cause in the Spanish civil war. All three fronts were international, backed by very important figures at home and abroad, and I was an officer in all. The Communists did not con-trol them, except indirectly through the strength of their participation: if they quit, the front would collapse, and in each of the three cases it did. I do not regret my participation, but it earned me quite unfairly a pro-Communist reputation in circles not entirely confined to the right wing. Not my public identification with anti-Communist agencies nor my efforts against Communist infiltration in other agencies seemed to counteract fixed impressions and repudiated quotes. No government agency blacklisted me, but I am on the lists of all of the self-styled patriots.

The greatest single change in my public life came at the advanced age of sixty-three, in 1947, when I was quite unexpectedly invited by the War Department to go to Japan and Korea to assist in developing civil rights agencies. It was an amazing offer, but as I was to find out, the military occupation was using every resource it could find to democratize those peoples, American-style. Of course I accepted with a leave of absence from the Union gladly given. Objecting to a role as a government representative, I arranged with General MacArthur's consent to go as a private citizen dealing with Japanese private citizens. I was a little fearful that among generals my pacifism and radicalism would create difficulties; they must have known my record, but nobody in Japan or Korea ever mentioned it or treated me other than as the VIP I rated.

The three months in Japan and Korea, where General MacArthur and General Hodge opened every door for me, were the most edu-cating I ever spent, keeping me keyed to the top of my abilities. Every minute I was occupied with interviews, inquiries, and conferences on every aspect of occupation policy and Japanese practice on civil rights. I had to learn a lot fast. I was invited to meet the Emperor and found him a friendly and understanding simple man. Twelve years later his chief chamberlain invited me again to the palace in the Emperor's absence in the country, and he with other old friends of 1947 gave me a banquet. I had established a Japanese Civil Liberties Union, stimulated both the occupation and Japanese government to protect civil rights, and they seemed to see in me a different American. A few years later the Japanese government awarded me the Order of the Rising Sun at the embassy in Washington, with jewels and ribbons to match.

Following the Japanese experience in 1947, which had drawn me into a new world of activity, I was invited next to Germany by Gen. Lucius Clay to do the same service of waking up the Germans to protect their own rights. The invitation was for the Civil Liberties Union's delegating, so I was accompanied by Arthur Hays and Norman Cousins. General Clay was as cordial and helpful as General MacArthur, but I did not find in him or any other general the stature of General MacArthur, with whom I had enjoyed hours of private discussion. Vain, the critics said, but I found him free from pride and self-importance. General Clay was the executive who got things done. He laid the way for me to return to Germany, as I did three times in the following years to the new German organization, far less effective than in Japan because of the division of Germany, and the traditional dependence on government and authority.

These experiences under American occupation strengthened my international interest, already expressed in the human rights ambitions of the new United Nations. I had worked in Geneva with the defunct League of Nations on its mandate and minorities commissions, but they were useless; no government would heed them. But the United Nations held better prospects and the work was in New York where we already were functioning under French refugees in an International League for the Rights of Man. So when I retired from the Union in 1950, I was quite prepared for the international field. I became the League chairman and held the post for fifteen years, devoting my major time to its work at the United Nations. It has taken me far afield, too, in one trip around the world in 1959 under UN auspices to examine the activities of non-governmental organizations, in trips to the Middle East and Arab Israeli refugees, in trips to Cuba, Venezuela, Costa Rica and Peru in behalf of Latin American democracy, many trips to European conferences, one to West Africa to celebrate Nigerian independence under my old friend, Dr. Zik (Azikawe) and in 1967 after a UN conference in Warsaw a return after forty years to Moscow.

Ever since 1954 when the issue of Puerto Rican self-government came before the UN, I have visited that island regularly as the guest of my old friend, Gov. Luis Munoz Marin. First I helped him set up a study of civil rights and liberties, then a commission to protect them. To that was added an appointment at the University of Puerto Rico law school to help handle a constitutional rights seminar, so that I've been going to Puerto Rico, happily in the winters, for the last ten years. I've taken on the Virgin Islands, too, where I have helped with getting more home-rule.

It seems to me amazing that the late years of my life should be the most exciting and varied, if not the most productive. Not only in my public life but private, too, they have been the most rewarding. I had married Evelyn Preston, also divorced with two little boys, who soon chose to take my name, though she as a good feminist did not until years later. Then we had a daughter, Helen, as ordered, who with the boys grew up in our houses in New York for the school year, New Jersey for week-ends, and Martha's Vineyard for summers. It was a happy family, acquired after I was fifty, with the children at home and away at their schools and colleges, and Evelyn and I always busy and devoted. Then Carl married and the first grandchildren came, and then Roger with a ready-made family of girls to which he added two of his own. Helen went off to Rome for graduate study after Radcliffe, and was there when a fatal illness struck Evelyn, in 1962, at the age of sixty-four. Her death left me alone until my daughter, who had gone back to Italy, returned and married her Roman fiancé. We resumed life together, my daughter and her husband and later two little girls, in the same house in which she was born and where the family had lived in Greenwich Village for over thirty years.

I have been blessed always with health and energy. My ills have been so few I cannot remember them, I am eternally busy at something, never retired nor tired, I have my discouraged moments, and I know the pain of failure. But extroverts recover fast.

It's been a varied and satisfying life with a single direction in a dangerous and confused world of the greatest wars, revolutions and inventions in all history. Despite armed power, I am sure the forces of law and freedom are growing, and I am grateful for the chances I have had to play a part in the struggle. I keep my faith in mankind's progress toward an ordered world of peace, law, and freedom. It will be that or nothing.

Anyhow, I've enjoyed the show; I wouldn't have missed it for the world.

COMMENTARY
Remembering Roger Nash Baldwin
WILLIAM J. VANDEN HEUVEL

He was almost sixty-five when I first met him. I was just eighteen, in my first year of college. His stepson who proudly bore his name had invited me to stay at the family home on West 11th Street while I was representing the debate team of Cornell against Columbia University. It was my first visit to New York City. He welcomed me into the living room of a spartan double brownstone, excused the fact that he had to speak at a public meeting on postwar Japan, and he was gone. It was October 1948. It was the beginning of a friendship that profoundly influenced my life. He became a mentor, a guide, and most of all a beloved friend for more than thirty years.

Roger Nash Baldwin's life on earth came quietly to an end in the early morning hours of August 26, 1981. He was in his ninety-eighth year. His life had spanned half of the presidential history of the United States (Chester Alan Arthur was president when he was born in Wellesley, Massachusetts, on January 21, 1884). The family called him Bunkle, a sobriquet combining Baldwin and uncle, reflecting a relationship that afforded many young people a shelter of affection and support. Since humanity was truly his family, I have no doubt that Roger, Carl, and Helen sometimes felt shortchanged in the attention they were entitled to as his children, but the devotion he gave to so many was certainly intended for them in greatest abundance. I knew him to be heartbroken twice—in 1962 when his wife, Evie (Evelyn Preston Baldwin), the commanding center of the family, died of cancer, and in 1979 when the same disease claimed his daughter Helen's life at much too early an age. He told me one day that he had an incurable illness, but I was not to worry. What, Bunkle, is it? What can we do? Then, with the wit and humor that crinkled his face and wrapped around his words, he replied: "It is old age—and no doctor has a cure."

He always spoke of life as a journey, believing the travel to be more important than the arrival at a destination. He never sought the comfort of institutional religion. Having been raised in the spiritual home of Emerson, Thoreau, and the great Unitarian-Congregationalist preachers of the nineteenth century, his creed was self-reliance, a beneficent regard for the goodness of mankind, and a conviction that life was to be lived on earth and that any judgments would depend on whether generosity and love or selfishness and arrogance dominated our earthly existence. "It is easy in the world to live after the world's opinions," said Emerson; "it is easy in solitude to live after our own; but the great man is he who in the midst of the crowd keeps with perfect sweetness the independence of solitude." Roger Baldwin was such a man. His opinions and judgments were his own—independent and carefully reached. He avoided absolutes except in his personal commitment against violence. Tolerance, common sense, and a passion for justice were the qualities of his temperament.

He was a great teacher and a wise adviser, believing that each of us is entitled to make our own mistakes in plotting life's journey. The Korean War was stalemated in 1953 when Gen. William J. (Wild Bill) Donovan invited me to join him as his executive assistant while he was serving as U.S. ambassador in Thailand. Bunkle advised: "Do it! Do it without hesitation. Donovan is an extraordinary man and you will have a front seat at the drama of your times—and maybe you will get on the stage." Donovan was a legendary citizen soldier, the most decorated American hero, a conservative Republican, a great lawyer. He and Bunkle were opposites in so many ways, yet each held the other in high regard. Bunkle did not try to dissuade me from military service. He was a pacifist and hated war but he respected that American forces were in Korea under a UN flag, responding to an unprovoked aggression from the North. He trusted Donovan's decency and integrity—and he was always ready to encourage me to be my own person, to agree or disagree with powerful influences, and remain on my own chosen course. During my years with Donovan both in Asia and New York, Bunkle and I were in frequent contact. He welcomed the new nationalism of Asia. Anticolonialism was the abolitionist movement of his lifetime. Nehru especially, both father and son, were his good friends. Nonviolence defined in the teachings of Mahatma Gandhi was a cornerstone of Bunkle's character. In those days, not many Americans even knew where Indochina was located. But seemingly Bunkle had traveled everywhere. I was a willing student of his worldview, opposing colonialism, welcoming the United Nations, and urging America to lead the democracies, not command them.

With General Donovan, I went to Hungary in 1956 and stayed for some weeks in Austria organizing the movement of refugee Freedom Fighters to the United States through the International Rescue Committee (IRC). Bunkle had a special sense of concern and responsibility for refugees from totalitarian governments. He had helped organize relief efforts for refugees of the Spanish civil war and worked with Eleanor Roosevelt and others to help the IRC bring Jewish refugees from Naziism to the United States. Bunkle helped me understand the meaning of being a refugee—the sense of homelessness, of coming to a country whose language you do not speak, of having the courage to overcome the loss of everything and begin life again. Later, as president of the IRC, I expanded its work to include refugees from Angola fleeing colonial Portuguese oppression. How pleased he was that Africa was being recognized and helped.

We often discussed and debated the threat of Communism. His disillusionment with Soviet totalitarianism was complete, but he profoundly opposed the political forces in America that invoked the threat of Communism to diminish our own civil liberties. We went together for a day of observation of the second trial of Alger Hiss, whom Bunkle had known over the years. He believed Hiss was guilty of perjury and had served some covert espionage purpose for the Soviets. The [Senator Joseph R.] McCarthy era and the influence of the senator from Wisconsin was a brutal price to pay, and in Bunkle's judgment, diminished our strength in confronting the Soviets around the world.

In the summer of 1950, I was invited to be part of a Baldwin family trip to Europe. We crossed the Atlantic on the French liner *de Grasse*, landing at Southhampton to be met by Michael Straight [then publisher of *The New Republic*], who drove us to his mother's home at Dartington, then and perhaps now the most progressive educational center in the United Kingdom. Having never been to Europe, I nevertheless had been an avid student of British politics—and Bunkle provided incomparable opportunities to meet the leaders of the Labor Party—Aneurin Bevan, Jennie Lee, Sir Stafford Cripps, David Lowe, Clement Atlee, Michael Foot, Lord Pakenham, Michael Scott—it was an endless discussion of world politics that confirmed my commitment to public affairs and political involvement.

Party politics, elective politics, were not career directions that Bunkle encouraged. He had voted four times for FDR as president, often lightly referring to "Franklin" as his classmate at Harvard, and he regarded the New Deal as the most progressive era in his lifetime for the defense of civil liberties and the pursuit of an egalitarian society. In his opinion, most politicians glowed with their self-importance, and personal opportunism was an unavoidable necessity for their success. When I ran for Congress in New York City's Seventeenth Congressional District, Bunkle's support was the loyalty of a friend, not the energetic encouragement of a mentor hoping to see a destiny fulfilled. He was a reformer who believed that government and political leaders had to be pushed, constantly pushed, to do the things for "the people" that common sense and decency should have assured without pressure. The strength of reformers was that they were outsiders. The civil rights movement was led by intrepid reformers who risked their lives, not by politicians. He was delighted when I was appointed special assistant to Attorney General Robert Kennedy. Bunkle followed my work to open up the public schools in Prince Edward County, Virginia, and applauded the creative use of governmental power to give meaning to the great desegregation decisions of the Supreme Court. "You couldn't have done that if you were a member of Congress," he would say.

Bunkle disliked being labeled in any political context except that he regarded right-wing attacks on him as "a radical" as an honor. Along with Eugene Debs, Norman Thomas, and Clarence Darrow, Roger Baldwin was certainly one of the great (and successful) radicals of the twentieth century. He saw himself as a pragmatist, forever consistent in his struggle to emancipate humanity from the arbitrary oppression of government or any group that sought power at the price of an individual's freedom. But he saw good government as being essential to a well-ordered society that ultimately is the guarantor of individual rights. He once said that he was "pro-state in all of its functions save oppression—alas, a vast area still."

"Go West," the great Brandeis had told him in 1905. He needed a break from family, establishment, and Boston tradition. For ten years he was teacher, chief probation officer, and director of the progressive Civil League in St. Louis. He admired the democratic attitudes of the Middle West and waged his first successful battles there to protect free speech. His involvement in the problems of criminal justice never lessened. It was a family joke that ex-cons whom he had met in various courts or prison situations would come knocking at the door of the Baldwins' West 11th Street house—and always be welcomed with a meal and sometimes an overnight stay. When Mayor John Lindsay appointed me chairman of the Board of Correction, the oversight body for the New York City prison system, Bunkle had no doubt that I should accept. We had endless conversations over the years about the role of prisons in a well-ordered society, about how they should be organized to best protect the community, about the rights of prisoners and the difficult responsibility of correction officers, about the dangers to life and rights when one person has total, arbitrary, and often unwitnessed power over other human beings. Bunkle had been sent to a county penitentiary in 1918 as a conscientious objector. Anyone who hopes to make the criminal justice system more effective prays to have a prisoner like Roger Baldwin. He always believed that an individual could change the world whatever the time or place of his being. In jail, he had organized a Prison Welfare League. He was a one-man Legal Aid Society, raising money from the wealthy prisoners (mostly gamblers) to hire lawyers to defend the poor awaiting trial. He established a prison library, learned to play the piano, lectured on the possibilities of democracy, and managed the prison garden. His challenging of the system never stopped.

There were two experiences in Missouri that always stayed with Roger Baldwin. We discussed them often. One was meeting Emma Goldman, whose intelligence and maternal warmth stood in sharp contrast to her notoriety as an anarchist revolutionary. He was inspired by her resistance to arbitrary authority, unjust laws, and insistence on the supremacy of individual conscience. She introduced him to a larger world of thought and experience, just as Bunkle did for so many of us. Her personal integrity in the struggle against oppression would always be an important example for him. He rejected, however, both Emma Goldman's anarchism and its willingness to accept violence as an instrument to achieve her ideals. Roger Baldwin's passion was against injustice, against the fanatical ideologues who never know doubt, against the arbitrary corrupt exercise of power.

The second experience was his introduction to Missouri's rivers. He would often say that his happiest days had been on rivers, his most contented, deeply spiritual moments of unity with the universe had been in a canoe, alone or with a silent companion. "Life and the river went by and I remained still, a point in time and space," he wrote. The canoe, the river, and Bunkle remained inseparable as symbols of joy and strength. My father died in 1957. Bunkle called and suggested a week of flatboating on the Current and Jack's Fork Rivers with the great American artist Thomas Hart Benton, his close friend of forty years. It was a challenge for me, but those two, both nearing seventy, were as happy as Huckleberry Finn. Bunkle would do the cooking, Tom would play the harmonica and keep warm with Jack Daniel's bourbon, and the evening dusk would come over our campsite as worldly discussions and American folk songs filled the air. How many times did we navigate the Ramapo River in his beloved New Jersey countryside! Every turn, every sound was part of his magical guidance.

For Bunkle, the United Nations was his second home. All his life he had fought against racism, for the end of colonialism, for the equality of women, for a true league of nations, for universal peace and justice. He saw the United Nations as being a powerful opportunity to secure those objectives. No one knew the faults and weaknesses of the United Nations better than he did. The bureaucratic quagmire of the organization, the stalemates of the Cold War, the destructive division into national blocs were painful for a visionary to witness. He had hoped for an International Court of Justice to protect human rights everywhere in the world. Explaining the obstacles to progress at the United

Nations, he told me that "few things in history happen at the right time." He thought it a miracle that the world organization had traveled so far. His was the long view. War must be avoided. Peace must be secured. Disarmament must begin. The United Nations had the possibility to achieve these purposes. There was no alternative. The boring, repetitious rhetoric of UN monologues would have to be endured. Meanwhile, he worked fervently in his own country and abroad to advance the cause of a just world through the only organization that brought all of mankind together. Those were the lessons of his mentoring, and I never forgot them.

President Carter appointed me as U.S. ambassador to the European Office of the United Nations in 1977. Geneva, Switzerland, was a place that had special resonance for Bunkle. His father had spent years there, and Bunkle had visited often. In 1950 on the family trip, Geneva was an important stop. The Palais des Nations was familiar territory as he met with UN and nongovernmental organization leaders. The Korean War was in its first weeks. The nuclear threat had escalated with the announcement of Soviet testing. India was newly independent, and the voice of Nehru was dominant in the Third World. Bunkle went from meeting to meeting, as effective a lobbyist as I have ever seen for UN principles. Later, when I was the U.S. deputy permanent representative in New York, we exchanged views constantly. One of my greatest pleasures was to represent the president of the United States in awarding Bunkle the nation's highest civilian honor. At a White House ceremony on January 16, 1981, President Carter said: "I would like to say before I present the last medal here that Roger Baldwin, a great civil rights leader, is in the hospital in New Jersey. At 3 o'clock this afternoon, the same time as we begin our ceremony here, he was presented with a Medal of Freedom by William vanden Heuvel, deputy ambassador to the United Nations, on my behalf." After I presented the Presidential Medal to him, Bunkle literally leaped from his chair, no longer old, without a suggestion of infirmity, and without a note before him, he gave a ten-minute response on the struggle for liberty and human rights. No one who heard him that day will forget his eloquence. My journey with Bunkle had come full circle.

On my last visit with him as the end approached, he sat up and in his strong and vibrant voice repeated faultlessly from memory a verse by Robert Louis Stevenson that he cherished:

> Under the wide and starry sky
> Dig the grave and let me lie.

Glad did I live and gladly die,
And I lay me down with a will.
This be the verse you gave for me:
Here he lies where he longed to be;
Home is the sailor, home from the sea,
And the hunter home from the hill.

The place "where he longed to be," that spot in the Ramapo Hills where a hemlock and sycamore are grown together, now belongs to him. I spoke at his memorial and said: "Those who light a campfire, who hear the woodlark sing, or marvel at the bursting crocus on a forest walk, or slip a canoe silently into a river's water where space, time, fear, suffering no longer exist, where everything becomes simple, where the calm says there is something indestructible in us against which nothing shall prevail—Roger Baldwin will be at their side." He is always at mine.

———

William vanden Heuvel, a protégé of Roger Baldwin's, helped him launch the International League for the Rights of Man as a member of the advisory board. Vanden Heuvel served as Deputy U.S. Permanent Representative to the United Nations in the Carter administration and as U.S. Ambassador to the European Office of the UN. Now of Counsel to the law firm of Stroock & Stroock & Lavan, he is also Senior Adviser to Allen and Company, a New York investment banking firm.

———

COMMENTARY
He Would See Civil Liberties Today as Deeply Threatened
ALAN F. WESTIN

———

If Roger Baldwin could awake in 2006, twenty-five years from his passing away in 1981, what would he think of the state of civil liberties in our nation? And would his ideas as the preeminent civil liberties advocate and organizational leader in America from World War I into the 1970s still be relevant now, in the Internet age and in a post-9/11 nation?

Absolutely.

I knew Roger first when I was on the National Board of Directors of the ACLU in the 1960s. He was no longer running the ACLU, but was leading international activities for the Union and for the International League for the Rights of Man. He came to many ACLU Board meetings, though, and was quite interested in the new issues of personal privacy, which I was then exploring as chair of the ACLU's first Privacy Committee.

In 1975, when I was serving as founding editor of the *Civil Liberties Review*, a semischolarly ACLU publication, we asked Roger to work with us to create a memoir of his life. We were able to draw on and expand a set of fine recollections Roger had done in 1972 for Columbia University's Oral History project.

I spent half a dozen fascinating days interviewing Roger in his Greenwich Village townhouse and also at his New Jersey retreat, going over each of his then–six decades of work in the civil liberties vineyard. CLR published the memoir in 1975, in two articles entitled "Roger Baldwin: Recollections of a Life in Civil Liberties."

And so, if a youthful Rip Van Baldwin could be awakened in 2006, how would he see the current scene, and what might he do to update his role?

1. He would see civil liberties as being deeply threatened and under siege in the United States today, with the dark forces of authoritarianism he had always fought now riding high in the [Texas] saddle.

Because he defended outspoken civil liberties in the World War I and World War II contexts, and in the Cold War/McCarthy days, Roger would be thoroughly familiar with both the legitimate and the overreaching actions of American government in crisis times. To the arguments that post-9/11 security required major reductions if not suspensions of civil liberties and due process, he would say—Nonsense. Yes, he would accede to realistic and measured new investigative and surveillance powers. But he was always skeptical—a "show me" respondent—when it came to programs that reached far beyond what he would see as being necessary steps. He would be pressing for disclosure of government surveillance and watch list programs and restoration of fundamental due process procedures in detentions.

2. He would be entirely pleased and proud of the current role of the ACLU in attacking what it condemns as dangerous threats to our liberties, from both government and businesses.

When Roger led the ACLU, from 1920 to 1950, it was a deliberately small and elite-based organization. Its members were drawn from the ranks of activist social workers, union leaders, socialists, pacifists, teachers and professors, lawyers, and similar slices of the American left-of-center ranks. Using test cases very effectively, along with Roger's unique contacts in elite circles, the ACLU waged vigorous educational, advocacy, and litigative campaigns from its small base.

In the 1960s and thereafter, the ACLU's new leaders transformed the ACLU into a much broader organization, larger and more reflective of the broad liberal citizenry rather than just the professional and organizational elites. Roger had already seen and accepted the wisdom of that organizational expansion in the 1970s. And, he would surely be a cheerleader for the kind of mass media advocacy campaigns, large test case docket across the nation, and participation in left-right coalitions that mark the ACLU's modus operandi today.

Roger believed in the pendulum concept of civil liberties. Crises arose, governments overreached, one worked to defend as much liberty as possible. Then the crises receded, allowing greater civil liberties to be restored, and also documenting, hopefully for later valuable use, the overreachings done in the name of necessity.

3. He would be very pleased at the spread of democracy in formerly authoritarian regimes in Eastern Europe, the Russian empire, and the Middle East, and at the vigorous human rights movements throughout the world.

Given Roger's primary focus on international human rights between 1950 and 1980, and his strong support for international human rights monitoring, he would view the global scene today as highly promising. Though he would surely have opposed the Iraq intervention, we can see him supporting the early stirring of popular democracy in Iraq (and elsewhere). But he would also surely be worried about whether these new democracies would include or exclude meaningful civil liberties in their new regimes. Free speech, free press, and due process do not come automatically with free elections and representative government, he would remark. But he would point to all the spontaneous human rights demonstrations and protests springing up across the past decade as a force that would—in his always optimistic view—make slow but steady headway in the twenty-first century.

4. He would find a way to adapt his principled-patrician leadership style and pacifist credo to the very different but also, he would say, the very similar civil liberties fights of the twenty-first century.

Roger was correctly perceived as being a civil liberties "absolutist," opposed to the usual "balancing of interests" approach of most courts, legislatures, and more mainstream liberal groups. He was always ready to be the tip-of-the-drill advocate of pure positions, understanding that even if the ACLU position was rejected, it sometimes led to a more civil liberties–respecting outcome because of the ACLU's stance.

In many situations, however, Roger was ready to discard absolutist positions when he saw events justifying change. He supported the

1930s Popular Front movements, like most liberal-left leaders at that time. But he turned against the Popular Front after Stalin's purges and the 1939 Nazi-Soviet Pact. He engineered the expulsion of Communist members from the ACLU national board (the Elizabeth Gurley Flynn episode in 1940) when he decided that Communists would not support civil liberties for all, just for themselves and their allies.

Marrying his absolutist and pragmatic sides, I believe Roger would say—and he did say in some of my interviews with him in the 1970s— that there was rarely anything new under the civil liberties sun. The cycles of civil liberties advances, government repression in times of assumed crises or fears of societal excesses, religious and conservative hostility to vigorous freedoms, and appeals to the best in the American heritage, he would say, are here in the Internet age and in the post-9/11 nation.

Were he awakened in 2006, Roger would throw himself into the good fight in such a spirit, ready to adopt the new techniques needed to assert the old verities of freedom.

He is missed.

––––––––

Alan F. Westin is Professor Emeritus of Public Law and Government at Columbia University, where he taught for thirty-seven years, retiring in 1997. Born in 1929, he earned his B.A. from the University of Florida; his LL.B. from Harvard Law School; and his Ph.D. in political science from Harvard University. He is the author or editor of twenty-six books, a member of the District of Columbia Bar, and has been listed in *Who's Who in America* for three decades.

Introduction to Chapter 2

The denial of the rights of one threatens the rights of all.
—Roger N. Baldwin, 1970

The founding of the American Civil Liberties Union by Roger Baldwin was not an accident of history. Rather, it was a direct result of the unrest in America immediately following World War I—the increase in racial strife resulting in a record number of lynchings in the South, and in the North an outburst of race riots in more than twenty-five cities. The anticipation of an improvement in the lives of black people—hopes raised by their military service in the war as well as the optimistic rhetoric of President Woodrow Wilson—brought them to a new level of expectations that, sadly, were not met.

During the war itself, Baldwin had been in St. Louis employed as a social worker in a settlement house. He also headed the St. Louis branch of the newly created American Union Against Militarism (AUAM) in 1915. Two years later he was summoned to New York to serve as the AUAM secretary, where—a pacifist himself—he took up the cause mostly with the rights of pacifists. The AUAM planted the seeds of the modern civil liberties movement.[1]

Labor had similar hopes for an improved life after all the talk of democracy and freedom during the war, when workers had received better wages, worked shorter hours, and enjoyed improved working conditions. Following the Armistice, however, employers and big corporations resumed their all-out attacks on the workers' right to organize. Tension between management and labor resulted in an outbreak of crippling strikes in cities across America. Adding to the chaos was the movement of radicalism, which evoked great anxiety among many

Americans who had already developed an antagonism toward immigrants.

It was against this backdrop that Roger Baldwin in 1917 set up a separate branch of the AUAM called the Civil Liberties Bureau. As Baldwin described it, "It was the first time the phrase 'civil liberties' had been so used in the United States. It was borrowed from a British wartime Council for Civil Liberties." "Finally, in 1920, a small group of visionaries came together to discuss how to start the engine," an ACLU briefing paper states. "Led by Roger Baldwin, a social worker and labor activist, the group included Crystal Eastman, Albert DeSilver, Jane Addams, Felix Frankfurter, Helen Keller, and Arthur Garfield Hays. They formed "the American Civil Liberties Union and dedicated themselves to holding the government to the Bill of Rights' promises."[2]

The first meeting of its newly chosen board of directors was held in New York City on January 20, 1920. From that modest beginning, the Union has for eighty-six years steadily grown in numbers and resources—and, most important, become part of the fiber and body politic of the American justice system.

—W. K.

NOTES

1. The precedents for such an organization can be found in the National Defense Association, founded in 1878, and in the Free Speech League founded in 1902.

2. From ACLU briefing paper, "In the Public Interest" (Number 9, undated), American Civil Liberties Union, 125 Broad Street, New York, N.Y.

CHAPTER 2

ACLU: WATCHDOG FOR THE UNDERDOG

Civil liberties, asserted as a principle, become legal rights when they are embodied in enforceable law, as they are in the Bill of Rights.

—Roger N. Baldwin, 1970

Author's Note: The term "civil liberties" has broadened in its application since the inception of the ACLU in 1920, when the rights of labor was its main focus. When the possibility of America becoming involved in World War I arose, the ACLU quickly came to the aid of conscientious objectors—those who held religious beliefs that, they argued, should not permit them to engage in violence or killing. Baldwin himself was a conscientious objector during World War I and served time in prison, an experience he seemed proud of in terms of standing up for what he believed in. Since it was founded, the ACLU has broadened its mission to include defending the rights of those who espouse many unpopular causes such as the Ku Klux Klan, the Nazis, and Native American groups—they had the constitutional right to protest and to assemble in public to air their grievances against the government of the United States, according to the ACLU. Although it is now recognized by many Americans as the most effective independent organization to support the Bill of Rights, especially through the courts, the ACLU also is perceived in the minds of many as a "left-wing" organization. To this day, many well-educated, intelligent, well-read people in the United States react negatively when they see the ACLU going to court to defend an individual or group. The most recent example, of course, is the USA Patriot Act, which, no doubt, Baldwin would have vehemently opposed. The question of just how far the government can go in the interest of preserving national security is a critical national issue today and will no doubt continue to be fiercely debated for some time to come. Nonetheless, progress in applying the Bill of Rights across the board up until Baldwin's death in 1981 was palpable, and he often said so—always expressing his philosophical qualification that "the fight for civil liberties never stays won." Following are some of Baldwin's most insightful observations about the ACLU as "watchdog for the underdog."

—W. K.

<hr>

In Baldwin's Words

ACLU NONPARTISAN (1935)

To the Editor: The union, founded in 1920, is a strictly nonpartisan organization for the defense of the rights of free speech, free press and assembly. It acts on any issue in the United States, regardless of whose rights are attacked. The charges that the union is a "Communist defense organization" grows out of the easy and false assumption that those who defend Communist rights must be Communists at heart. By such logic, since we have defended Fascism, Catholics, Ku Klux Klanners and atheists, our organization must have a chameleon-like facility in changing its faiths and convictions. The fact of the matter is that we are called upon to defend such a wide variety of movements that it would be utterly impossible to take sides with any. (Roger N. Baldwin, letter to the editor, *The New York Times*, October 4, 1935, p. 20.)

RACE FRICTION IN THE MILITARY (1944)

The unspoken sense of friction between Negroes and whites is everywhere the same—the white man's assumption of the superiority of his race and the Negroes' resentment at being treated on the basis of his color. He has always resented it, but the war has intensified his feelings, and he is vocal and determined now to play his part as a citizen on his merits. I heard repeated warnings from whites that the "Negro is pushing us too fast," but the plain facts are that the white communities are far too slow in meeting the most elementary needs of Negroes for decent homes and jobs fitting their skills.

What whites mean when they object to being "pushed too fast" is that Negroes no longer accept without protest the pattern of segregation fixed for them, or the white man's claims to superior rights. The

resentments of whites, which I picked up everywhere, have no justification except in tradition. The resentments of Negroes, universal and
articulate as never before, rest on perfectly legitimate claims in law and
morality. The ways which they are mistreated clearly violate their
constitutional rights to equal protection of the laws under the Fourteenth Amendment.

Whatever complaints stood out locally as the causes of friction—and
they varied considerably—I found everywhere [in the country] an
underlying resentment against discrimination in gaining admission to
many of the units of the armed forces, and in the segregation of almost
all of them. It is rather the sense that they [Negroes] are not recognized
as citizens like others, deserving of equality of sacrifice for their
community. In almost every city I visited, I heard evidence of the
immediate provocation on furloughs. They tell their folks, and they
speak in churches and at meetings, recounting how they are pushed
around by white officers, how they are treated in towns around Southern training camps, the endless difficulties in getting places on buses
and trains, the arrogance of white MPs. In one city, numerous unjustified arrests of Negroes on furlough by white MPs were reported,
resulting in such indignation that the army replaced them with Negro
MPs. The arrests and trouble stopped at once.

But the grievance is too deep to be reached by any measure short of
a reversal of the segregation and discrimination practiced by the War
Department and there is no hope of such relief in the midst of a war.
Yet from the clashes between Negro soldiers and white police officers
may come the spark, as it did in Harlem, to set off other riots, reflecting
the sense of frustration in a war for democratic goals denied to Negroes. (Roger Nash Baldwin Papers, Seeley G. Mudd Manuscript Library, Princeton, N.J. box 22, folder 23, article draft for the *New York
Post*, January 4, 1944.)

ON NATIVE AMERICANS (1950)

I was moved to organize an ACLU Committee on Indian Civil
Rights by rereading a book, *Massacre*, by Robert Gessner, a young
instructor at New York University, who had become interested in
Indians in his native Michigan and had visited the northwestern reservations. Gessner became secretary of the Committee, and with me
arranged the conferences in Washington at which the principles of a
bill [in Congress] were formulated. Interior Secretary Harold Ickes, a

devoted friend of the Indians, long active in Indian affairs, promoted it at once. With the legislation on the books we aided in its application. My own concern was more than official; I had a personal emotion toward the Indians from a college experience spent among them with my professor of anthropology from Harvard, William C. Farabee, who led an expedition of some fifteen students among the Navajos and Pueblos. Ever since, the Indian problems of rights had gripped my attention. The old slogan, "Let my people go," from Dr. Montezuma and his followers struck a responsive echo in me. (Roger Nash Baldwin Papers, Seeley G. Mudd Manuscript Library, Princeton, N.J., Memorandum to file, 1950.)

Defending the Ku Klux Klan (1969)

After the war [World War II], the press began to report incidents of Ku Klux Klan meetings with the fiery crosses, hoods and shirts directed not only against Negroes but any minority, Jews, Catholics, radicals. I knew we would have to defend their right to meet on private property, burn crosses and wear their nightshirts, but I knew a limit had to be set for public property. The first conflict with the law was not long in coming; meetings even on private property were barred in Southern cities as likely to endanger the peace. I offered our aid on behalf of our board by telegram to the Imperial Wizard in Atlanta. It was not a gesture; we meant it, unpleasant as the duty was. We hardly expected an answer to Yankee intervention but one came promptly and in the most courteous language, full of appreciation; but no thanks, we can handle our own business. After that we made several offers when the Klan's freedom of speech and assembly was denied, but never was an offer accepted. We protested to officials with little effect. The Klan got too strong to need any outside help; it was not long before it controlled state and local governments over a large part of the South and West.

As it grew, it got bold in its lawless attacks on its victims, and, acting under cover of darkness and hoods, it was impossible to identify the guilty Klansmen even in the rare cases where arrests were made. I took satisfaction in one in which we succeeded in getting a conviction in Texas of a Klansman who had beaten members of the International Workers of the World attempting to organize longshoremen. It was remarkable to convict Klansmen anywhere in the South, and even more when the victims were members of the most radical and hated labor organization.

I would figure that over the period of 1920 to 1940, more civil liberties violations and personal assaults could be charged against Klansmen in the South and West than to any other single source in recent history. Not even the violence of the struggle for trade union rights was as great. I felt helpless to take any useful action. Nobody did, not even the law enforcement agencies, some of which were corrupted by Klansmen anyway. I assume that offers of aid to the Klan and our protests on its behalf surprised many who regarded us as partisans of the left. It was a healthy surprise, for it proved our integrity; we meant everybody's rights, not somebody's rights. Nobody resigned; maybe some joined. The Klan shriveled after it aroused formidable opposition by its lawlessness, and though it still functions, its violence no longer threatens anyone. (Roger R. Baldwin Collection, excerpt of remarks by Roger N. Baldwin at commencement exercises at Brandeis University, 1969, on the school's twentieth anniversary. Address: "Human Rights: The Past Twenty Years in the U.S.")

THE MEANING OF CIVIL LIBERTIES (1970)

The phrase "civil liberties" has a long history in English and American political usage, but it was the ACLU that first adopted it in an organization's title and so brought it into a wider public vocabulary. "Civil liberties" had always described the freedoms of the people in a democracy to speak, publish, and organize. They were so central to the ACLU's concerns that ACLU letterheads in the early years carried "Free Speech, Free Press, Free Assembly" as the organization's slogan. To this day, as the "First Amendment" freedoms, they have the preferred place for us and the Supreme Court alike.

They are what many schools of political thought call natural rights; the inherent desires of people to express themselves and as a society with their fellows. The ACLU recognizes that the principles existed long before constitutions embodied them, and so is not bound by whatever limits are fixed by constitutional guarantees or Supreme Court decisions. Its lawyers must work within those limits, or seek to extend their scope, but law cases are not the sole function of the protection and defense of citizens' liberties against abuses of official power.

The ACLU has not formulated definitions or declarations of the meaning of civil liberties; they are assumed, based on the principles of the Bill of Rights. If strictly defined, they would, I think, come out thus: Civil liberties, asserted as a principle, become legal rights when they are embodied in enforceable law, as they are in the Bill of Rights. The Bill of Rights covers all the protections of citizens against government power abuses of the liberties of the people. It includes all the elements of fairness in the area of criminal justice embodied in the phrase "due process." The phrase "civil rights" is not the same as civil liberties. In accepted U.S. usage it designates the post–Civil War amendments to the Constitution for the equality of all citizens regardless of race. It is so used by the ACLU, burdened to also include equality regardless of creed, national origin, sex, or economic status.

All rights of the people are restraints on government or guarantees to the people by government. They are individual, personal, or collective as the right of association. They find their political sanction in the supremacy of a sovereign people over their governments in a democracy. They find their judicial sanction in the protection of minority and personal rights against the majority. They find their philosophical sanction in the natural right of every individual to the fullest opportunity to develop his capacities. This purpose led Justice Brandeis once to observe "the fundamental human right is the right to be left alone." Only recently has the Supreme Court formulated a right of privacy, not to be found in the words of the Bill of Rights, but inherent in its concept of the relation of citizens to government. Obviously, the application of these general principles raises constant and highly controversial questions: conflicts of rights, the precedence of one right over another, the proper powers of government, the social limits of personal freedoms—to name a few. These questions form the stuff of ACLU policy decisions as to what civil liberties and rights mean in practice. The years have produced over four hundred such decisions to use as guides in deciding particular cases, and there are still new problems demanding new guides. How difficult decisions can be in the complexities of a democratic society is evident in the debates and dissents among the Union's large and representative Board of Directors. Decisions by narrow majorities reflect the kind of conflicting arguments that so often split by a single vote U.S. Supreme Court justices.

Democracy is choice: freedom of choice demands dissent, diversity, difference, all the contradictory counsels through which a majority arrives at a decision through public debate by press, radio, TV, and meetings of parties and organizations. This is the assumption underlying the ACLU activities for political freedom. Personal motives may differ for supporting democratic freedom, but they do not qualify the common agreement on its necessity. Conservatives among our colleagues may support civil liberties as insurance for private property; radicals may support them as an aid to socialization of property. But all agree on the rule of law against violence, on democracy, political, and civil, on fair procedures in applying all rights—economic and social as well as political.

Disagreement arises mainly in drawing lines when one right conflicts with another. We have followed for years Thomas Jefferson's dictum that it is time enough for the rightful purposes of "government to intervene when principles break out into overt acts against peace and good order." Deeds may be unlawful, but not words apart from deeds. The distinction presents problems. We accepted for a long time the "clear and present danger" test of words leading to action the government has a right to prohibit. The Supreme Court found it handy if vague enough to arouse dissent among the justices. We found it vague, too, and fell back on the law of incitement to an act committed or attempted. Advocacy of the overthrow of government by force without any act, however shocking to many, seemed to us a protected right, but the Supreme Court outlawed it when used by Communists. "Surely," said Benjamin Franklin, "the abuses of freedom of speech should be suppressed, but to whom dare we entrust the power to do so?" Better run the risk, we hold, that no speech, no mere words, no expression should be criminal save as part of an unlawful act. The history of civil liberties is marked by the acts of courageous men and women who put moral claims of conscience ahead of obedience to law, and who by their acts, often at the price of their freedom, helped win legal recognition of their claims.

Without courage to assert rights, they weaken. The test of progress in American liberties is to be found in the determination of organized citizens to get and hold the rights they are presumed to have. Every minority won such rights as it had only by struggle, by organization, by insistence that its claims be recognized. "When liberty dies in the hearts of the people," wrote Judge Learned Hand, "no constitutions and no laws will save it." The task of the ACLU is to help nourish that spirit of liberty in the American people. (Roger N. Baldwin, "The Meaning of Civil Liberties,"

The Bill of Rights covers all the protections of citizens against government power abuses of the liberties of the people. It includes all the elements of fairness in the area of criminal justice embodied in the phrase "due process."

introduction in Volume 1, *American Civil Liberties Annual Reports*, published by Arnow Press and *The New York Times*, New York, bound in 1970.)

DEFEND THE THOUGHT WE HATE (1970)

The tests of the loyalty of the ACLU to its principles lie in the impartiality with which they are applied and the character of its leadership—no favorites in defense of rights for all, no contradictory loyalties in the minds of the leaders. These are hard tests to impose and apply against natural sympathies and prejudices; harder, perhaps, to determine the consistency of anyone's loyalties and beliefs; even harder to defend the thought we hate.

But the leadership has always kept in mind the necessity of impartiality as the basis of good faith in carrying out its purposes. Not much appears in the reports to indicate the efforts required to stick to principle in the midst of pressures and controversies; resisting temptations to think of "friends" and "enemies" in applying principles, steering clear of alliances with partisans, avoiding involvement in the merits of clients or ideas. To hold together both staff and board composed of people with varied prejudices and politics, and hold them true to their common basis always tests tolerance and mutual good faith. Without those qualities the Union would long since have split apart.

It is quite true that the reality of impartiality has not been matched by its appearance. It could hardly be, because publicity emphasizes the unusual or the dramatic and so our concerns sometimes seemed to be with the "reds," and "pinks" and the extremists—always good copy for the press. It is also true that some of us in the leadership contributed to this impression in the 1930s by our personal associations with united fronts for good causes in which Communists and Socialists and other "disreputables" took part. The opposition never let us forget it even after we had long since abandoned such associations. The opposition of right-wing advocates of repression was able to mislead and confuse the uninformed, but it was unable to influence officialdom and the press into questioning the Union's good faith. Recent years have seen so few leftist issues and interventions that the attacks have died down in the face of so many other activities, though the American Legion conventions right up to the mid-1960s faithfully went through the futile ritual of calling on federal officials to investigate the ACLU's "subversive" role.

An examination of the record would reveal what might be reasonably expected in failures to take some cases and issues, or mistakes in taking others. There were matters which at the moment seemed worthy but which later hindsight proved otherwise. Integrity does not require consistency. One matter that troubles me was a failure to see in lawless prohibition enforcement the violations of rights that should have concerned us, a failure due to a notion that since prohibition was outside the concerns of democratic processes it was not ours.

Drawing a line between what rights we would defend and lawless acts we would not has posed difficulties for us and misunderstanding for others. Why should we defend the rights of the Ku Klux Klan or the American Nazi Party to meet peaceably and publish their propaganda when violence is their hallmark? If we do, are we not parties to lawlessness? *But we insist that the only practical test for the exercise of civil liberties is between expression and deeds* [Italic the author's]. And that lawless deeds do not ban lawful expression. Only so could we keep the integrity of our principles. The enviable record of integrity in applying principles suffered some exceptions as applied to its leadership before a policy was adopted which assured complete loyalty of boards, committees and staff to civil liberties for all persons everywhere. The occasion for such a policy arose twenty years after the Union's founding in the passions aroused by the Nazi-Soviet Pact at the outbreak of the Second World War. The Union had cooperated with Communists who professed support of civil rights. The Nazi-Soviet Pact showed how baseless were the professions; it made association impossible. The Union had never elected to its board, committees or staff any known Communists, but it had tolerated two otherwise elected who had become Communists. One had resigned. The other one refused to resign on request. A policy was then adopted requiring loyalty to the principles of civil liberties. Under it a board hearing was held on charges of disloyalty to the principles, and the member was expelled—the only expulsion in the Union's history.

Opposed only to all repression of civil liberties and to any distortion of the equality of all citizens under law, the Union champions no cause but its own. If time brings new concepts of citizen rights, new visions arising from old principles, the Union welcomes them as an obligation inherent in its integrity of purpose. (Roger N. Baldwin, "The Meaning of Civil Liberties," introduction in Volume 1, *American Civil Liberties*

Annual Reports, published by Arnow Press and the *New York Times,* New York, bound in 1970, xxv–xxxi.)

ORIGINAL MISSION (1974): AN INTERVIEW WITH THE CIVIL LIBERTIES REVIEW

Q. When you organized what has now become the institution of the ACLU, I'm sure you had certain concepts in mind of what constituted civil liberties. Have those concepts changed over the years?

A. I think they've grown enormously because our original concept was really confined to the First Amendment and the First Amendment expanded in itself, but many things have been added to it and I think in a complex society like ours that you go on and keep finding new issues and new conflicts—you do expand, so not only has the concept expanded, the practice has expanded and the spirit of it affects the country's thinking. I don't know. But the elitist thinking in this country is certainly quite different from what it was fifty years ago, for that reason. They would never have talked about privacy, abortion, abolition of the death penalty—we wouldn't have conceived to be within the compass of civil liberties then.

Q. We're now entering an age where computers and telecommunications systems and people talk about a technocratic society. Do you think there will be major changes in the way people work on problems of liberty?

A. I cannot conceive that the basic demands of people for freedom and equality and justice is going to change in any society. I think a great deal depends in the future on our freedoms—in our freedoms—on what happens to the world. Because if the world is headed for another catastrophe like a world war, we needn't discuss these matters because we'd all be finished, anyway. But if the world is headed for some kind of law—I wouldn't say world government—but some kind of world order, if we're going to settle our disputes and conflicts by rational means instead of by killing people, then I think an entirely different future looms for the United States because we'll be part of a whole and not an isolated country as we have been isolated by our riches and our wealth and our arms and rather reluctant partner in the world. Instead of that, we'll become probably a very essential part of it, by the virtue of our power. (Columbia University, Oral History Research Office, A Conversation with Roger Baldwin with Alan F. Westin, editor, the *Civil Liberties Review,* and professor of Public Law, Columbia University, December 18, 1974, pp. 88–89.)

THE QUESTION OF PRIVACY (1974)

Q. How about privacy?

A. I have welcomed the ACLU's interest in privacy a long time ago with birth control. Of course, birth control goes back to my very earliest experience with civil liberties, because it was a meeting of Margaret Sanger in St. Louis in which I, for the first time in my life, appeared in public to protest the closing of a hall. And, I've been an exponent myself anyhow of every possible aspect of non-interference with private lives. Whether it's sex relations, or whatever, gambling or whatever it was, the right to read a book on "dirty" literature at home if you like, any sex performances you're interested in: government stay out. It was a long time before I read Brandeis's Law Review article way back in 1890, the resurrected leader of the right to be alone, and I realized when I read that, that he really had enunciated a great principle. And it is a principle that has been sanctified by all history. That's been the attitude of people toward government: You let me alone. The government says you've got to support us. Swell. All right, we support you, but that's enough.

Q. The ACLU has really been a defender of the right to privacy in a whole number of areas.

A. I thought we had, although in the beginning we didn't formulate that concept. It was rather instinctive with us that the Bill of Rights is predicated on the notion that Congress has no right to interfere with a whole series of citizen activities; then it also follows that the spirit of the Bill of Rights must enter into the relations of government and people in their private lives. I suppose that assumption accompanied any concept that I had of civil liberties from the very beginning. ("Reminiscences of Roger Nash Baldwin," in the Columbia University Oral History Research Office Collection, with Alan F. Westin, editor, the *Civil liberties Review*, and professor of public law, December 18, 1974, pp. 51–52.)

COOPERATION WITH THE JEHOVAH'S WITNESSES' COUNSEL (1975)

At the other extreme from the Communists and their defense was our participation in the defense of Jehovah's Witnesses and our cooperation with their lawyers. I was never able to establish wholehearted relations with them. They were a remote sort of people, anyhow, wrapped up in their otherworldliness, but determined to get their rights. I had first run into them in the First World War as International Bible Students opposed to conscription and war, but not pacifists, since they were prepared to a man to fight in a war for Jehovah. I had offered our services in their early tangle with the law, and had backed them up by public statements.

Willing to accept us as an ally among the infidels, they were a bit skittish about open cooperation. But they relented. One day I got a telephone call—this must have been in the early or mid-1920s—from the headquarters of the Witnesses in Brooklyn, advising me that their head, Judge Joseph Rutherford, would like to call on me. An appointment was arranged. Judge Rutherford appeared at my office with a retinue of women followers—the very picture, I presume, of Jehovah Himself to his faithful, tall, benign, courteous, dressed in a cutaway with wing collar, spats and carrying a gold-headed cane. He occupied the office as if it were his own. He made his mission clear at once. He said, "I have come to see you to express our appreciation of what you are doing to help our people. I want you to be able to continue it without cost, and so would want to make a contribution for that purpose." I explained that it was our business to help anyone get civil rights and that our supporters expected to use their money for that. "No, no," he said, "I don't want you to tax them for us." He then turned to his secretary and asked if they had any money in the bank. The secretary thought they had. "Well, in that case," he said, "write out a check for a thousand dollars for Mr. Baldwin, and send him another whenever he asks for it." I was somewhat taken aback, but, not being in the habit of refusing honest money for the cause, accepted it. I never asked for the other thousands, though the Witnesses' cases over the years cost us much more than the contribution. (From Collection of Roger R. Baldwin, manuscript draft from Roger N. Baldwin to Alan F. Westin, editor, the *Civil Liberties Review*, for an article on himself, 1975.)

COMMENTARY
Roger Baldwin's Legacy
AN INTERVIEW WITH ANTHONY ROMERO,
EXECUTIVE DIRECTOR, AMERICAN CIVIL LIBERTIES UNION

Q. How would you describe Roger Baldwin's legacy in terms of his founding the ACLU in 1920 as its first executive director—the seat that you now have?

A. It's very humbling to be occupying the job of Roger Baldwin.[1] Roger would have to be a model as one of the greatest American geniuses in his initial vision of what was necessary, his initial belief in what would be possible, in his dogged determination, and his understanding about what was wrong in American society and what could be possible in America. He is one of the true giants of the American twentieth century. The idea that, when you think about it, we have these great founding documents—you go back to the Declaration of Independence in 1776, the Constitution in 1787 and, the ratification of the Bill of the Rights in 1791—but it almost took 140 years before anyone came up with the idea that in order for these to be more than just paper guarantees, someone had to give them life. You have to give them teeth—an enforcement mechanism to take what were principles and convert them into practice. And that was Roger's genius. It was his belief and his understanding about seeing that we were not measuring up to what we had set for ourselves as a nation— at a time when women were not allowed to win the right to vote, at a time when racial segregation was the law of the land, when you had inequality all across the country, and the suppression of dissent and freedom of association, which was not all guaranteed, and the perception and the belief that it could change—that someone had to do something about it, some entity needed to take seriously the enforcement of those rights. We could not leave it to the government for those rights to be self-executed. That is the genius of Roger Baldwin, which continues to this very day—eighty-five years later. That is still the ACLU raison d'etre—we are here to defend everybody's rights and all of their rights. A very simple mission and a very daunting task.

Q. Baldwin left a trail of writings, speeches, letters, messages, interviews—all of his words—what do you think of them?

A. Let's go back. I remember reading some of Roger's earliest papers. When I first came on board, I spent time with our archivist, and the archivists in Princeton. I am the first executive director to come from outside the ACLU in more than thirty years. I felt it was important for me to understand the history going back to Roger's earliest papers. They were vital to my understanding of the mission and history of the ACLU.

Some of the earlier pieces that Roger wrote, especially on World War II, were prophetic. For example, in a press release from "Roger Baldwin, director," on March 1, 1942, right before the Japanese internment issue, Roger mandated that the "West Coast offices of the ACLU assist in protecting the civil rights of Japanese-American citizens." He goes on to write: "The Civil Liberties Union does not have the slightest intention of interfering with moves to protect the West Coast areas. We recognize that as a first and necessary consideration. But we believe it can be done without injustice and abrogation of the civil rights of American citizens. The situation's admittedly delicate, with public prejudice and hysteria demanding action. We are confident, however, that between the public authorities and private agencies, means can be found to obtain the desired results without sacrificing those rights to which American citizens are entitled." The ACLU was one of the few organizations with the courage to challenge President Roosevelt's executive order authorizing the internment of more than one hundred thousand individuals of Japanese ancestry. A full two-thirds of these individuals were American citizens. No charges were brought against them; no hearings were held; no one was told where they were being taken, or how long they would be gone. This issue was not without controversy, even within the ACLU. In fact, it almost tore our organization apart. Thanks to the leadership of our West Coast offices, the ACLU represented Fred Korematsu, a Japanese-American who had been arrested for resisting evacuation. His case went to the Supreme Court in 1944 and was lost in a six-to-three decision in favor of the government. He was forced to join his family in a holding facility for Japanese-Americans on their way to internment camps in Utah. Although he was released after swearing his allegiance to the United States in order to take a job as a welder in Salt Lake City in 1943, it was not until 1983—more than thirty-nine years after the fact—when his case was again presented to the Supreme Court that it correctly decided that the U.S. government had no substantial basis to intern its citizens of Japanese descent.

The wartime internment of Japanese-Americans demonstrated what happens when popular fear and prejudice are allowed to dictate policy, and even good men and women to lose their faith in the Constitution and the Bill of Rights. Let's never forget that this shameful action was approved by three of the greatest names in American liberalism: President Franklin Roosevelt; Earl Warren, who at the time was attorney general of California, and Supreme Court justice Hugo Black. This is almost the same Faustian bargain that we confronted in the United States after 9/11 with the detainees in Guantanamo—and even in the United States itself.

Q. You went to Guantánamo Bay in August of 2004 to see for yourself firsthand what the situation was with the detainees. What did you find?

A. For more than two years, I had been trying to persuade the Pentagon to provide access to Guantánamo Bay, where suspected terrorists were being held amid extraordinarily tight security measures that span the U.S. naval station there. In 2004 the Pentagon granted the request, inviting the ACLU and several other groups to witness the historic military trials. I witnessed history in the making. I was one of forty-nine people inside the military commission courtroom allowed to observe the first military commission in the sixty years since World War II. America's system of justice was on the world stage. The problems that the ACLU had identified from the beginning were borne out in concrete detail.

First, the issues with the lack of an independent review outside the chain of command became particularly clear. Several commissioners had very active roles in the government's war on terror: two with regard to operations in Guantánamo and one with substantial experience in the battlefields in Afghanistan. Second, I found that the rules of evidence were still confused. What we do know is that they are inferior to what's used in military courts-martial. The third problem concerned the inability of defense lawyers to adequately represent their clients' interests, notwithstanding their heroic efforts. The deck is still very much stacked against the defense—the prosecution has many more resources. Another problem that became painfully clear was that only the presiding officer is a lawyer, whereas the other four commissioners are not. The defense counsel did its best to explain concepts like jurisdiction and post hoc, but this wasn't easy and it's certainly put the presiding officer in a greater position of power vis-à-vis the other commissioners. Interestingly enough, all of their votes are supposed to count equally. How can that possibly happen when only one is a lawyer and that lawyer is the presiding officer?

I want to say a word about the good men and women in uniform. Sometimes we civil libertarians see members of the military with suspicion. But let me tell you, some of the best civil libertarians I've met recently are soldiers who believe in due process and are doing their best to conduct a fair trial despite the fatal flaws in this system. They make America look good, because even though they've been dealt a terrible hand, they're defending their clients with all the zeal of a Johnnie Cochran. The prosecution was also quite thoughtful and even-tempered and evenhanded. They make the best of a terrible situation, but our government shouldn't have put them in this situation in the first place. We have a good system of military justice that we should be proud of and we should have used it. The fact that there are men and women in uniform who support this president, who support these commissions, but who also understand the important role of the ACLU, should give all civil libertarians hope. Remember, Ben Franklin was asked after leaving the Constitutional Convention: "What have you wrought?" "A Republic," he answered, "if you can keep it." With patriots like the defense counsel, we may have a fighting chance.

Q. Getting back to Roosevelt and the Japanese, would you say there was an analogy between the Japanese internments of the 1940s and the internment of the detainees in Guantánamo?

A. To some extent. America's leaders unwittingly fanned the flames of prejudice against the detainees, most of whom were captured in Afghanistan. Americans began to express an animosity toward Arabs, in general, in the post-9/11 era. Similarly, Roger Baldwin talked about racial hatred against the Japanese. He wrote in a letter to President Roosevelt on March 20, 1942:

> We are greatly concerned over the execution of your order of February 20, 1942, giving the military authorities power to evacuate from any designated area in the United States all aliens and citizens alike. This unprecedented order, in our judgment, is open to grave question on the constitutional grounds of depriving American citizens of their liberty and use of their property without due process of law. It would appear reasonable to assume that the protection of our country in wartime can be assured without such a wholesale invasion of civil rights and without creating a precedent so opposed to democratic principles.
>
> But quite aside from the constitutional aspect, your order is obviously open to great abuses in administration, for it clothes the military authorities with unchecked power to remove vast populations from areas which in their uncontrolled judgment are declared to be defense zones.

I keep the Baldwin letters right next to my 9/11 files, when I think about people telling me I've got to be "pragmatic" or I've got to be "politically expedient" or "don't you understand the context of what's happening?"

Q. You are using Baldwin's writings as a guide for the present and future?

A. Absolutely. You've got to remember the lessons from the past, and you've got to remember that the mistakes this country has made are ones we ought not repeat, willingly or easily. It took an enormous amount of courage for Roger Baldwin to write this letter on March 20,

1942, where he had the ability to ask this president, saying, I understand you have to protect our country and that you've got a war to
fight, but quite aside from the constititutional aspect—the big "But" he
starts the second paragraph with—that courage has proven an inspiration to me during some of the most difficult periods in my short
tenure here. I just hope to make him proud.

Q. What else did you learn from his writings?

A. I read about the beginning of the ACLU and the types of circumstances Roger Baldwin was confronting—the rise in the Bolshevik
Revolution in 1917, this hostile power that was completely antithetical
to American interests, the way they were challenging fundamentally
American ideology and the American way of life, the thirty-three
bombs that went off in the cities all across the country in 1918, one
going off on the doorstep of the U.S. attorney general, a man named
Mitchell Palmer. You had a growing immigrant population, a bur-
geoning union movement that was beginning to get active, sometimes
violent, and in the middle of that you had this increased unrest and
disorder as a result of the bombs and the immigrant growth. And you
had Palmer unleash the full fury of the Justice Department on immigrants. And it was precisely at that time, in 1918, that Baldwin and
others said we've got to make sure that we create some type of organization that stands up to government excess and to government
abuse. In 1918 they founded the National Civil Liberties Bureau that
two years later was renamed the American Civil Liberties Union.

When you think about that set of circumstances and context, it
is very much the same as the one I confront eighty-odd years later on
9/11. I am on the job a week, where again you have this collapsing law
and order, bombs going off—in this case airplanes being used as bombs
in New York, in Washington, D.C., and in the field in Pennsylvania—
where again there was a concern about some hostile force antithetical
to American interests and American values, where the initial focus of
government scrutiny and the government's efforts were again immigrants—but this time they were not the Russians or the Poles or the
Jews of the Palmer raids. But this time they were Arabs, Muslims,
Asians, and other immigrants.

When you see this, we are precisely confronted with some of the
same sets of challenges that Roger Baldwin confronted in the immediate days of the Palmer raids. And you see that is exactly the fire
out of which the ACLU was born. That's exactly what our missions
is—to defend civil liberties and civil rights at some of the most difficult

periods in our nation's history and to remind the American public and our government and ourselves what it is that we are fighting *for* and not just what we are fighting *against*. And that the mistakes of the Palmer raids, which later on were discredited—were widely supported by the public and Congress at the time because they were seen as a necessary accommodation to deal with collapsing law and order. It was only after the history books were written that we were to learn that a very young, energetic Justice Department official, J. Edgar Hoover, was in charge of the Palmer raids—it was only after we rewrote that history that we realized they were some of the darkest moments in American history, when we deported five thousand plus immigrants who had nothing to do with the bombs. It is ironic that eighty-five years later I am in the same job as Roger, trying to remind the American public of exactly the same lessons. It brought home about why it is that no matter what happens in this country, you're always going to need an ACLU. This isn't a mission that comes and goes. This isn't a mission that will "solve" the problems of our generation and we can call it quits. For as long as you have an American democracy, as long as you have a concern for the Bill of Rights and the Constitution, you are going to need an ACLU. This is a permanent fixture in the American political landscape. Now that is a remarkable accomplishment for Roger to have structured for us. The idea that as long as this country is around, you are going to need an ACLU to take seriously those guarantees and to keep fighting some of the same battles over and over again because every generation comes up against the same set of questions and you need someone with the vigilance and the doggedness, and the determination and the memory to engage it with the same principles that he would want.

Q. What do you think he would say today if he were to suddenly come back for a day in your seat and face all the problems you face?

A. He would probably say, "You've got to do more." He's right. I think he would be proud, but I think he would feel we have a lot more work to do.

Q. What is the line that should not be crossed in defending national security against foreign or domestic terrorism?

A. I think you have to start with wanting to advance both. Because if you set them up as an either/or, you are setting up a Faustian bargain where you are asked to give up one in return for the other. You have to remember that you need to keep the American democratic experiment alive and well. You certainly need safety. You certainly need security. You need to make sure that that's an obligation that only the government can fulfill. The ACLU does not quarrel with the fact that the government has to play that role. It has that responsibility to us. But—and ours is a very important but—if it does so, it must do so in a way that comports with the best of American values. It must do so in a way that is in line with the Constitution, and that safeguards our freedoms and other liberties, and shows that our courts and that our judges and that our freedoms and our liberties were not the cause of 9/11. They are not the obstacle in the war on terror. They are part of the solution. And that as you engage the war on terror, you need to have as much regard and as much engagement with those core democratic institutions—congressional oversight, judicial review, protection of due process, a system of checks and balances. That's got to be as much a part of the government's effort in fighting terrorism as any national intelligence information, any search or any seizure. If we cut corners on these core values, then we will do much more damage than we should.

Q. How are you going about taking this heritage that you have inherited and trying to make the impact that you want?

A. I think the fact that the whole debate now is one that focuses on national security and civil liberties is a sign of our success. And that is a real testament to Roger Baldwin and his vision and his genius. The fact is that there is now enough recognition that you've got to keep these issues alive and well in the public debate, that if you give it short shrift you will do damage to some core American values. That's a sign, I think, that we have come a long way in four years. And I say that with enormous pride in the work of this organization. Now that the debate has been framed on our terms, where you don't have to run and catch up and say, "Wait a minute, what about civil liberties?"— the fact that they willingly now have to engage you on a national concern for civil liberties shows you how far we have come. That has everything to do with the success of the ACLU and our allies. Now, where we end up is another matter. There are still ways at times in which politicians will use popular fear and prejudice to give ammunition to an agenda that has the people give up their civil liberties and basic rights. That's the war we are fighting. Now we've got to talk about it much more clearly to the American public—how we achieve both. Making sure that we not give up more than we should, that we strike the right balance between making sure that we protect our freedoms and that we advance national security.

Q. You must be chagrined by the reputation that the United States has today compared to when you took office just prior to 9/11 in 2001. How do you see this damage and how can it be repaired?

A. The damage to our reputation worldwide is something that I don't think in my life I will see be fully restored, frankly. I've talked with friends and colleagues who still talk about, for instance, some of the human rights violations that happened during World War II, where public sentiment against Germans or the Japanese or the Italians is sometimes very hard to undo because people remember. What will we say to future generations of Iraqis who remember how American soldiers tortured their men and women? How will we be able to justify that when we stare the world community in the face and we say that we uphold the best of the values of human rights, so that they don't think us to be hypocrites, that those are rules that don't apply to others, they only apply for us? And I think it will be a long time before we regain some of that lost ground. This administration has squandered so much that was possible, so much that was good in the midst of the tragedy of 9/11.

Frankly, I find it remarkable that the Bush administration has always had hostility to the rule of law and to international law in a way that was truly un-American. We have to remember where these documents came from. The Universal Declaration of Human Rights is one of the great patrimonies of American foreign policy. It was Eleanor Roosevelt who was deployed in 1948 as an extension of the American government, which said, "Okay, let's take the best of these principles that we find in our Constitution in the Bill of Rights and let's talk about these universal values and let's enshrine them in this Universal Declaration of Human Rights and its two international covenants— Civil and Political Rights, and Economic, Social, and Cultural Rights. Those were documents that emerged from the American democratic experience. And now we have this administration trying to shun those documents, trying to shun those universal values, trying to undo what was the genius of American foreign policy and American leadership in a very difficult period when the world required that leadership of us. We fought World War II for human rights and that's why we got into the war. We fought it because of the gross violations of human rights and that part of the rebuilding that was necessary after World War II was not just the rebuilding of Berlin and the cities of Western Europe— part of the rebuilding was the rebuilding of the fabric for the protection of human rights. And we did so by putting in place institutions and legal documents that articulated the best of those values.

Q. Where did the detainees in the U.S. military installation at Guantánamo Bay, Cuba, fit into your priorities?

A. Our priorities have to be about defending civil liberties in the United States. But controversies like the detainees held at Guantánamo were high on my list as well. I went to Guantánamo in August of 2004 to observe the proceedings. The ACLU was one of the groups invited to observe the military commission on Guantánamo. We have serious doubts that the commissions—the way they were constructed—were giving sufficient due process protections to the accused men in front of these commissions. Hundreds of people called enemy combatants by the U.S. government languished in legal limbo at Guantánamo Bay. With no access to the courts, or legal counsel, these policies were fundamentally lawless and trespassed on our most deeply held values of fairness and basic due process. I observed them firsthand. We went to see for ourselves. I observed the first series of preliminary hearings for the commissions, which are different from the hearings that opened for business in July of 2004. Those dealt with the status of several detainees and found that they were all rightfully detained indefinitely as "enemy combatants."

While granting the public limited access to the military commissions is a step in the right direction, that alone will not fix the serious civil liberties problems: Key evidence can be kept secret by the prosecution, the only venue for appeal is up the chain of command, and defense attorneys will be hamstrung by bad procedure and lack of privilege. These are not full and fair trials in keeping with the best of American traditions.

Q. Has your membership gone up as a result of 9/11 and the ensuing government actions affecting civil liberties?

A. Yes, it has. When I took over, the membership was about 300,000. Today we estimate it stands about 450,000 or so; we have seen almost a 50 percent growth in membership since September 11. What that shows us is the fact that people are concerned, that this is a time when they realize what's at stake. Members are much more than checkbook participants, not just people who write a check to a charity. They joined the ACLU because they believe in its cause and they are joining a mission, they are taking a stand. People really do see it as being more than just giving to a charity. This is about joining a political movement for civil liberties, and that political movement is not partisan, it's immigrants and it's citizens, it's young and old, it's male and female, it's black, white, and Latino, and that is the power of this, of the card-carrying members of the ACLU that gives us strength. Just like we don't para-chute in and out of local communities, we're also not a funded special interest group. We represent hundreds of thousands of Americans. And when we lobby on their behalf, we speak for a bigger audi-ence than just ourselves. That's what gives us the political muscle in Congress—to say, you cross paths with the ACLU and you cross paths not just with a powerful, litigating, lobbying, public education group, you cross paths with its hundreds of thousands of members. We will hold you accountable. We will hold your feet to the fire. We will kick up the dust if we need to. Politicians of either party who avoid discussion of the critical issues, who avoid taking a position, and who avoid criticism are doing a disservice to the American people. They are rob-bing the people of the opportunity to understand the issues clearly and meaningfully. They are also depriving the nation of the opportunity to build a broad consensus in defense of freedom and liberty.

Q. What are the four or five most important issues that you spend your time on?

A. Number one is the erosion of civil liberties in the name of national security. That has permeated much of what we have done.

I'd say, number two would be a shutting down of dissent and de-bate in America in a way that is most unfortunate for the democratic process, that no matter what happens, you have to make sure you have robust debates. We've all heard of the FBI surveillance and in-terrogation of people who protested at the conventions, the Secret Ser-vice corralling people into free speech zones, the denial of protesters who want to protest the wars, protest the conventions, the sending home of teenagers from high school because they say, "Bush is a ter-rorist." It's a lockdown of dissent and debate, a tone set at the very highest levels of our government.

Third would obviously be the continued persistence of race and the unequal playing field in America based on race and national origin. We are still not a society where the playing field is equal. That's be-come even more apparent in the aftermath of 9/11, where race and religion are used as proxies for suspicion.

Fourth, I would say with the encroachment of government into re-ligious life, where you have the government funding religion, and the government meddling with religious affairs, and activities of religious institutions. That is a very dangerous thing for a country as diverse and pluralistic as this one. The reason why you don't want the government to meddle into the religious affairs of its people is because once it begins to meddle in those affairs, you lose religious freedom and religious independence. The best way to observe diversity and the ability to worship any God you want or no God at all is to make sure that the government is not involved in those personal transactions. We have now an administration that seems unconcerned about the political fallout of involving itself in the private affairs of Americans.

I would say those are the top four. There will always be a need to fight issues as they come up and as this generation proceeds. For us now, we have continuous struggles right over the rights of lesbians and gay men, whether or not they are afforded full equality, full equal rights in a way that is appropriate given our democracy. That struggle has come a long way in my short life, but we have a long way to go still. We're still fighting over some basic privacy issues, that have to do with surveillance, through the computer or private entities or through the government, or even still efforts to erode personal privacy in the context of reproductive freedom and reproductive rights where this administration is challenging a woman's fundamental right to choice. So the battles are on many fronts. We have to fight them all. We don't have the luxury of other organizations, which say, it's not my issue, it's not my target group. Not my problem, when your mission is to defend everybody's rights and defend all of those rights, you've got to do the best you can. You have to prioritize; you have to fight a smart battle and you have to find allies where you can get them. You have to take that mission at its core.

Q. How worried are you about our government tipping toward an autocratic, all-powerful entity that strikes fear in the hearts of its citizens? What is there to prevent such an outcome?

A. I think the safeguards reside with the people. They reside in informed democracy, where dissent and debate is encouraged, where a system of checks and balances and judicial review and congressional branch action is alive and well. I think if you begin to let those important checks fall, then you are going to find that this is not the democracy you know and love.

Q. What do you say to the image that some critics have of the ACLU as a bunch of longhaired, pot-smoking hippies who haven't grown out of the 1960s?

A. I think this organization stands for the most basic of American values. These are mainstream values. These are not radical, fringe "lefty" values, these are basic values about defending the Constitution and the Bill of Rights. No matter who you are, you have certain rights that nobody can take away from you. That no matter what you believe, or what you think or what you say, you have a right to think and say and believe what you will. The role of government is not to intrude upon the private lives of its people, but to allow each of us to live life with dignity. That doesn't seem to be a left or liberal ideology. That applies as much to the Ku Klux Klan or the Nazi marchers as it applies to business leaders as it applies to the NAACP or the Republicans or the Democrats.

Q. The ACLU has defended other unpopular groups under the umbrella of defending everybody's right to speak. How do you see that in terms of your image?
A. We need to do a better job of explaining who we are, and what we do and how we do it and why we do it so a larger portion of the American public understands it. Sometimes we are up against very deep odds because most people don't fully know the work we do. For instance, yes it's true we have been fighting this whole question of prayer in the schools because we think there should not be an official prayer, that this is a country of many different religions and viewpoints and you can't have one religion governing the population. But we also recently took a case of a local ordinance that was banning a religious group from conducting baptisms in a river in a state park. We say that if you allow people to bathe in that water, and if you allow people to go swimming, then you've got to allow people to perform baptisms. Most folks won't know about that second case. That's a case my mother cites when she says the church ladies are concerned that the ACLU is antireligious or anti-God. I say, Ma, let me explain this case. I think we have to do much more.

Some of the history of the ACLU I am very proud of. I am not going to run away from the fact that this is an organization that grew its strength as an opposition movement, in opposition to the war in Vietnam, in opposition to J. Edgar Hoover, the McCarthy scare, and that some of the people who were courageous enough to stand up to the government at that time came from a certain political ideology, came from a certain viewpoint, willing to take a stand. We ought not be embarrassed by that. That is as much about who we are as the investment bankers who are now part of the ACLU. We are as much the ACLU of the hippies and the pot-smoking antigovernment section of society as we are for the button-down, Greenwich, Connecticut, multibillion-dollar investment bankers who say, "But for the ACLU, government power and government abuse could be much greater and could fall on my head as well."

That is the ACLU. We are everybody's ACLU. If we are not perceived as reaching all the people, not perceived as reaching that broad orbit of individuals who span the political spectrum, span the religious and ethnic and racial spectrum, then we have work to do to help them realize that's what we are all about.

Q. Since you took this job in 2001, what have been your biggest surprises?

A. I came in very enthusiastic, a little afraid, did not know what to expect. I remain very enthusiastic, a little less afraid, but what I realize is that this organization is the secular church for a lot of people. The ACLU is their defining value system. It's not just a nonprofit. It's not just a bunch of lawyers and lobbyists and grassroots organizers. This is about the best of our defining values and for many of our members this is what they most believe in. If there is one surprise I have had, it is just how much trust is given to those of us who are privileged enough to serve the ACLU. People not only expect it of you, they demand it of you, and that is a very humbling job to have. It's not just humbling because I follow in the footsteps of some great giants, people like Roger Baldwin, Ira Glasser [executive director, 1982–89] and Aryeh Neier [executive director, 1970–78]. That's daunting enough. But when you think about how much is vested in the mission and cause of the ACLU, how much people believe in it, how much people expect the ACLU to lead in difficult times no matter what the circumstances or what the controversies, that is a remarkable endeavor.

Q. Have you dared to dream of what kind of things you see possible in the future? What is it that you are a little bit afraid of?

A. The odds are so daunting. The work is so expansive to accomplish and, you know, when you have a mission set out for you in terms of defending everybody's rights, that's a mission that should make anybody afraid. That's your job description, your job mandate. But I do see an enormous opportunity. I have an echoing voice of Roger. He was very old in life, in his nineties at this point, in one of the videos that gives the history of the ACLU, where I, too, "travel hopefully" with the ACLU. As Baldwin put it: "I have been traveling hopefully and I am still traveling hopefully. And so is the ACLU. And someday, sometime—for the goal is clear—and the road is hard and progress painful, will we ever approach, we are beginning to approach a tolerable world of peace, order and justice."

That is what Roger said. When I think about how far we have come in eighty-some-odd years and where we will be eighty more years hence, it's daunting, it's scary to think about how much we have yet to realize. But when we think about how much we have accomplished, and realize that with the strength of this history and with the best and the brightest of the country we must get this work done, you understand that failure is never an option.

NOTES

1. Interview with the author on August 16, 2004, updated on September 2, 2005.

COMMENTARY
Roger Turned Out to Be the Realist
IRA GLASSER

On the day Roger Baldwin died, in 1981, I wrote a statement for the ACLU that attempted to encapsulate his importance. "Roger Baldwin," I wrote, "was in a way one of this country's Founding Fathers. They invented the Bill of Rights, and he invented a way to enforce it."

What did I mean by that?

The Bill of Rights was ratified as part of the Constitution on December 15, 1791. Nearly 130 years later, in 1920, when Baldwin and a few colleagues started the ACLU, the Bill of Rights was a dormant document. James Madison had fretted, during the original debate over whether to have a Bill of Rights, that even if passed, it would likely be little more than a "parchment barrier" to tyranny, least useful when it was most necessary. And indeed, until relatively recently in our history, he was right.

Only seven years after the Bill of Rights, including the First Amendment, was passed, Congress passed the Alien and Sedition Act, one of the most blatant violations of First Amendment rights in our history. Yet the First Amendment provided no relief; it was indeed a parchment barrier.

And what was true in 1798 remained true. At the time the ACLU was founded, the Supreme Court had never once struck down a single law or government action on First Amendment grounds. And in the years immediately preceding the founding of the ACLU, another Sedition Act had been passed and, along with the Espionage Act, used brutally to repress and imprison antiwar activists and labor activists.

And local laws everywhere repressed dissent on other issues; for example, Margaret Sanger, the founder of Planned Parenthood and a friend of Baldwin's, was regularly arrested on the streets of New York in the years before the ACLU began for distributing information about birth control.

What was true about the First Amendment was also true about the full range of rights ostensibly protected by the Bill of Rights. Illegal searches were common, for example, and the Fourth Amendment was not as a practical matter available to help.

Finally, entire groups of people most in need of the Bill of Rights were initially excluded from its protections: blacks, whom the law did not even see as human prior to the Civil War; women, who were denied the right to vote until 1920; and everyone whose rights were violated by state and local officials (because initially the Bill of Rights applied only to the federal government).

What was missing from the Founders' initial formulation was a mechanism for enforcement. If one looks at all the Supreme Court cases between 1791 and 1920, there are virtually no civil liberties cases invoking the Constitution to be found, except in a small number of cases, where constitutional issues were raised during the course of commercial corporate litigation. The reason is not hard to discern: The people most in need of the Bill of Rights were so pervasively powerless and vulnerable that in most cases, they did not know they had rights; were not able to hire a lawyer or afford the considerable costs of litigation; and in any event, few lawyers in private practice were prepared to take on the discomfort of defending pariahs and unpopular causes.

Baldwin changed all that when he established the ACLU. Along with the NAACP, established in 1909, and the rise of labor unions, after 1920 cases began to be brought into court systematically raising, for the first time, questions involving limits on government authority set forth in the Bill of Rights and the Civil War Amendments.

Because all these organizations were small and had few resources, it took awhile for the tide to begin to turn. But turn it did, so that by the mid-1970s, the Bill of Rights was the source for a wide range of enforceable rights nearly unimaginable in 1920. Many would say that the ACLU came of age shortly after it was founded when, in 1924, Baldwin got Clarence Darrow and Arthur Garfield Hays to agree to defend John Scopes, who was being prosecuted for teaching evolution in Dayton, Tennessee—a case that would probably not otherwise have been defended, certainly not vigorously. With that case, the ACLU was off and running. It was for many years the ACLU's most famous case, and nearly six decades later, shortly before he died, Baldwin liked to tell me, with a mischievous gleam in his eye, that it was *"still the ACLU's most famous case!"*

Indeed, on the day in March 1981 when *The New York Times* published a story about Arkansas having passed a law requiring the biblical story of how God created the world to be taught in science classes wherever evolution was taught, Baldwin called me at ten minutes past nine that morning and asked whether I had seen the story. When I said I had, he said, loudly and accusingly: "Well, what are you doing about it?" I laughed and said it was only a few minutes after 9:00 A.M., but that we would undoubtedly challenge it. He harrumphed and left the phone, making me feel as if I had betrayed not only his legacy but Jefferson's and Madison's as well by my failure to have arranged to strike down the statute that same morning!

Later, after we had taken the case and months had gone by, Baldwin called again to get a status report, and I mentioned that we had ten lawyers working on the case. "TEN lawyers!" he boomed. "We only needed two." Yes, I replied, by then finding it fun to joust with this extraordinary man whose passion was, in his ninety-eighth year, undiminished, "Yes, Roger, but you lost the Scopes case!"

Eventually we won the Arkansas case and struck down the statute, but by that time Roger had died and he never knew the result. A couple of years later, when a similar ACLU case from Louisiana reached the U.S. Supreme Court, which ruled in our favor and struck down the creationist laws as violations of the separation of church and state, I was quoted in the press as saying that "Somewhere in heaven, John Scopes is smiling." And later I would think that it would be nice to imagine Clarence Darrow, Arthur Garfield Hays, and Roger toasting the victory over a glass of sherry.

The path from Scopes to the creationist cases demonstrated Roger's incredible persistence, and his irrepressible optimism as well. He had, as a young man, held a press conference in 1924 to announce that the ACLU—then a tiny, little-known new organization—would be defending John Scopes' right to academic freedom, during a time of stifling fundamentalism and in the teeth of a Supreme Court that was yet to even once vindicate the First Amendment in its rulings. Fifty-seven years later, I asked him to be the spokesman to announce our challenge to the Arkansas creationism case, and he agreed, relishing the ACLU's stamina and his own.

A few weeks before he died, I visited him on his farm in New Jersey; he was pretty much chairbound by then by terminal emphysema brought on by a bout of double pneumonia a year earlier that would have killed most men his age. He offered me a glass of sherry and apologized for the fact that I would have to get it myself. I asked him how he was doing and he said, "Aside from the fact that I can't breathe, I'm feeling fine."

I noticed that even this close to death, he was reading a very long and dense book, Henry Kissinger's autobiography, looking forward, not giving an inch more than he was forced to give. I remember wondering whether he was likely to finish it, and whether I would be bothering with such a book at such a moment in my life.

He asked me how the ACLU was doing—it was 1981; Ronald Reagan had just been elected; Ed Meese was the attorney general; Strom Thurmond had just become the chair of the Senate Judiciary Committee, and Jerry Falwell and his Moral Majority were riding high. I expressed a bit of despair about the future of civil liberties and received an upbeat response from Roger, full of optimism.

It was then that I realized how demoralizing it can be to view things over a short term during troubling times, and why a realist like Roger could be so optimistic. He simply saw further than the rest of us. We realize that today more than ever as we contemplate his vision and his words in perspective.

He looked back upon a time, when he was about my age, when Jim Crow segregation, and the state-sponsored terrorism that enforced it, seemed unlikely ever to be undone; when women could not even vote, much less enjoy equality of opportunity in education and employment; when reproductive freedom yielded to arrests for the distribution of information on birth control; when dissent was an enforceable crime; when the rights of gay people were so far below the radar that they were impossible even to discuss; and when the U.S. Supreme Court seemed so hopeless as a protector of civil liberties that early ACLU strategies advocated not going into court.

By the time Roger faced death, all that had changed, in ways nearly unimaginable when he and the ACLU began. His vision in 1920, and his persistence in carrying that vision forward in the decades after, might well have seemed delusional to most "realists" back then. But it was Roger who turned out to be the realist, and it pleases me that he lived long enough to know it, and to pass that lesson on to those of us left to face other terrible, but hardly hopeless, times.

————————

Ira Glasser, immediate predecessor of Anthony Romero—current executive director of the American Civil Liberties Union—worked with Roger N. Baldwin for many years.

Introduction to Chapter 3

> *The chief danger to American democracy today arises from the
> demand that dissent be suppressed in the interest of defense and
> national unity.*
>
> —Roger N. Baldwin, 1941

Roger Baldwin's periodic warnings all during the twentieth century of
the dangers of curtailing civil liberties in time of war were reflected in
his writings, his speeches, and in his public role as executive director of
the American Civil Liberties Union. This theme occurs again and again
during the many decades in which he represented the ACLU and,
subsequently, the International League for the Rights of Man, later
known as the International League for Human Rights. At the dawn of
this twenty-first century, with Baldwin having passed on, his warnings
of the danger of infringement on individual rights in time of war still
echo in the hearts and minds of those who continue to defend the Bill
of Rights. There have been many presidents in American history who
have, in time of crisis, violated the rights of citizens during wartime.[1]

All of America's previous wartime presidents—Abraham Lincoln,
Woodrow Wilson, Franklin D. Roosevelt, Harry S. Truman, Lyndon B.
Johnson, and Richard M. Nixon—each took different approaches in
very different circumstances to managing the delicate balance between
protecting the nation from foreign threats and the constitutional responsibility of maintaining individual freedoms. But the one thread
that can be found in all of them was that while the issue was thrashed
out again and again over the years, our nation as a people was strong
enough to withstand the challenges and to restore, inevitably, the
generations-old American heritage of living up to the foundation of

our democracy—the Bill of Rights, the foundation upon which Roger Baldwin built his life's work.

Abraham Lincoln's prime mission, history has shown, was to keep the Union together. Above all, Lincoln feared that a civil war would not only destroy the union, but also basically reduce the U.S. Constitution to mere words without meaning. After the eleven Confederate states had seceded, Lincoln took what these days would appear to be unthinkable steps: starting with the raising of funds by issuing bonds as well as imposing many unpopular taxes on the masses—a grab bag of measures that included increased tariffs, excise taxes, and taxes on virtually everything that was sold daily to the public. With the increased revenue he was able to create an enlarged fighting force, through conscription as well as volunteers, armed with the best equipment money could buy in those days. It logically followed that Lincoln took additional steps to beef up internal security so that the government and the people would be safe from spies, bomb-throwers, armed dissidents, and other treasonous individuals or groups. Strange as it may sound today, Lincoln was arguably the first president to establish a Secret Service to ensure his personal safety, and a cadre of federal marshals and an informal organization of informants to keep him aware of threats against the Union as well.

In 1862, Lincoln issued two directives that forever changed the face of America: first was the Emancipation Proclamation; the second suspended the right to be brought before a court to decide the legality of a charge against a defendant—known as habeas corpus—and ordered military trials for all "Rebels and Insurgents [and] their aiders and abettors within the United States, charged with discouraging volunteer enlistments or revisiting the drafts or found guilty "of any disloyal practice."[2] Lincoln also imposed martial law in some states and instructed marshals to arrest and detain in jail without trial anyone—including elected public officials, and even some judges—who appeared to obstruct the Union's war measures.

As a result, Lincoln was accused of everything from being a dictator and a tyrant to encouraging the Negroes and white races to mix—a repulsive concept totally abhorred by the vast majority of whites in America at that time. The war got worse before it got better. By 1864—when Lincoln was up for reelection—the Union's commanders had taken extraordinary steps that would leave a permanent stain on Lincoln as arguably the most vilified president in American history. Some Northerners, in sympathy with the South, took actions that make the administration of George W. Bush look relatively harmless in terms of civil liberties: They closed down newspapers. So, too, did the War Department, which barred what it called "treasonable" papers from the mails because they contained stories about the military. Interestingly, despite imposing measures that would seem drastic and virtually unacceptable today, Lincoln was later seen by historians as relatively mild in suppressing what he perceived to be opposition to the Union. The reasoning: his strong public commitment to adhere to the Constitution, especially when it came to civil liberties and his opposition to discrimination and prejudice. There had been no judicial precedents laid out by the United States Supreme Court and there was no background of judicial records on the nature and limit of civil liberties in wartime.

Woodrow Wilson may have been the worst offender when it came to civil liberties. He was the first president to commit American troops to an overseas war and, as such, came under fire for not fully explaining to the voters why he had gotten the United States involved in World War I in the first place. His entry into a European war, as many historians saw it, came after a generation of Americans had emigrated from European countries, including Germany. Thus by allying America with England against Germany, many Americans held the view that Germany's imperialism in Europe was not that much different than that in Great Britain and France.

In order to fight this war, Wilson took certain unpopular measures including denying use of the mails to publications that might "embarrass" the government, a major mobilization of American troops, and a vast enlargement of industrial production. Further. He also took steps to regulate aspects of the economy such as pricing in certain defense businesses, controlling war-related factories, and empowering the government to operate rail and water transport. All of these actions turned the United States into a country on a war footing similar to Germany, France, and Great Britain.

Freedom of expression was also curbed by the government—the postmaster general confiscated anything that even remotely appeared to show disloyalty to the country, the secretary of war rounded up conscientious objectors and assigned noncombatant jobs to those who did not wish to fight. Worst of all, perhaps, two major pieces of legislation were passed by Congress at Wilson's request, both of which became historical examples of stringent violations of the Constitution: First was the passage of the Espionage Act in 1917 that completely suppressed any opposition to the war, including publication of any information that could be helpful to the enemy; the second was the

Sedition Act of 1918, which gave the attorney general the power to find and arrest anyone who publicly verbally or in writing criticized the war effort, the government's policies, the armed forces, the Constitution, the military uniform, and even the United States flag. A brand-new Bureau of Investigation, forerunner of the Federal Bureau of Investigation, was formed to seek out a variety of perceived threats to the war effort, including those identified as pacifists, members of socialist and Communist parties, the International Workers of the World, a trade union of which Roger Baldwin was a member, and various other organizations that had spontaneously been formed to defend citizens' rights.

Yet another legislative inhibitor was the Trading with the Enemy Act of 1917, which "authorized the government to confiscate and hold enemy property in the United States; regulate the conduct of enemy aliens residing in the country; censor communications by mail, cable, radio, or otherwise with foreign countries; and control the nation's foreign language press, a provision falling heavily on Yiddish and German papers in particular."

In addition, the Alien Act of 1918 permitted the deportation of alien anarchists—those who believed in the violent overthrow of the government, or advocates of assassination of public officials. The Wilson administration even had its own internal security program. One day after declaring war on Germany, the president ordered the heads of departments and independent offices to remove any employee whose behavior provided "grounds for believing that his retention was inimical to the public welfare." Even after the Armistice on November 11, 1918, the Wilson administration was still at risk on the home front, where many leaders became intensely concerned about rebuilding the economy, on strikes and on continued deportations of enemy aliens. One frightening incident, a bomb explosion in front of Attorney General A. Mitchell Palmer's home, gave birth to a General Intelligence Division inside the Justice Department to find and arrest radicals.

Then came the famous "Red scare" raids by Attorney General A. Mitchell Palmer, led with precision attacks by a young agent, J. Edgar Hoover, against labor leaders, anarchists, socialists, and Communists, using widespread beatings, thousands of arrests, and hundreds of deportations. When Warren Harding and the Republicans regained the White House in 1920, the suppression finally let up and, with the assistance of Supreme Court decisions—principally the "clear and present danger" doctrine of Justice Oliver Wendell Holmes and Justice

Louis Brandeis—the administration laid the groundwork as safeguards for the future.

Franklin Delano Roosevelt, revered in American history as one of its greatest presidents, himself succumbed to questionable tactics—at least from a civil libertarian's viewpoint—even before the official outbreak of World War II. After the Germans conquered France and were in a life-and-death struggle with the British, Secretary of State Cordell Hull got Roosevelt's blessing to fingerprint aliens applying for visas, and also persuaded the president to sign the Smith Act, which required aliens to register; it also authorized wiretaps against "anyone suggested of subversive activities."[3]

Following the unprovoked Japanese attack on Pearl Harbor on December 7, 1941, FDR gave some thought to creating a system of censorship against those who would criticize the government, but he thought better of the idea and dropped it. However, he did direct FBI director J. Edgar Hoover to investigate any publications that were pacifist, socialist, pro-fascist, or even isolationist. In fact, Attorney General Francis Biddle used both the Espionage Act and the Sedition Acts against more than one hundred individuals for abusing their right to free speech—an action that undoubtedly would be frowned upon today, and certainly rejected by the U.S. Supreme Court. Roosevelt, arguably the first of the "great communicators" in the White House, created an Office of War Information, which "sold" Americans on the war and produced the well-remembered "Why We Fight" documentaries.

What stands out today as one of the worst violations of individual civil liberties—aside from slavery—in the nation's history was what looked like a routine wartime executive order issued by Roosevelt in February 1942 directing Secretary of War Henry Stimson to select military sections of the country where "people of Japanese origin should be excluded." With the nation—and the West Coast in particular—in such a state of high anxiety following the attack, the order was carried out by the military in the extreme. Some 120,000 Japanese-Americans, living normal lives, were deprived of their personal liberty, rounded up in every community in or near California, and banished to detention camps. A few brave souls—most notably Fred Korematsu[4]—eventually backed by the ACLU, challenged the constitutionality of the detentions, but without immediate success. Italian and German aliens were required to register as aliens of "enemy nationality" and were dispersed throughout the nation, but no practical action was taken to contain them. Years later, in 1976, Baldwin would admit in an interview: "One of the few persistent criticisms of the ACLU record has been that we initially failed to challenge the government's wartime executive order to remove the entire Japanese population, aliens and citizens alike, from the West Coast states."[5]

The United States fought World War II by drafting 10 million soldiers and signing up an additional 6 million who volunteered. There were those, of course, who tried to get out of serving—the government convicted 16,000 found guilty of evading the draft—and other controls, upheld by the Supreme Court, were put upon the civilian population, such as investigations by the army's newly created Counter-Intelligence Corps of individuals working in defense plants or in sensitive defense industry jobs.

Harry S. Truman sent American troops into an altogether different kind of war—overseas in Korea, a tiny nation little known to Americans, but which faced a hostile takeover by Communist North Korea. The "domino theory" was the rationale for going to war in that distant land. But instead of declaring war, Truman called it a "police action," under the auspices of the United Nations. He reinstated the draft, raised taxes, and expanded government regulation of industry. With a draft in effect, thousands of Selective Service draftees sought conscientious objector status (in the tradition of Roger Baldwin's refusal to serve in World War I) and thousands of others were granted academic deferments for pursuing graduate degrees in college and universities.

Truman not only defended his reason for going to war, he emboldened the soldiers in battle by calling it everyone's "patriotic duty" to support the troops. He also initiated a "loyalty program" for federal employees and insisted on prosecuting draft-dodgers. On the plus side, Truman goes down in history as the president who integrated the armed forces. His executive order on July 26, 1948, stated, simply: "It is hereby declared to be the policy of the president that there shall be equality of treatment and opportunity for all persons in the armed services without regard to race, color, religion or national origin."[6]

Lyndon B. Johnson will always be remembered by historians as the president who escalated the tragic Vietnam War, even though his early focus was on President John F. Kennedy's original bill to secure voting rights for blacks. The Civil Rights Act of 1964 and the Voting Acts of 1965 were milestones, which Johnson was able to get Congress to pass. Still, it was the antiwar protest movement that gained most of the attention in the late-1960s. Johnson took little action to repress the demonstrators, mostly because his succession of three progressive attorney generals—Robert F. Kennedy, Nicholas deB. Katzenbach, and

Ramsey Clark—were themselves highly sympathetic with the antiwar movement. Johnson's Great Society program over time dissipated as the war took center stage.

———

During Richard M. Nixon's tenure in the White House, shortened by the threat of impeachment when he resigned in 1974, the power of the presidency was illegally used to shield him from the "Watergate" scandal, which erupted into a congressional inquiry. But aside from his own personal abuse of power and bad-mouthing of protesters involved in the anti–Vietnam War movement, he was not seen as a president who violated the civil liberties of the citizens in wartime.

Many political observers have charged that the administration of George W. Bush has intruded on Americans' civil liberties in the post-9/11 years of his presidency. The USA Patriot Act ("Uniting and Strengthening America by Providing Appropriate Tools Required to Intercept and Obstruct Terrorism") was designed to favor the protection of national security over individual rights. However, it was seen by many as containing dangerous invasive powers that gave the attorney general the legal grounds to eavesdrop on suspects, conduct searches, and track Internet communications and library records of individuals. These constraints alarmed civil libertarians because the act compromised an individual's constitutionally guaranteed right to privacy. In addition, the military tribunals for trying "unlawful combatants" who are not American citizens were viewed by White House watchers as raising serious questions about presidential authority eclipsing the jurisdiction of the federal courts; further, the issue of the U.S. military's treatment of enemy combatants in Afghanistan and Iraq, as well as thousands of men sent to Guantánamo, raised serious questions of a possible breach of international law and the Geneva Convention's rules prohibiting torture. At home, the Bush administration was seen as arbitrarily protecting the president against criticism by screening crowds wherever he traveled to make certain that only those individuals who supported the president could gain entrance to so-called "town meetings." In addition, protest-free zones were created to prevent any individual or crowd from getting too close to the president's motorcade when he made appearances across the nation at so-called "Republican-friendly venues."

In addition, the president aroused the ire of civil libertarians with his secret, warrantless wiretapping spying program by the National Security Agency of e-mail and phone calls between American citizens and suspected terrorists overseas. The president's action was uncovered by *The New York Times* and touched off a firestorm across the political spectrum. Bush defended it by labeling it a "terrorist surveillance program" and argued that Congress' authorization to use force in Afghanistan and Iraq in 2002 allowed him to take such measures. He said Congress gave him the authority to use "all necessary force" to protect the American people. He also argued that he had such powers under the constitution as commander-in-chief. Critics pointed out the irony of Bush fighting in behalf of liberty in Afghanistan and Iraq while abusing precious liberties here at home.

Yet, as concerned as the civil libertarians were about what appeared to be drastic measures to prevent terrorists from operating within America's borders, it is clear from looking back in history that the Bush administration's actions were the latest in a series of historical precedents that revealed a pattern of favoring internal security over individual rights in the name of "national security" in time of war.

Perhaps the most important lesson that history has taught us about the endangerment of civil liberties when America is at war is summed up by Roger Baldwin in his writings on the following pages: "Only the most scrupulous defense of every attack on the Bill of Rights can guarantee in time of war as in peace that we will emerge . . . with our testimony to our democratic faith intact."[7]

—W. K.

NOTES

1. Revised and adapted from *America's Wartime Presidents: Politics, National Security, and Civil Liberties,* by Jerome M. Mileur and Ronald Story, pp. 95–127; chapter 3, "Civil Liberties," in *Politics of Terror: The U.S. Response To 9/11,* ed. William Crotty (Boston: Northeastern University Press, 2004).

2. Ibid., 97.

3. Ibid., 106.

4. Ibid., 108, 144–45. Fred T. Korematsu, a native of Oakland, California, and one of four sons of Japanese-born parents, was jailed on May 30, 1942, in San Leandro, having refused to join family members who had reported to a nearby racetrack that was being used as a temporary detention center. Korematsu had been working as a welder and simply hoped to be left alone. A few days after his arrest, Korematsu was visited in jail by a California official of the American Civil Liberties Union who was seeking a test case against the government's internment

program that came as a result of President Franklin D. Roosevelt's Executive Order 9066, which sent 120,000 Japanese-Americans on the West Coast to internment camps, without evidence of any wrongdoing, after the Japanese attack on Pearl Harbor. Roosevelt's order authorized the designation of military areas from which anyone could be excluded "as protection against espionage and sabotage." In the summer of 1942, Korematsu agreed to sue. He was found guilty in federal court of ignoring the exclusion directive and was sentenced to five years' probation. He spent two years at an internment camp in Utah with his family. In December 1944, in *Korematsu v. the United States*, the Supreme Court upheld internment by a vote of six to three in a ruling that declared, in part, that Korematsu was not excluded "because of hostility to him or his race but because the United States was at war with Japan, and the military feared an invasion of our West Coast." In dissenting, Justice Frank Murphy wrote that the exclusion order "goes over the very brink of constitutional power and falls into the ugly abyss of racism."

Some forty-one years later, Judge Marilyn H. Patel of Federal District Court in San Francisco overturned Korematsu's conviction in November 1983. In her decision, Judge Patel wrote, "Korematsu stands as a constant caution that in times of war or declared military necessity our institutions must be vigilant in protecting constitutional guarantees." "I didn't feel guilty because I didn't do anything wrong," he told *The New York Times* in 1983. "Every day in school, we said the pledge to the flag, with liberty and justice for all, and I believed all that. I was an American citizen, and I had as many rights as anyone else."

Korematsu maintained that his constitutional rights were violated by internment and that he had suffered racial discrimination. Korematsu helped win a national apology and reparations for internment camp survivors and the families in 1988. Koremsatsu returned to California after the war, worked as a draftsman, and raised a family. Korematsu gained vindication when President Bill Clinton presented him with the Medal of Freedom, the nation's highest civilian award, in January 1998. The president likened him to Linda Brown and Rosa Parks in the civil rights struggle.

In recent years Korematsu expressed concern about civil liberties in the United States after the September 11, 2001, terrorist attacks. He said at the time: "There are Arab-Americans today who are going through what Japanese-Americans experienced years ago, and we can't let that happen again." He filed an amicus brief in the U.S. Supreme Court on October 3, 2003, asking the high court to review the constitutionality of prolonged executive detentions under the Bush administration's war on terror. Korematsu died on March 30, 2005, at the age of eighty-six. (Associated Press, *New York Times*, University of Chicago press release, April 2, 2005.)

5. The interview was with this writer at Baldwin's home in Greenwich Village.

6. Kenneth B. Clark, "The New Negro in the North," in Matthew A. Ahnman, ed., *The New Negro* (Fides Publishers, 1961), 27.

7. Roger N. Baldwin Archives, Box 24, Folder 5,1943, Seeley G. Mudd Manuscript Library, Princeton University, N.J.

CHAPTER 3

CIVIL LIBERTIES
IN WARTIME

We affirm that a war for democracy cannot be won if we sacrifice the very liberties we not only profess to defend at home but to extend to all the world.

—Roger N. Baldwin, 1943

Author's Note: With signs of war on the horizon after the first decade of the beginning of the twentieth century, Roger Baldwin—true to his public position of opposing militarism in any form—wrote to his draft board telling it that if called, he would refuse service in a war because he was against killing and war. He said in a letter to the board: "I am opposed to the use of force to accomplish any end, however good. I am, therefore, opposed to participation in this war [WWI] and any other war. My opposition is not only to direct military service, but also to survive whatsoever helps prosecute the war. I am furthermore opposed to the principle of conscription in time of war or peace, for any purpose whatever. I will decline to perform my service under compulsion regardless of its character." Subsequently, Baldwin was jailed[1] as a conscientious objector (CO) and actually enjoyed the experience by bonding with his fellow COs—he went on to found the ACLU after World War I and made one of its basic tenets the right to be a conscientious objector. From the outset, Baldwin consistently opposed war as the solution to any problem. As a result, he defended the Jehovah's Witnesses, whose conscientious objection to saluting the flag and to accepting military service provoked widespread hostility. He also spoke out repeatedly about the compelling need to protect individual liberties over the need for national security in a time of war; although widely criticized, Baldwin and the ACLU also fought for the right of Nazis to march peacefully in the United States. However, the ACLU belatedly opposed the government's actions in rounding up all Japanese-Americans, citizens or not, and placing them in internment camps during the war. Consistent with his beliefs, he was among the first to oppose the war in Vietnam. He even warned of the hazards to civil liberties if the attorney general of the United States and the Justice Department are not inclined to support civil liberties. It is striking how the views he held, cited below, are all the more relevant in today's post-9/11 America. Following are his commentaries from pre–World War I to Vietnam.

—W. K.

In Baldwin's Words

REPRESSING DISSENT (1941)

The chief danger to American democracy today arises from the demand that dissent be suppressed in the interest of defense and national unity. Even a distinguished committee of liberal lawyers in the American Bar Association, which has done valiant work for civil liberty in recent years, warns that we may have to surrender in part established liberties for the period of the emergency. The press and radio are unresponsive to the appeal of minority rights. Protests against their denials are more and more confined to the small circles of defenders of civil liberty on the principle, and of the partisans of the movements attacked.

Yet the real dangers to American democracy arise more from these comparatively insignificant minorities, not from foreign propaganda from the dictatorships, but from powerful forces intent upon destroying the right of dissent. Congress reflects them. The Martin Dies [Senate] Committee is their mouthpiece. No democracy can endure unless every element in making public opinion has the right to be heard. All organizations with international political connections, however peaceful and legal their purposes, have been forced to register with the Department of Justice, subject to investigation by G-men. Communists and Bundists have been denied employment in public service, with the threat of ousting them by law even from private employment.

The justification alleged for these measures is the preservation of democracy. Yet how can democracy be saved if civil liberty is sacrificed? And how can civil liberty be protected if the rights of any movement to freedom of speech, press and assembly are denied? No democracy can make any distinction in protecting the rights of those who uphold and those who deny its principles. It may legitimately engage only in the suppression of acts, conspiracies or conduct aimed at the government or the public peace.

The preservation of civil liberty in this crisis will depend largely upon the attitude of the Department of Justice. The vast powers in the hands of an attorney general unsympathetic with civil liberty may easily be used to stifle criticism and dissent. The federal government has the obligation, not only to refrain from violating civil rights, but to protect them. The test of our faith lies in the degree

> *The vast powers in the hands of an attorney general unsympathetic with civil liberty may easily be used to stifle criticism and dissent. The federal government has the obligation, not only to refrain from violating civil rights, but to protect them.*

to which, in the midst of crisis, we practice the principles we profess. (Roger Nash Baldwin Papers, Box 22, File 1, "Liberty Repressed," *Presbyterian Tribune,* January 1941, Seeley G. Mudd Manuscript Library, Princeton, N.J.)

CHALLENGES TO CIVIL LIBERTIES DURING WORLD WAR II (1943)

The ACLU's work is conducted in wartime as in peace on the general principle that civil liberties are essential to the preservation of democracy and that we must not suspend in wartime the very principles for which the country is fighting. The Union recognizes of course the necessity for controlling military information at its source; for restricting the activities of criminals of enemy countries; for registering foreign agents and identifying their propaganda; and for censoring communications with foreign countries.

It is opposed to any proceedings under cover of war measures against utterances or opinions that do not present a "clear and present danger" of inciting to illegal acts. It opposes all restraints on public discussion. It is opposed to censorship of domestic mails and press; to government ownership or censorship of domestic radio news in areas under military control; and to racial discrimination, especially in the armed forces, trade unions and defense industries.

Freedom of speech and the press has been under attack on several fronts. Government control over communications abroad has produced unwarranted censorship of opinion on the grounds that it might yield material for Axis propaganda. The Union has been among the many to protest unreasonable restrictions on the transmission to allied nations of fact and opinion concerning race discrimination and other non-military matters. The Union has supported the defense of several publications against proceedings to remove their second-class mailing privileges for alleged violation of the Espionage Act, because the postal authorities have failed to apply the "clear and present danger" test in regard to the alleged effect of the published material. The Union has also protested the procedures by which the Post Office has excluded individual issues of publications without specifications or hearings. (Roger Nash Baldwin Papers, Box 21 File 3, Seeley G. Mudd Manuscript Library, Princeton, N.J., January 30, 1943.)

CIVIL LIBERTIES VERSUS NATIONAL SECURITY (1943)

Those of us who insist on maintenance of the Bill of Rights in wartime are constantly confronted by the argument that we should suspend our liberties until victory is won. But we deny that any such sacrifice is necessary. On the contrary, we affirm that a war for democracy cannot be won if we sacrifice the very liberties we not only profess to defend at home but to extend to all the world. If the first two of the Four Freedoms mean anything, freedom of speech and religion, they mean that the United States must set the example that we want the world to follow.

Not only that, but the very morale on which success in the war so largely depends is strengthened by the degree to which we practice and extend in wartime the principles of the Bill of Rights. And this applies not only to the major freedoms for all of press, radio and motion pictures, but to the rights of minorities of all sorts to carry on their activities freely. We concede the necessary controls of military information at home and abroad, of enemy aliens, of activities presenting a clear obstruction of the war, and of industrial conflict, but we do not accept controls of opinion nor of non-military news, nor of debate and dissent on the critical issues.

The government has moved under the Espionage Act to bring criminal charges of sedition and to revoke the mailing privileges of publications construed to cause disaffection in the armed forces. Unhappily, the government appears not to have applied to many of these cases the "clear and present danger" test laid down by the Supreme Court in World War I, the only satisfactory yardstick we have for distinguishing between sedition and legitimate freedom under the Bill of Rights. While the overall record of civil liberties so far during the war is surprisingly to the good, we are constantly faced with the uncertainties of the war itself and the effect of international efforts on domestic opinions. Mounting casualty lists or reverses might change the public temper on which the action of government so largely depends. The balance of forces that now keeps debate free may be upset. Only the most scrupulous defense of every attack on the Bill of Rights can guarantee in time of war as in peace that we will emerge from this unprecedented catastrophe with our testimony to our democratic faith intact. (Roger N. Baldwin, Abstracts of remarks by; ACLU Archives, New York, March 1943, Box 24, Folder 5, Seeley G. Mudd Manuscript Library, Roger Baldwin Papers, Princeton University.)

CIVIL RIGHTS PRINCIPLES APPLIED IN JAPAN (1953) INTERVIEW

In 1947, General MacArthur invited Baldwin to visit Japan and inspect the state of civil liberties under the Occupation. Baldwin accepted, with the stipulation that he went as a private citizen, so that he might be free to criticize. This precaution turned out to be unnecessary. He and MacArthur took to each other right away. "We saw the problem of civil rights eye to eye," Baldwin recalls. He traveled all over Japan conferring, asking questions, speaking at meetings, giving interviews, and laying the foundation for a Japanese Civil Liberties Union, which came into existence the following year. His general impression was extremely favorable. Someone in Tokyo asked him: "How did you get in here? Aren't you some kind of revolutionary?" "Yes," answered Baldwin, "and this is the greatest revolution I've seen, and General MacArthur is leading it."

Baldwin's Japanese trip was a turning point in his political life. After he got home, he wrote an informal report on it, which he called "A Balance Sheet of the Occupation," and sent copies of it to the War Department and to MacArthur and his aides. He also wrote several magazine articles that recall his 1934 *Soviet Russia Today* outburst their manner of reporting seemingly unfavorable data without taking a particular gloomy view of it. He recorded MacArthur's quelling of certain Communist-led strikes and quoted approvingly of his retort to a Russian general: "Since when has the Soviet government permitted a strike?" The trip also challenged Baldwin's ideas about generals. "Imagine an antimilitarist like me falling for MacArthur," he says, wonderingly. "Why, on civil liberties he's as liberal as I am!" (Dwight Macdonald, Profiles-I, "The Defense of Everybody–II," *New Yorker* [July 18, 1953]: 47–50.)

THE JAPANESE AND GENERAL MACARTHUR (1954)

One does not hear much criticism of General MacArtrhur among either Americans or Japanese. Respect and admiration are the current attitudes. Why not, when the achievements of the Occupation and its "superb psychological handling," as [author] John Gunther says, make it stand out as one of the most remarkable efforts in all history to reorganize democratically the whole life of a defeated people suffering from the domination of militarists and autocrats? Gunther concludes that MacArthur is a "great man with a great job done." The general says that "it is the greatest reformation of a people ever attempted," and he believes the Japanese are already "democratized."[2]

Nobody can know until the Japanese are on their own. The general with his sure faith and sense of mission is given to overtly optimistic interpretations. But Gunther points out what any student of the Occupation must realize at once are enduring reforms buttressing democracy—the distribution of land to the peasants who work it, the right of trade unions to a powerful position in Japanese life (despite the Occupation's "Taft-Hartley" policy in banning strikes by all public employees), the emancipation of women, the dissolution of the great family trusts, the humanization of the emperor-deity, and the decentralization of national controls over education and the police.

Back of these institutional reforms, which have laid the basis for wide popular power, stands the historic receptiveness of the Japanese to new ideas, heightened by MacArthur's trust in them. Never has he by word or act treated the Japanese as an inferior people; never has he reminded them that they as a people are a defeated nation to be ordered around by a conqueror. He is credited with rare understanding of the "Oriental mind," a bit of nonsense as it doesn't exist.

Critics of the occupation charge that MacArthur has done the artificial job of attempting to remake an entire civilization in our own image. Gunther refutes it. He says that MacArthur's purpose has been to "prove to Asia that democracy is better than Communism," and that he has done it. If the recent suppression of the Communist Party and its press in Japan seems to refute the thesis of open competition between systems, it is evident that after the outbreak of the Korean

War a "clear and present danger" existed that justified departure from five years' tolerance of Communist propaganda.

Way back in 1947, MacArthur openly stated that the time had come for the occupation to end in a peace treaty. Occupations, he said, tend to defeat their own purposes after a few years by becoming established bureaucracies, checking native initiative. All alien controls of any civilization bear the heavy burden of evil and error. Considering that, it is a miracle that so much that is so good seems to have taken root in Japan. Gunther cites the criticisms of leading Japanese that the Occupation has attempted too many reforms too fast, that the "lower echelon" personnel do not understand either democracy or the Japanese, and that the costs of Occupation to the Japanese are too great a burden.

When I returned from Japan with so favorable a report on the Occupation, I was twitted by friends everywhere who thought I had been taken in by MacArthur's charm and VIP luxury. Like Gunther, I circulated widely and freely, mostly among the Japanese. If I was deceived, so was he. It's a fair conclusion neither of us was, and that the facts make our case. For honest and colorful reporting, Gunther does the most illuminating job of all among the many books on MacArthur and the Occupation.

The general's faith in others was demonstrated upon his arrival in Japan, and I kept hearing Japanese delightedly comment on it. He arrived long before the troops and before the formal surrender in a single unarmed airplane against all advice as to the risks. He said he knew the Japanese; when the emperor said quit, they quit, and would receive him as a distinguished guest. They did. Next day when he was escorted to the office made ready for him, a carpenter happened to be in the elevator to take him up. When he saw the general, he rushed out in confusion. MacArthur called him back and rode up with him. "No Japanese general could possibly have done that," commented one of my Japanese friends. The story, published in the press, was Japan's first introduction to postwar "democracy."

When I got back to Washington, I called on Gen. Frank McCoy, head of the Far Eastern Commission and MacArthur's nominal superior in policy. He had known MacArthur for years. I told him of my experience and of my admiration for the job MacArthur was doing. General McCoy's comment was that MacArthur was Dr. Jekyll and Mr. Hyde. I had met Dr. Jekyll.

The Mr. Hyde came out later. I was distressed by MacArthur's fall from grace—my graces—a year later when he banned all strikes against the government and collective bargaining in government unions. I deplored his getting tough with the Communists and so driving them underground. I applauded my friends in the labor section who resigned in protest. I was stunned and disgusted with the general's political ambition to run for the presidency, influenced doubtless by flattery and false prophets who had been too long away from the American scene.

But I have never qualified my admiration for what I saw of his role in 1947. I have been a consultant or observer in all the other American occupations, and the occupation of Japan still stands out, as I think the facts justify, as a rare expression of the highest American principles, imperfectly applied but to a remarkable degree accepted and embodied in Japanese life and institutions, despite the post-peace anti-Americanism, a natural reaction.

I conceive that exceptional result is due in greatest part to the attitude, faith, crusading spirit, skill and forbearance of a Supreme Commander—and he was indeed that—who exactly fitted the role he was called upon to play.

When I got back in June 1947, I reported to the ACLU. We established a committee on occupied countries composed of men who, like me, had served in them. I kept up correspondence with my American colleagues in Tokyo, but rather for the record than for results. The best result was the formation after I left of what I had begun, the Japanese Civil Liberties Union, not a strong agency, but one that has made its impression since in Japanese life. The United Nations Association continued to grow. (Columbia University, Oral History Research Office, "The Reminiscences of Roger Nash Baldwin," interviews held by Dr. Harlan B. Phillips during the months of November and December 1953, and January 1954, pp. 487–503.)

THE REVOLT AGAINST THE VIETNAM WAR (1968)

The war in Vietnam escalated to become the chief preoccupation in American politics, the chief issue of citizens' rights for the American Civil Liberties Union, and the most disturbing of international conflicts at the United Nations.

Opposition to the war everywhere was based on the fear that it may erupt into a world catastrophe. The United States is blamed far more than North Vietnam for not taking steps to end the war. A great power fighting a little country is assumed to be the aggressor, able to stop the bombing. The United States calls North Vietnam the aggressor.

It refuses to recognize the war for what it has been for years, a civil war in the South against a government that cannot win the loyalty of its people. I was in Vietnam some years ago before the United States intervened and it was the same conditions that prevail today. The North helps the rebels; we run the war for the government.

The confrontation is the most dangerous in the Cold War cycle of confrontation because both Russia and China aid the rebels. Behind the revolt against the war in the United States is the feeling that the days of unilateral intervention by great powers should be over in view of our commitments to collective security. The United States should therefore bring the war to an end by unconditional cessation of the bombing and agreement to deal with the Vietnamese. The war is in the South, not the North, and the North's agreement alone will not bring the end. U Thant, who should know better than anyone from his recent consultations around the world, holds even more stoutly that the United States can end the war by stopping bombing permanently and unconditionally. This is the core of the position of those in revolt against the war: the senators, the few generals, the politicians, religious and peace organizations, and more ad hoc citizens' groups than I have seen in previous years.

The revolt of the intellectuals in the colleges has produced more agitation, demonstrations, paid advertisements, petitions and remonstrations than have marked other wars because the feeling against this one is more profound. They challenge its legality. They challenge the inhumanity of the use of napalm. They raise the defense of conscientious objectors on the ground of the principle declared at the trials of Nazis where refusal to follow orders to engage in inhuman acts was held to be a duty.

The Civil Liberties Union is defending objectors to this war who are not legally recognized, but it is defending the Puerto Rican young men in the federal courts who resist service on constitutional grounds. It is defending those who are inducted simply because of their publicly expressed opposition to this war. It defends men in the army who become conscientious objectors. I think the revolt against the administration in this unpopular and miserable war is more widespread and more profound than in the Korean War certainly, which became a political issue because of its unpopularity, ended by General Eisenhower's campaign promise.

Despite the opposition the administration does not yield. I charge it to a self-righteous spirit of obstinate adherence to a position thought to be highly moral. It is fighting for democracy, freedom, commitments to the military clique that runs South Vietnam, and of course against the aggressor of the North. Military victory is not the object, says the President, but the Pentagon is running the war.

What will break the administration's resistance to the pressure against it? Public opinion polls show decreasing popularity but substantial tolerance of the war's conduct. Powerful voices threatened the administration in an election year. They may conceivably prevail.

One way out should be through the United Nations. It has the obligation to handle threats to peace. It cannot when the parties are not members but it might bring to bear the pressure of world opinion. If China and the divided states were members, as even the pope advocated, the conflict could be controlled as others have been. The United States bears the burden of China's escalation. The revolt will continue; the war will end one of these days without world war, I believe, because the prospect restrains the combatants. There are those with more hope than may be justified who think that Vietnam may be the last of the Cold War armed confrontations, and the last great-power intervention in a civil war. It should be. There are vastly better ways at hand already agreed to by the nations in the United Nations Charter. The only road to peace is collective security based on progressive disarmament. Only through it can the goals of the charter for a world of peace and law be won. (Roger Nash Baldwin Papers, Box 24, Folder 5. Excerpts of remarks to the Puerto Rico branch of the Fellowship of Reconciliation, San Juan, Puerto Rico, March 5, 1968, Seeley G. Mudd Manuscript Library, Princeton, N.J.)

EXCLUSION OF THE JAPANESE FROM THE WEST COAST (1976)

One of the few persistent criticisms of the ACLU record has been that we failed to challenge the government's wartime executive order to remove the entire Japanese population, aliens and citizens alike, from the West Coast states. The Executive Order 9066 was issued on February 19, 1942, and after initial protests the ACLU board debated for several months the constitutional question of challenging in the courts the president's wartime powers. It was one of the major controversies in the Union's history because it involved a shocking and unprecedented exercise of military power. I had told a reporter of *The New York Times* who called me the morning the order was announced—the first news I had heard of it—that on its face the ACLU would oppose it. It was not so clear and simple to others; I soon found out that our Pacific Coast branches were divided, and board members reluctant to make a clear challenge.

We were all confused by the fears aroused by the war. The attack on Pearl Harbor, the presence of Japanese submarines off the Pacific Coast, the imposition of martial law in Hawaii and the complete ignorance in the majority of the Japanese minority against whom racial prejudice was latent everywhere on the coast and now was open and alarmed. But it was only the army that got so excited as to urge the president to issue so extraordinary an order. The navy advised against it; the FBI did—only the commanding general on the coast insisted, and Roosevelt responded.

I must therefore confess that I became ambivalent as my colleagues; it was my duty to poll them, advise them and keep us together. It took almost a month to formulate our first protest in a letter to the president on March 16, 1942. A week later we were considering the first test cases in the courts on constitutionality. But what were the arguments? The aliens were no problem; their rights were not those of their American-born children. Could the government legally order them to move just because of their national origin, the suspicion of sympathy with the enemy? No, we were quite sure, all of us, that at least they could not be moved without individual hearings before civilian authorities on their presumed danger. That was a nice idea, but it didn't get very far. Like many good ideas, it was too good for practical use.

All the Japanese on the coast were ordered to register for evacuation. They weren't yet forced; they could leave voluntarily for the interior but plans were in the wind for the remote concentration camps to which all those remaining after a fixed date were to be moved. When we learned that one young Japanese-American in Seattle refused to register, we backed his defense in the court. In 1942, twenty-two-year-old Fred Korematsu, then working in a California shipyard, refused to be put into an internment camp and, as a result, was arrested and jailed.[3] The U.S. Supreme Court upheld that conviction in 1944 stating that the government could jail him in wartime, without a hearing and without any judicial determination that he had committed a crime. (Roger N. Baldwin, Draft for *Civil Liberties Review*, 1976.)

Author's Note: It was not until 1983 that a San Francisco federal judge overturned the Korematsu conviction. He went on to become the recipient of numerous prestigious awards for his courageous stand, including the Medal of Freedom, the nation's highest civilian award, from President Bill Clinton in 1998, when Clinton likened him to Linda Brown and Rosa Parks in the civil rights struggles of the 1950s. In 2001 he was the recipient of the Roger Baldwin Medal of Liberty Award for being "a courageous opponent of the injustices perpetuated against Japanese-Americans during World War II, and lifelong human rights activists on behalf of Japan."

CONSCIENTIOUS OBJECTORS (1976)

I have always been a conscientious objector. I don't think war is the way to settle anything. The question arises, would I participate in it, and I won't, no more than I would be a policeman. You couldn't get me to be a policeman. The simple idea that I think is constructive, that has gripped me most strongly is that of pacifism, that goes under the heading of nonviolence as the rational solution to problems and of conflict without war and without collusion and without force. We expect human beings to get along together by persuasion and compromise without inflicting the doctrine of power of one over the other. Now this is the main thing I've been interested in ever since I began in my teens with some kind of social service and later with the periods that I went through the wars and through political movements— Communism and fascism afterward, I think that was the central feature. I was rather known as, if you ever wanted to characterize me. I'd rather be known as one who strove to try to effect order without collusion. (Roger N. Baldwin, interview with this writer, June 1976.)

NOTES

1. Baldwin in letter to Local Board 129, September 12, 1918, Roger N. Baldwin Papers, Box 2, Seeley G. Mudd Manuscript Library, Princeton University, N.J. Baldwin was eventually taken to the County Prison in Newark, which housed short-term prisoners—a year and under. Ironically, it turned out to be Armistice Day, November 11, 1918. Following that, he was taken to the county penitentiary in Caldwell, New Jersey. He served until July 1919, with time off for good behavior.

2. John Gunther, *The Riddle of MacArthur* (New York: Harper & Brothers, 1950), p. xiii.

3. From all appearances the organization, the ACLU, that Baldwin confidently characterized as "the watchdog for the underdog" was put in question at the outset of World War II. This was because of the national ACLU's uncertain posture when Baldwin and two other ACLU officials sent a letter dated November 3, 1942,

to Lt. Gen. John L. DeWitt of the Western Defense Command assuring the general, that, although they were opposed to "wholesale" evacuation, "we cannot refrain from expressing to you our congratulations on so difficult a job accomplished with a minimum of hardship, considering its unprecedented character. Never before were American military authorities confronted with a situation of this magnitude; and it is testimony to a high order of administrative organization that it was accomplished with so comparatively few complaints of injustice and mismanagement."

Baldwin enclosed the letter with a covering note to Ernest Besig, an attorney in San Francisco: "If you think this is not entirely improper, will you forward this and advise us?" Besig obliged, but curtly advised in a letter [November 7, 1942] to Baldwin that he had "better keep your letter of thanks for a form letter. In the years to come there may be many humane American army officers engaged in establishing ghettos." Besig replied by saying that officials should not be congratulated for not violating civil liberties. This contributed to the protracted conflict between Baldwin and Besig, and between their respective ACLU offices in New York and San Francisco. In the early months following Pearl Harbor many a warning cry came from the New York office as events audibly and visibly moved toward what the ACLU would denounce one day in 1943, safely after the fact, as *"the worst single wholesale violation of civil rights of American citizens in our history"* [italics mine].

Not until March 2, 1942, eleven days after President Roosevelt signed Executive Order 9066, did Baldwin speak out for the Union, perfunctorily criticizing the order, but accepting its legitimacy. It was, Baldwin said, "undoubtedly legal in principle, but may readily result in illegal action," according to an account in the *Northern California American Civil Liberties Union-News*, dated March 9, 1942. Two weeks later, Baldwin appealed to Roosevelt directly in a letter that urged modification of the order so that citizens and aliens alike could have individual hearings and thereby "minimize injustice," according to an ACLU press release, March 16, 1942.

Although at first the New York office had invited a legal test of exclusion, it changed that policy after four months of acrimonious debate, with the board of directors split into two definite factions, one led by Norman Thomas and the other by Whitney North Seymour, a Wall Street lawyer who gave the war effort precedence over civil liberties. By a two-to-one joint vote (51 to 26) the board and the national committee accepted Seymour's assertion that Roosevelt's order was constitutional. To implement this decision Baldwin drafted a statement, called the Seymour Resolution, that ultimately was accepted by the warring factions, that committed the ACLU not to participate, "except where fundamentals of due process are denied, in cases where, after investigation, there are grounds for belief that the defendant is cooperating with...the enemy." In the *Christian Century* a month later [July 29, 1942], the discouraged Thomas bewailed this spectacle of individuals boasting of their liberalism while taking the lead "in justifying the presidential assumption of dictatorial power."

In San Francisco, Ernest Besig also had to contend with those Thomas called "totalitarian liberals." When polled, a slight plurality of Northern California ACLU members (120 to 117) and of its executive committee (9 to 8) were of the opinion that the union should not challenge the exclusion, according to the *ACLU*

News, April 1942. Besig managed to swing the committee around, so that on June 4, 1942, he could be instructed to provide legal defense for Fred Toyosaburo Korematsu, "citizen of Japanese extraction, arrested for remaining illegally within a Military Zone." In response to notification of the Seymour resolution by the New York office, the committee adopted the following motion on July 2, 1942: (a) that the new national policy be followed in any future cases; (b) that in view of the reliance of the local branch on existing policy when it intervened in the Korematsu case, we cannot in good conscience withdraw from that case at this late date."

Baldwin and his board tried but never budged Besig and his committee from their commitment to Korematsu. Baldwin began by requesting them politely to withdraw from the case. Besig replied in a letter (July 8, 1942) to Clifford Forster, a staff attorney in the New York office and the national director's right-hand man: "We don't intend to trim our sails to suit the Board's vacillating policy. Surely the Corporation's members could not have intended us to be faithless to our client."

Acting Chairman Walter Frank shot back a telegram (July 10, 1942) from New York: "OVERWHELMING VOTE OF NATIONAL COMMITTEE ON THE WEST COAST ORDER IS A MANDATE LAYING DOWN POLICY WHICH MUST BE FOLLOWED UNDER BY LAWS BY ALL AFFILIATED COMMITTEES." As the controversy boiled over into the autumn, Frank went over Besig's head to the Right Reverend Edward L. Parsons, the Episcopalian bishop who was chairman of the Northern California ACLU Executive Committee, urging him to "conform" to national policy in handling Korematsu's appeal:

"Your attorneys could file a brief amicus which would not raise the issue of the underlying presidential power and would raise only the points authorized under our national policy. Personal counsel can, of course, raise whatever points he may desire.... We ask you now that in the handling of the case on appeal both in the briefs and in publicity the position of the Union be made clear: as distinguished from contentions which may be made on behalf of the defendant by his own counsel. *It should be emphasized that the Union does not attack the underlying presidential power* [November 9, 1942].

Replying (November 11, 1942) for the bishop, Besig restrainedly pointed out that Korematsu had no money for legal fees, no counsel other than Wayne M. Collins, who had taken on the case for the NCACLU, and no place to turn after having been assured "before he accepted our help that in the event he was convicted, we would undertake an appeal, if necessary, because we regarded his as a test case. Our policy at the time conformed to your own."

And so the contention continued on into the next year and the next; but we already have before us ample evidence to lay to rest the misleading claims of Baldwin's successors on this score. On November 2, 1981, for instance, Edward J. Ennis appeared before the Commission on Wartime Relocation and Internment of Civilians as spokesman for the union and testified that, "as soon as it was known that an evacuation program was being considered, the ACLU, both the national organization with its headquarters in New York, and its West Coast affiliates, immediately, vigorously and continuously opposed the evacuation as unnecessary and unconstitutional." On the contrary, after initial inertness the national organization continuously and with relative vigor did precisely the opposite. (Richard Drinnon, *Keeper of Concentration Camps* [Berkeley and Los Angeles: University of California Press, 1987], pp. 118–22.)

In 1983, Korematsu's long journey to clear his name ended successfully when his case was reopened on the grounds that Korematsu's attorneys did not have all the facts at hand when they presented his case at each stage. In legal terms, this is called a writ of error *coram nobis*, a Latin phrase meaning an error committed in the proceedings "before us." On January 19, 1983, Korematsu's attorneys filed a motion in the U.S. District Court for the Northern District of California in San Francisco, almost forty years after his conviction. Judge Marilyn Hall Patel granted the *coram nobis* motion because critical information had been kept from the courts at every level during Korematsu's trial and appeal process. The judge called it "a complete miscarriage of justice," and ordered that Korematsu's forty-year-old conviction be set aside. She pointed out that the real value of the Korematsu decision was a warning for times of war. It should be noted that, despite some opposition, on August 10, 1988, Congress passed a bill granting reparation payments to all the Japanese who had been illegally evacuated. In the bill, the government admitted that a "grave injustice" had been committed. (Karen Alonso, *Korematsu v. United States, Japanese-American Internment Camps* [Enslow Publishers, 1998], pp. 88–106.)

COMMENTARY
Safeguard Every American's Civil Liberties
RUSSELL D. FEINGOLD

Roger Baldwin's lifelong crusade to safeguard every American's civil liberties should always be remembered as a lasting contribution to maintaining our country as a strong and viable democracy. Wartime has sometimes brought us the greatest tests of our Bill of Rights, as Mr. Baldwin has written in this chapter. What he said in the past still resonates today during yet another war brought on by a new enemy.

September 11, 2001, irrevocably changed so many lives. We all had our own initial reactions, and my first and most powerful emotion was a solemn resolve to stop these terrorists. And that remains my principal reaction to these events. But I also quickly realized that two cautions were necessary, and I raised them on the Senate floor within one day of the attacks.

The first caution was that we must continue to respect our Constitution and protect our civil liberties in the wake of the attacks. As the chairman of the Constitution Subcommittee of the Judiciary Committee, I recognize this is a different world with different technologies, different issues, and different threats. Yet we must examine every item that is proposed in response to these events to be sure we are not rewarding these terrorists and weakening ourselves by giving up the cherished freedoms that they seek to destroy.

The second caution I issued was a warning against the mistreatment of Arab-Americans, Muslim-Americans, South Asians, or others in this country. Already, one day after the attacks, we were hearing news reports that misguided anger against people of these backgrounds had led to harassment, violence, and even death.

During those first few hours after the attacks, I kept remembering a sentence from a case I had studied in law school. Not surprisingly, I didn't remember which case it was, who wrote the opinion, or what it was about, but I did remember these words: "While the Constitution protects against invasions of individual rights, it is not a suicide pact."

We must redouble our vigilance to ensure our security and to prevent further acts of terror. But we must also redouble our vigilance to preserve our values and the basic rights that make us who we are. The Founders who wrote our Constitution and Bill of Rights exercised that vigilance even though they had recently fought and won the Revolutionary War. They did not live in comfortable and easy times of hypothetical enemies. They wrote a Constitution of limited powers and an explicit Bill of Rights to protect liberty in times of war, as well as in times of peace.

There have been periods in our nation's history when civil liberties have taken a backseat to what appeared at the time to be the legitimate exigencies of war. Our national consciousness still bears the stain and the scars of those events: the Alien and Sedition Acts, the suspension of habeas corpus during the Civil War, the internment of Japanese-Americans, German-Americans, and Italian-Americans during World War II, the blacklisting of supposed Communist sympathizers during the McCarthy era, and the surveillance and harassment of antiwar protesters, including Dr. Martin Luther King Jr., during the Vietnam War.

These past anomalies in history—many opposed by the noted civil libertarian Roger N. Baldwin in his writings during his long and distinguished career—must not be permitted to happen again.

Now, some may say we may hope that we have come a long way since those days of infringements on civil liberties [during Roger Baldwin's years]. But there is ample reason for concern. I have been troubled by the potential loss of commitment to traditional civil liberties. As it seeks to combat terrorism, the Justice Department is making extraordinary use of its power to arrest and detain individuals, jailing hundreds of people on immigration violations and arresting more than a dozen "material witnesses" not charged with any crime. Although the government has used these authorities before, it has not done so on such a broad scale. Judging from government announcements, the government has not brought any criminal charges related to the attacks with regard to the overwhelming majority of these detainees. Even as America addresses the demanding security challenges before us, we must strive mightily also to guard our values and basic rights. We must guard against racism and ethnic discrimination against people of Arab and South Asian origin and those who are Muslim. We who don't have Arabic names or don't wear turbans or headscarves may not feel the weight of these times as much as Americans from the Middle East and South Asia do. But as the great jurist Learned Hand said in a speech in New York's Central Park during World War II.

"The spirit of liberty is the spirit which seeks to understand the minds of other men and women; the spirit of liberty is the spirit which weighs their interests alongside its own without bias." Of course, given the enormous anxiety and fears generated by the events of September 11, it would not have been difficult to anticipate some of the reactions, both by our government and some of our people. And, of course, there is no doubt that if we lived in a police state, it would be easier to catch terrorists. If we lived in a country that allowed the police to search your home at any time for any reason; if we lived in a country that allowed the government to open your mail, eavesdrop on your phone conversations, or intercept your e-mail communications; if we lived in a country that allowed the government to hold people in jail indefinitely based on what they write or think, or based on mere suspicion that they are up to no good, then the government would no doubt discover and arrest more terrorists.

But that probably would not be a country in which we would want to live. That would not be a country for which we could, in good conscience, ask our young people to fight and die. In short, that would not be America. Preserving our freedom is the reason that we are now engaged in this new war on terrorism. We will lose that war without firing a shot if we sacrifice the liberties of the American people.

The antiterrorism bill that we considered in the Senate highlights the march of technology, and how that march cuts both for and against personal liberty. Justice Brandeis foresaw some of the future in a 1928 dissent, when he wrote: "The progress of science in furnishing the Government with means of espionage is not likely to stop with wiretapping. Ways may some day be developed by which the Government, without removing papers from secret drawers, can reproduce them in court, and by which it will be enabled to expose to a jury the most intimate occurrences of the home. Can it be that the Constitution affords no protection against such invasions of individual security?"

We must grant law enforcement the tools that it needs to stop this terrible threat. But we must give them only those extraordinary tools that they need and that relate specifically to the task at hand.

We must maintain our vigilance to preserve our laws and our basic rights. We have a duty to analyze, to test, to weigh new laws that the zealous and often sincere advocates of security would suggest to us. This is what I have tried to do with the so-called antiterrorism bill. Protecting the safety of the American people is a solemn duty of the Congress; we must work tirelessly to prevent more tragedies like the devastating attacks of September 11. We must prevent more children from losing their mothers, more wives from losing their husbands, and more firefighters from losing their brave and heroic colleagues. But the Congress will fulfill its duty only when it protects *both* the American people and the freedoms at the foundation of American society.

So let us preserve our heritage of basic rights—a heritage that is very much the legacy of Roger Baldwin. Let us practice that liberty. And let us fight to maintain that freedom that we call America.[1]

Russell D. Feingold, a Democratic Senator from Wisconsin, cast the lone vote against the USA Patriot Act when it was passed immediately in the aftermath of September 11, 2001.

NOTE

1. This commentary is a shortened, updated version of a speech delivered by Senator Feingold on October 12, 2001, to the Associated Press Managing Editors Conference in Milwaukee, Wisconsin, in which he explained why he was the sole member of the U.S. Senate to vote against the Bush administration–sponsored "USA Patriot Act." Feingold was then chairman of the Constitution Subcommittee of the Judiciary Committee in the Senate. (Reprinted by permission of the office of Sen. Russell Feingold, November 18, 2003.)

COMMENTARY
Roger Baldwin: Willing to Stand Up for Values
PATRICK J. LEAHY

Security, liberty, and privacy are always in tension in our society, but rarely as acutely as since the terrorist attacks of 9/11. It is the role of each new generation and its policy-makers to do the best they can to continually sort things out and try to strike the right balance.

Today's security-saturated environment, coupled with rapid advances in complex new technologies that more easily collect, digitize, and distribute personal information about each and every American have quickened the pace, straining the fault lines between technology on one side, and freedom and privacy on the other, as never before.

Ben Franklin and Roger Baldwin would recognize the policy dynamics of today's security and civil liberties debates. In the aftermath of the attacks of 9/11, there have been many temptations to trade away liberty in pursuit of security. The Founders, and later lights like Roger Baldwin, did not consider liberty a sunny-day American value. The test of our commitment to our values is our willingness to stand up for them not when it's easy, but when it's not.

I am proud to have been able to slow the speeding train when Congress considered the USA Patriot Act, to buy time for inclusion of checks and balances that were not in the initial draft. I also joined with former House Majority Leader Dick Armey to override the White House's objections to the sunset provisions that he and I included in the final version of the bill. We felt that sun setting some of the law's most sensitive provisions would raise the prospects for meaningful congressional oversight and for cooperation from the administration in the oversight process.

When the Bush administration asserted the right to imprison people without counsel and without access to the courts, several of us stood in opposition, and I was gratified when the Supreme Court agreed with our view that such a stance was inconsistent with our constitutional framework.

Holding true to our ideals is an ongoing legacy that each generation of Americans owes to the next. Our example also can inspire reformers and opponents of terrorism and oppression around the world. As Roger Baldwin said during a different momentous struggle, "A war for democracy cannot be won if we sacrifice the very liberties we not only profess to defend at home but to extend to the entire world."

Openness and accountability in government are crucial to preserving our fundamental civil liberties in wartime. Where freedom and security are in tension, the checks and balances of our system help us find the right balance. Congressional oversight provides essential accountability from the Executive Branch, and the Freedom of Information Act allows individual Americans to demand answers from their government. Sunshine is a potent antidote to abuse of power by government.

Unfortunately, cooperation from the Bush administration has been sparse and grudging. Former attorney general John Ashcroft rarely appeared before Congress to answer questions, testifying less frequently than any of his predecessors of modern times, and he was extraordinarily slow even in answering oversight letters from members of Congress. He even went so far as to equate questions from Congress and the American people about the liberties of the American people as giving aid and comfort to our enemies.

Of course, the opposite is true. Questioning our government and fighting to preserve our liberties are the hallmarks of our system of government, and have been since the adoption of the Bill of Rights. As Roger Baldwin said, "Freedom and equality are not the gifts of governments. They are the possessions of people who love and cherish them and are willing to sacrifice and fight for them."

Senator Patrick J. Leahy (D-VT) is the ranking member of the Senate Judiciary Committee.

COMMENTARY
Willing to Stand Up for What He Believes
CHRISTOPHER J. DODD

Since the attacks of September 11, 2001, America has grappled with serious questions about how to keep our nation safe, while maintaining the basic rights and liberties for which so many have fought and died over the years. Sometimes, the answers to these questions can be easy. Nearly every American will accept government security cameras at airports and federal buildings. None of us would allow them inside our own homes.

Often, though, the answers are quite complicated. To what extent do we restrict public access to potential terrorist targets? Is "profiling" of any kind acceptable, and if so, under what circumstances? What measures can be taken when our government learns of a possible impending attack?

Liberty and safety are not, and must not be, mutually exclusive. It is critical that our nation not allow its eternal principles to be tailored to the conflict of the moment.

It is deeply concerning that some in our nation appear to believe otherwise. Over the past few years, the phrase "national security" has, at times, been used as a blanket response to justify significant restrictions on liberties—including those which relate minimally, if at all, to terrorism. Dissent and free speech have been decried by some as giving aid and comfort to the enemy. American citizens have been detained without trial, and without access to legal counsel. The Department of Justice and the White House have supported policies that allow for the torture of suspected terrorists. These developments should not be tolerated—even by Americans who are not directly affected by them. As Dr. Martin Luther King said so eloquently, "Injustice anywhere is a threat to justice everywhere."

As we confront the threat of terrorism, it is important to remember that our nation has faced deadly enemies before. And it is critical that we consider not only how our actions will be viewed now, but how we will be judged in the future.

World War II is the source of two striking examples. Toward the beginning of the war, citing security concerns, our nation forced Japanese-Americans into internment camps. This decision—one approved by our Supreme Court at the time—is now regarded by most in our nation as shameful, shortsighted, and wrong.

Conversely, at the end of the war, we chose not to summarily execute Nazi war criminals—but to place them on trial for their heinous crimes. In doing so, we honored our nation's historic commitment to justice and the rule of law—even though the parties involved were not even United States citizens.

It is my hope that we continue to take steps to secure our nation from terrorists, while holding fast to the principles of liberty, justice, and freedom that have sustained our nation for two-and-a-quarter centuries. In doing so, we will honor the legacies of individuals like Roger Nash Baldwin, who taught us through his speeches and writings that the strength of a nation is measured not merely by its might, but by its willingness to stand up for what it believes.

Senator Christopher Dodd (D-CT) is a senior leader in the U.S. Senate. A recipient of the Edmund S. Muskie Distinguished Public Service Award for leadership in foreign policy, Dodd has also fought to protect people's basic right to privacy, authoring legislation to protect individuals' financial, medical, and genetic records.

Introduction to Chapter 4

I'm a radical in defense of the Bill of Rights.
—Roger N. Baldwin, 1978

The Bill of Rights seemed to be written in broad language that excluded no one, but in fact, it was not intended to protect all the people—whole groups were left out. Women were second-class citizens, essentially the property of their husbands, unable even to vote until 1920, when the Nineteenth Amendment was passed and ratified. Native Americans were entirely outside the constitutional system, defined as an alien people in their own land. They were governed not by ordinary American laws, but by federal treaties and statutes that stripped tribes of most of their land and much of their autonomy. The Bill of Rights was in force for nearly 135 years before Congress granted Native Americans U.S. citizenship. And it was well understood that there was a "race exception" to the Constitution. Slavery was this country's original sin. For the first seventy-eight years after it was ratified, the Constitution protected slavery and legalized racial subordination. Instead of constitutional rights, slaves were governed by "slave codes" that controlled every aspect of their lives. They had no access to the rule of law: They could not go to court, make contracts, or own any property. They could be whipped, branded, imprisoned without trial, and hanged. In short, as one infamous Supreme Court opinion declared: "Blacks had no rights which the white man was bound to respect." It would take years of struggle and a bloody civil war before additional amendments to the Constitution were passed, giving slaves and their descendants the full rights of citizenship—at least on paper:

- The Thirteenth Amendment *abolished slavery.*
- The Fourteenth Amendment guaranteed to African-Americans the rights of *due process and equal protection of the law.*
- The Fifteenth Amendment gave them *the right to vote.*

But it would take a century more of struggle before these rights were effectively enforced.

———

Reprinted from ACLU Briefing Paper No. 9 by permission of Ira Glasser, former executive director of the ACLU.

CHAPTER 4

THE COURTS AND
EQUAL JUSTICE

As the powers of government grow so does the need to challenge their abuses. Whether that need is met depends on the courage of citizens exerted on courts and legislatures. The result has been to extend liberty and to restrict power.

—Roger N. Baldwin, 1968

Author's Note: From his youthful days as a social worker in St. Louis in the early 1900s until his death in 1981, Roger Baldwin was a "work in progress," growing as he did with changing times to cope with more and more complex issues. The ACLU, too, has become better accepted as a part of mainstream American life. As Baldwin himself said about the ACLU in 1951, shortly after his retirement as executive director: "Our Supreme Court has affirmed in a long series of decisions those years [of the ACLU] from a position of suspected subversion to one of unexpected respectability."[1] Baldwin threw himself into his work from the outset, working with juvenile court reform and with labor unions; as a firm opponent of censorship of any kind; as an advocate of the theory of evolution as opposed to "divine creation" in the so-called Scopes "monkey Trial" in 1925 (see chapter 10, "Separation of Church and State"); as defender of Sacco and Vanzetti, accused alien anarchists executed in 1927; and of the "Scottsboro boys"— Southern blacks accused of raping a white woman, who went to trial in the early 1930s; as an opponent of the death penalty for Julius and Ethel Rosenberg who were tried, convicted, and executed for spying for the *Soviet Union*, the only atomic spies who were executed, in 1953; as critic of police brutality against prisoners; as outspoken opponent of sedition laws; as defender of free speech and assemblage, including espousing a neo-Nazi group's right to march in Skokie, Illinois, in 1979; as an outspoken opponent

of the McCarthy era witch hunt of Communists allegedly in the U.S. State
Department; and, finally, as an international statesman for human rights as
head of a nongovernmental organization working closely with the United
Nations. Baldwin, a charming and charismatic man who sought out people at
all levels of government to explain the ACLU's goals to them, knew every
president personally during his years of public service. His favorite: John F.
Kennedy. "I've always had a soft heart for the Boston Irish," he said in an
interview in 1974.[2] "I never had any of the prejudices that most of the Boston
bluebloods and old patricians had, who thought they had gotten there first
and had a monopoly of the place and resented newcomers. There was a little
superiority and a sense of snobbism among a lot of my friends, but I always
liked them, the Kennedys, especially. There was a brand called the 'Harvard
Irish' who were different. There were some classmates of mine who became
judges and mayors; I don't know, senators, maybe. I don't know who they all
were; but there was a type of the intellectual, moralist, aristocratic, Irish
Catholic politician, whom I trusted. And I trusted the Kennedys with it
because John Kennedy had a veneer of scholarship about him, too. I think he
was a fellow who read a great deal and kept his thoughts right up to date. He
was very familiar with literature." Baldwin's views on the law and equal
justice reveal the breadth of his knowledge and compassion.

—W. K.

In Baldwin's Words

ULTIMATE RELIANCE ON THE COURTS (1930)

Civil liberties comprises that group of personal and public rights set
forth in federal and state constitutions that are commonly accepted as
the fundamental attributes of a democratic state. The essence is freedom of speech, press, and assembly, guaranteeing to minorities as well
as majorities protection against interference with liberty of expression
on public issues whether by agencies of the government or the private
action of citizens. The political purpose of these democratic rights is to
insure orderly change without resort to violence or revolution, and to
keep government responsive to the popular will. Separation of church
and state is also conceived as an essential of a free democracy.

In addition, to the guarantees of freedom of expression, civil liberties
also include the body of personal rights set forth in our constitutions,
including the rights of defendants in criminal trials and equality before
the law regardless of race or religion.

Civil liberties as the mainspring of democracy gain increasing attention as democracy itself is challenged today by the forces of reaction and dictatorship. The invasion of any group's civil liberties is recognized as threatening the democratic process itself, leading ultimately to dictatorship. . . .

The commoner types of violations of civil liberties are (a) by private violence, particularly in the field of conflict between capital and labor, and in the repression of Negroes in the South, (b) in lawless police action, notably by the third degree, and (c) by laws making mere language criminal, as do sedition and criminal syndicalism acts, or by injunctions curtailing freedom of speech and assembly in strikes. The chief victims of repression are the weaker economic classes and the racial, and rather infrequently religious, minorities. Negroes, aliens, strikers, and Communists are the groups whose rights are most commonly invaded both by legal restraints and private violence.

Defense of civil rights is organized by the groups attacked, confined of course to their own interests. The broad social principle of civil liberty for all without distinction is defended by a few non-partisan agencies, by sections of the press, by the larger national associations in the religious field, and by many public officials. The ultimate reliance for their defense in law is of course the courts since the basic theory of American constitutional guarantees is the protection of the citizen by the courts against invasion of his rights by legislatures, executive authorities, or the action of fellow citizens.

Although every democracy confronts a ceaseless conflict between economic classes and political parties, the test of the strength of democratic institutions lies in the freedom of the weaker and more unpopular forces to organize and carry on their activities and propaganda. Judged by that standard, progress in civil liberty in the United States has shown marked advance in the months since the Supreme Court upheld the National Labor Relations Act guaranteeing to workers the right to organize free from interference by employers. The Act established in law the rights which have long been most widely attacked, and which have constituted by far the most numerous issues of civil liberty.

Civil liberties generally, with conspicuous exceptions, have shown steady improvement, due to more liberal decisions by the courts, to the stronger organization of labor, and to more vigorous support by influential sections of public opinion. The United States Supreme Court in a series of decisions has given new strength to civil rights, voiding ordinances interfering with hand-to-hand distribution of literature in public places, making inadmissible in the courts evidence obtained by tapping telephone wires, prohibiting state courts from enjoining picketing even where no strikes exist, voiding convictions in state courts where the defendants were not represented by counsel. State and lower federal courts have also rendered decisions noteworthy in advancing civil liberty. (Roger N. Baldwin, "Civil Liberties Comprise," *Social Work Yearbook* [New York: Russell Sage Foundation, 1930], 76–79.)

PERSONAL LIBERTY (1936)

No word in common political use is more ambiguous or equivocal than "liberty." Liberty for whom, and to do what? "Personal liberty" at once arouses the concept of freedom from restraint in habits of living. Its most vivid recent application involved the attempted philosophy that justified violating the Prohibition amendment. Its loudest immediate application concerns the rights of private property in the conflict between rugged individualism and state control. Less vocal but more in the American tradition are the genuine libertarians whose political thinking, running back to the Founding Fathers and beyond, regards liberty as the priceless possession of free men to agitate, to alter governments, to remold economic systems.

These conflicting concepts of personal liberty are ancient. Abraham Lincoln once put them better than any of the philosophers. Said he:

> The world has never had a good definition of the word "liberty," and the American people just now are much in want of one. We all declare for liberty, but in using the same word we do not all mean the same thing. With some the word "liberty" may mean for each man to do as he pleases with himself and the product of his labor; while with others the same word may mean for some men to do as they please with other men and the product of other men's labor. Here are two, not only different, but incompatible things, called by the same name, "liberty." And it follows that each of the things is by the respective parties, called by two different and incompatible names— "liberty" and "tyranny." The shepherd drives the wolf from the sheep's throat, for which the sheep thanks the shepherd as his liberator, while the wolf denounces him for the same act as the destroyer of liberty, especially as the sheep was a black one. Plainly, the sheep and the wolf are not agreed upon a definition of the word liberty; and precisely the same difference

prevails today among us human creatures, even in the North, and all
professing to love liberty.

Today both the sheep and the wolves appeal to the constitutional
guarantees of liberty to protect them. The wolves speak in terms of
property; the sheep in terms of human rights, of social control of property, of the welfare of producers, of change by democratic methods.
Their interests are irreconcilable on the economic field. On the political
side, the reconcilable issue they present is whether democratic liberty
offers a means of progress from where we are to where we must go if
the evils of a competitive economy are to be overcome.

The personal liberties set forth in the Bill of Rights, adopted not by
the Founding Fathers but by the pressure of the people themselves,
rest on two sets of guarantees—those protecting freedom of agitation,
and those protecting defendants on trial. Important as are the rights of
defendants, they are not a political issue, nor are they seriously under
attack. But the rights of freedom of agitation are beset today as rarely
in American history. Those who defend the *status quo*, rich and powerful as they always are, are deserting the democratic method for direct action. It is they who in Europe have abandoned parliamentary
government for fascism through fear of revolution. It is they who here
are the masters of strike-breaking, the organizers of vigilantes to crush
trade unions, the inciters of Red scares, the promoters of gag laws, and
the financiers of semi-fascist patriotic organizations and propaganda
sheets. It is they who are the enemies of American democracy, the
instigators of violence, the subverters of liberty.

Personal liberty to speak one's mind, to print one's views, to assemble, to be free of unlawful searches, to organize, strike, and picket,
is the heart of the Bill of Rights. It rests on the necessity for unrestricted
agitation as the only workable means for peaceful progress in a
democracy. The principles of our Bill of Rights are universal in democratic lands, whatever their schemes of government. They grew
naturally out of the system of liberal capitalism, which needed these
political rights to buttress its power and protect its freedom to exploit
wealth and labor. Our Constitution is unique only in being the first to
embody these rights as formal protections of the citizen against his
government.

Thus in the very origin of the guarantees of personal liberty is evident the economic conflict which produced them. And on the whole it
has worked well in the interests of the rugged individualists. Their
"free" competition is reflected in our political parties, representing one

or another section of capitalist power. Where popular revolt seemed to threaten the economic system at times, they have been able to manipulate the machinery to hold control. And while with the exception of the Alien and Sedition Laws of 1798, the Bill of Rights came through fairly intact to the world war, its liberties of agitation never really threatened the property interests of a pioneering and expanding economy. The growing United States did not develop those working-class political movements that in Europe have long threatened capitalism with an alternative system, socialism. Such anti-capitalism as has marked American life has been fragmentary and transitory—and largely imported.

Conflicts such as that over slavery, and in less degree that over women's rights, have put strains on the Bill of Rights and its guarantees of political agitation. But they did not produce either Supreme Court decisions or statutes violative of its principles. It remained for the great pressures of the world war to do that. It was not due so much to anti-war agitation as such that the casualties of free speech and free press were so numerous, but to the radical economic purpose that underlay the Socialist and IWW opposition to the war. Thus the courts, moved by the property interests which courts consciously or unconsciously reflect, sensed in the dominant radical anti-war agitation a threat to capitalism. Economic heresy was the essential crime for which hundreds went to prison for exercising what the Bill of Rights seemed to guarantee.

The war cases began the whittling away of the traditional legal concept of personal liberty to speak and print. When the United States Supreme Court laid down the rule that Congress could, in violation of the First Amendment, abridge free speech if there were in particular cases "clear and present dangers of the substantive evils which Congress has the right to prevent," the door was opened wide enough for legal suppression to enter. And it has come in and made itself at home since. The state sedition and criminal syndicalism laws have been sustained on the same general theory of protection against incitements. The post-office control of the press via the mails was approved. Rights of religious conscience were brushed aside in a series of cases from the draft act, through the denial of citizenship to alien pacifists, to refusal of exemptions from military training for college war-resisters. In a dozen ways the Bill of Rights has been emasculated by the Supreme Court. In a few unimportant ways, its provisions have been sustained. But outside the court, the drive for crippling rights by law goes on. (Roger Nash Baldwin Papers, Seeley G. Mudd Manuscript Library,

Box 22, Folder 1, reprint of article in the May issue of *The Annals of the American Academy of Political and Social Science,* summarized June 2, 1936, over a nationwide network of NBC in "You and Your Government," Series XIII, Lecture No. 18.)

Sacco-Vanzetti: Undying Symbols (1937)

Ten years ago, on the day after the execution of Sacco and Vanzetti, I was traveling from Leningrad to Warsaw in a compartment filled with Russians. I had started the night before, still confident that the execution would not take place, and was eager for the news but at a loss how to get it. One Russian who spoke some German answered my inquiries by showing me the morning paper, translating the tragic news spread in streamer headline across the front page. Everybody in the compartment joined in with indignant comment. Sacco and Vanzetti were in Russia symbols of capitalist justice. Even the German-speaking Russian, who turned out later to be quite anti-Bolshevik, shared the indignation.

Just a week before at a great Moscow meeting in a summer garden to protest the approaching executions, there had been a strong note of hope that international protest would stay the hand of the executioner. In the months I had been spending in Europe I had kept up a steady correspondence with both Sacco and Vanzetti, and though I could not bring myself to believe they would be put to death in the face of the grave doubts as to their guilt, their letters never reflected any hope. So sure was my long-distance faith in justice that I carelessly loaned the last letters from them, written in early August, for exhibition on some Soviet wall-newspaper. I never recovered them.

Sacco and Vanzetti were more to me than two victims of the hate and fear of radicals. They were friends whom I had come to know intimately from many visits to them in prison dating way back to before their trials—friends whose motives and high social principles I had come to respect and admire. Up to the end they were curious about my observations, in Italy, and Russia particularly, and their letters were far more devoted to comment on dictatorships than to their own fate. Anarchism as a philosophy of a society without violence or compulsion is even more consuming a faith than the disciplined creeds of socialism and Communism, for it demands intense personal feeling unsupported by organized power. Sacco and Vanzetti lived their faith in every word and act, and it sustained them to the chair. Vanzetti, much more the thinker of the two, sent me from prison for some months his penciled scripts of a translation from a work of Proudon's, so poorly done in his inadequate English that it could not be used, but testifying eloquently to the kind of passion that consumed him even in the face of death. What had struck me all along in the years I visited these idealists was the contrast between what they were in fact and what dominant Massachusetts opinion held them to be. No device of persuasion or interpretation could impress the unyielding conviction that they were dangerous men, anarchists, and Wops, who should be electrocuted on general principles. Shocking as such an attitude is to those who cherish a loyalty to impartial justice, it is tragically common wherever the emotions of class interest are aroused. It is the attitude of dominant California opinion to Mooney and Billings. It surrounds strikers arrested on criminal charges, however false or fabricated they may be. It was always the attitude to the IWW, and it is universally the attitude to Communists.

It is not enough to dismiss such a blind disregard for justice as an upper-class prejudice affecting only the occasional Mooneys, Saccos, and Vanzettis, for the history of the last decade or so is eloquent of the profound political consequences flowing from such a denial of democratic rights. Where democracy has disintegrated before the attack of fascist reaction, it has shown its first signs of decay in denying justice to those most hated and feared by the controlling class in power. First deny rights and justice to Reds, and it is a short step to the destruction of rights and justice for all. Thus does the democratic state go down.

Massachusetts in dealing with Sacco and Vanzetti furnished a perfect example of the process. The final touches to the long record of judicial prejudice, abundantly proved against the trial judge, were given in the appointment by the governor of three eminent citizens to review the evidence. The eminence of these citizens was directly due to their positions as representatives of the controlling class in Massachusetts. However dispassionately they approached their task, they were bound to carry so great a burden of unconscious prejudice against radicals and aliens as to weight their judgments of evidence. Could anyone reasonably expect a judge of the Puritan school, a president of the Institute of Technology, and a Brahmin president of Harvard University to throw overboard their traditions and caste fears in favor of justice? Even a casual understanding of the bitter conflict between the old Puritan caste in Boston and the alien newcomers would have fairly forecast their decision.

It may be unjust to assess blame when so many were involved in the tragedy, but I cannot escape the thought that the zeal of President A. Lawrence Lowell of Harvard as the most energetic member of the Governor's Commission made him the pivotal figure. If he had been able to rise above his prejudices, he could have carried the others along at least to the recommendation of a commutation, based on the doubt of guilt of one or both. And he is the perfect embodiment of that respectable opinion in Boston, which stood behind the judicial machinery, right or wrong.

Now ten years after, Sacco and Vanzetti live as undying symbols of the sacrifices exacted from a working class daring to dream of a world freed of exploiters. Their number the world over is legion. Wars, international and civil, are fought and will be fought over the rise of movements toward labor's freedom, bloodily contested at every step by the defenders of property. But when that historic conflict is done, Sacco and Vanzetti will be remembered as among its early martyrs and heroes. One day even Boston, I venture to predict, will erect to them a public monument in that spirit of historic justice so dramatically exhibited by the French republic, which placed in front of a church the bronze figure of a youth "executed for having refused to salute a religious procession."

In the ceaseless struggle today for the preservation of democracy as the one non-violent means of progress, Sacco and Vanzetti remain now, as ten years ago, an inspiration to defenders of liberty to see that such a tragedy does not happen again. (Roger Nash Baldwin Papers, Seeley G. Mudd Manuscript Library, Princeton, N.J. *Unity*, Monday, August 16, 1937, p. 222.)

> *The fight for liberty never stays won. We will have to keep winning it over and over again, we will have to amass our forces and resist.*

THE COMMUNIST TRIALS (1949)

They [the Communists] are not being tried for a secret conspiracy. They are being tried for openly advocating the Communist program and objectives. Even if they were tried for secret advocacies, the doctrine that secret utterances which may have an illegal object are in themselves criminal establishes a concept unknown in American law. The Civil Liberties Union adheres to its settled position that only a "clear and present danger" of unlawful acts justifies prosecution.

The government's indictment in the current case makes precisely that sort of charges . . . there is no indication yet that a secret conspiracy, apart from the vociferous Communist propaganda, is involved. The indictment alleges conspiracy to "teach and advocate" "the Marxist-Leninist principles of the overthrow of the United States by force and violence." There is no allegation of overt act. The prosecution rests solely on the utterances and publications of the Communist Party.

It has always been American public policy—and this has been embodied in many court decisions—that no language, publications or propaganda should be punished unless it constitutes, in Justice Holmes's language quoted above, a clear and present danger of unlawful acts. The Supreme Court has held that there must be great danger and the prospect of immediate action to justify penalties, which infringe freedom of speech and press. Nothing in the indictment suggests any such danger.

If the government knows of secret conspiratorial acts by the Communists, why did it not indict them for such acts? It could have done so, for example, under the General Conspiracy Statute, instead of the questionable Smith Act, which has been condemned in principle by such an authority on free speech as Professor Zechariah Chafee of Harvard University.

Many people believe, and there seems to be compelling evidence, that the American Communist Party is under the control of the Russian government, either directly or through a third group such as the Communist Party of France. If the U.S. government has evidence to support this charge, why does it not indict the Communists for failing to register as the agents of a foreign principal?

I hope I don't need to say, at this late date, that the American Civil Liberties Union has no sympathy with Communists, or with any other totalitarian doctrine. We would not oppose a federal indictment based upon overt acts by the Communists tending toward the violent overthrow of the government. But we do oppose action by any governmental body in this country that seeks to punish people for their beliefs and the mere expression of their beliefs. We opposed the application of the Smith Act against the Minnesota Trotskyites, at a time when the Communist Party was gleefully supporting that prosecution. We also opposed its only other use, the retrial of alleged pro-Nazis in the District of Columbia.

There are some who would say that certain ideas are so dangerous, so abhorrent, that the effort to spread them must be suppressed even though no connection with overt acts is shown. Such a notion seems to me dangerous in the extreme. Powerful influences will always tend to say that unpopular ideas are of this character and that advocating them is an illegal conspiracy.

The only fair test I can conceive would continue to be the "clear and present danger." Ideas alone should not be punished as incitements in the absence of acts of the immediate danger of them. As Justice Holmes once said, "Every idea is an incitement." The only safest rule is not to prohibit utterances of publications dealing with public questions unless they are, first, direct incitements to unlawful acts shown to have been either attempted or actually committed, or, second, advocacies of actions which immediately threaten great danger. If there is any evidence that the Communists now on trial engaged in such activities, the indictment does not say so and the case appears to rest on the dangerously shaky ground of making long-tolerated propaganda criminal. A conviction would in effect outlaw the Communist Party and drive it underground, a result I am sure the country does not desire. (Roger N. Baldwin, "Roger Baldwin's View," *New Republic* [January 31, 1949]: 8.)

THE CASE OF JULIUS AND ETHEL ROSENBERG (1953)

For many years I have served actively in the American liberal movement for the defense of civil rights, both as director of the American Civil Liberties Union, and more lately as its representative in international efforts for those guarantees embodied in the sacred texts of both the French and American declarations. In that work I am also president of the United Nations consultant agency, the International League for the Rights of Man, which has twenty-three affiliated national bodies all over the world. Neither of these organizations has any official connection with governments, and both of them stoutly resist any encroachments by governments on the civil rights of anybody. Though excluding Communists as well as other anti-democrats from our councils, we defend their rights as we do those of others.

It can be taken for granted, therefore, that if any question of civil rights under American law had been raised in the trial of the two Rosenbergs, man and wife, for wartime espionage for the benefit of the Soviet Union, we would have intervened. No such question arose. Nor has any such question been found by lawyers for the American Civil Liberties Union who examined the claims made against the death sentence imposed on them. They concluded that this extreme penalty was "not so disproportionate to the crime as to amount to a denial of due process (no corresponding phrase in French; better translate either *quille equivaut a un deni de droit* [justice] or *constitue une violation de droit*).

But that is of course a narrow view of law confined to the aspect of civil rights. There are other considerations, as the worldwide protests, even though inspired by Communist propaganda, show. Dozens of press comments and letters come to us from abroad indicating not only abhorrence of the death penalty but doubts as to the fairness of the trial. I should say at once that on both humanitarian and political grounds I am opposed to the death penalty in this case. Indeed, I am opposed to all capital punishment. But in this case especially I oppose it because I do not want to see the United States hand the world Communist propaganda two martyrs to what it represents as barbaric American justice.

So long as the issue is confused with false charges of anti-Semitic prejudice and a frame-up of Communists, it lends itself only too easily to anti-American prejudices. I have fought for many years against injustices in our courts, against the condemnation of Sacco and Vanzetti, of Tom Mooney, the labor leader, of the Negro Scottsboro boys and many others. But the Rosenberg case is not like them an injustice. There is no question in my mind as to the fairness of the trial.

<hr/>

The advocates of carrying out the penalty argue that the crime was terrible, as it was, and that the Rosenbergs are the only atomic spies who have not confessed their guilt. The opponents argue on varied grounds— humanitarian opposition to making Communists martyrs, and the speculation that if alive they might yet confess. The Communists doubtless figure that they win either way. If the Rosenbergs die, they are martyrs to the cause and an endless indictment of American barbarity. If their sentences are commuted to prison, their campaign won.

As a result of evidence turned up by the Federal Bureau of Investigation, a German-born British scientist, Klaus Fuchs, working at the atomic bomb plant at Los Alamos, New Mexico, confessed to espionage for the Russians. His confession implicated one Harry Gold, who had acted as a courier for him. Gold, arrested in Philadelphia, also confessed, stating that he had worked under the direction of a Russian consular official. He also stated that he had acted as courier for one David Greenglass, when serving as a machinist at the Los Alamos plant in 1944. Greenglass, arrested in New York in 1950, then confessed to espionage which he said was undertaken for his brother-in-law, Julius

Rosenberg; he and his wife [Ethel] were thereupon arrested, and later they with Greenglass and one Sobell (whom Greenglass implicated in other espionage for Russia) were indicted for conspiracy. Everyone of these involved in this chain of events was convicted. (Roger Nash Baldwin Papers, "The Rosenberg Case: An American Liberal on the Rosenberg Case" [January 1953], memorandum.)

McCarthyism: Its Cause and Cure (1954)

The game of cops and robbers played by our grand inquisitors into the Communist heresy is not new. It is just more intense as its political rewards appear profitable. It is a game dangerous to our liberties of debate, to our reputation abroad as a democracy, and to our national strength to tackle more pressing problems. Preoccupation with digging up long past blunders and associations of men in public life weakens our urgent present obligations.

In deploring and opposing the congressional and other hunts for Communist witches, I speak without personal involvement beyond a lifelong defense of the civil rights of all citizens. Neither I nor the American Civil Liberties Union which I serve are on any blacklist, nor have we ever been called to account by a committee of Congress. I do not guarantee continued immunity when we oppose, as we do, all governmental inquiries into the political views and associations of private citizens, including the Communist Party. The Communist Party is legal in the United States, and membership in it is no crime, though leadership has sent to prison several score of its officials for conspiracy to advocate the violent overthrow of government—in prosecutions, which we opposed in the name of free speech, and press and association. An organization of citizens devoted to our Bill of Rights must take, as we do, the unpopular and misunderstood stand against all restraints on freedom of opinion and expression. We oppose the futile pressures for patriotic conformity by loyalty oaths, which have caught more Quakers than Communists.

We oppose equally the futile effort to determine what organizations are subversive and thus subject to registration and restrictions. We oppose the bans on alien visitors or immigrants based on their political views and associations, however long past. We oppose the attempt to impose American concepts of loyalty on American employees of the United Nations, sworn to loyalty only to their international duties. And, above all, because most far-reaching, we oppose the

principles, methods and goals of the competing congressional committees hunting down anyone ever tainted by association with Communists. The committees have caught no spies and few real Communists.
But they have smeared with the Red brush loyal Americans who in the
days of the 1930s or in the war when Russia was an ally joined some
organization now listed by the attorney general as subversive.

So wide and loose a word has Communism become that the story
rings true of the cop arresting some street speaker who protested, "But
I'm an anti-Communist," and the cop replied, "I don't care what kind
of Communist you are. Come along."

When we seek the causes of this most disastrous period for our
freedom, we find them in the fears aroused by the Cold War—or the
hot peace—whichever it is—in the frustrations of people used to quick
results, in the excitements over a few spy trials, and in the habit of the
American press to play up the drama of the chase. International tensions, of course, stimulate it. A negative anti-Communism as dominant
policy feeds the fires of a Holy War. Fears of the new world obligations
imposed on the United States since the war turn large numbers of our
people back to isolationism. Going it alone is so much simpler than
going it with others.

Historically, the roots of McCarthyism go deep into the intolerances
of a new country made up of so many minorities and so many bitter
conflicts between the privileged and the people. Too many are not
conscious of our rights and liberties because they have never had to
fight for them; they assume them without recognizing that their price,
here, as everywhere, is eternal vigilance.

We have long defended civil liberties for all comers without distinction. We are on the defensive against the popular pressures, fears
and concern with internal security. We have few allies. Our hopes for
an effective resistance to McCarthyism are obviously premature. We
have hoped to see a strong stand by the president against the reactionaries in his own party. We observe with dismay his superior
concern with party unity. We have hoped to see the Democratic
opposition marshal a constructive attack on the destructive anti-
Communism which confuses Communism with New Dealers and Fair
Dealers. But we see them, too, playing it safe. We have hoped that the
Supreme Court would check the excesses of the inquisition. But it has
been timid and divided. Any relief now comes too tardily. We have
hoped for popular revulsion against the excesses, injustices and political shenanigans of the witch-hunters. Only feebly have voices with
courage been raised, and more feebly heard.

But the revulsion will come. I have seen the United States go through such periods before, not so extreme it is true, and recover. We savagely suppressed all dissent in World War I; we succumbed to the white, Protestant Nordic nonsense of the Ku Klux Klan in the 1920s; and we regained our democratic balance. We will do so again when either international tensions relax or when the political rewards of witch-hunting fall off.

I do not surrender my professional optimism, although as someone put it, I am worried about it. I have seen enough of the ups and downs of our democracy to keep my faith in its strength to repudiate false saviors. We have had a lot of them, one sort or another, and they have all failed. I keep the kind of faith implicit in Churchill's remark that "Democracy is the worst system of government ever devised by man— except for all the others." We shall just have to put up for a while yet with the corruption of democracy that goes under the label of Mc- Carthyism, confident that the damage to our liberties, alarming at the moment, will leave no enduring mark on our hard-won heritage. (Roger Nash Baldwin Papers, Seeley G. Mudd Manuscript Library, Princeton, N.J., Box 23, Folder 9, January 17, 1954, excerpt of speech on CBC Trans-Canada, "McCarthyism: Its Cause and Cure.")

ON THE FIFTH AMENDMENT (1958)

The protection of citizens against incriminating themselves by testimony in a court or before a legislative committee is one of the oldest rights in both English and American law. It arose from experience with forced confessions by torture or the Third Degree, which showed that many confessions so extorted were false. Prosecutors have thus been forced to make their cases stick without compelling the accused to testify against themselves.

This is sound law and good policy. But it has been called into question recently because of the refusal of witnesses before the congressional committee investigating Communism to answer questions that anyone refusing to say whether he is or ever has been a Communist must be guilty. But that easy conclusion as to these Fifth Amendment Communists ignores others quite tenable.

A witness who has never been a Communist may fear that if he answers honestly, he may be caught for perjury if the congressional committee can dig up a couple of informers to testify that they knew him as a Communist. Or he may have objections to inquiries into the political beliefs and associations of private citizens, if he is not in a government job, and the only way his lawyers tell him he can voice his objections is by invoking the Fifth Amendment. He may wish to invoke the First Amendment protecting free speech, but his lawyers tell him that the courts will not sustain him. Or he may have joined long ago Communist-front organizations and is fearful that some violation of the Smith Act or other anti-Communist legalization might be construed from his membership. Or he may be willing to testify frankly about his own beliefs and associations but unwilling to testify about his friends and colleagues. But his lawyers tell him he can draw no such line; that if he answers about himself, he must answer about others or face contempt charges. Or he may regard the questions asked him as not authorized by a congressional committee's powers, and his lawyers may tell him he has a fair chance in the courts to make that objection stick. It will cost him money to find out, and he will run a risk; but it has been done.

Thus with these many objections to testifying, it is clear that no witness can be readily assumed to be what his refusal to answer seems to imply. But we cannot confront evils greater than the difficulty of exposing Communists by refusal to testify. Those greater evils lie in the very laws we have adopted which make crimes of opinions and associations without proof of any unlawful overt acts. They lie, too, in the assumption that congressional committees have a right to inquire into the beliefs and association of citizens not working for the government, a right which is denied by the whole concept of the freedom of political belief as the source of all democratic power. They lie also in the notion that it is the business of congressional committees to expose Communism anywhere it can be found and to gather evidence of it. The business of congressional committees is to gather evidence for legislation only, or to inquire into the conduct of government and the expenditure of federal funds. It should have no other authority to inquire, without trespass on the executive or the courts.

I oppose all congressional inquiries into the beliefs and associations of citizens. I oppose all such inquiries of public employees except those in sensitive areas where divided loyalties make them unsuitable or dangerous. I oppose repressive laws which make crimes of opinions and associations alone. The Fifth Amendment issue has arisen in recent years only because we have as a nation embarked on the un-American policy—judged by our traditions—of penalizing political opinions and associations. We have gone now to the extreme, attempting to force by law self-accusation by pledging immunity for so testifying. But it is doubtful if federal law can guarantee immunity from state prosecution under their many anti-Communist laws. Whether the courts sustain that position or not, it is bad policy thus to impair a constitutional guarantee of protection of such general significance. It is far better to suffer the evils of a tiny movement of Soviet supporters than to give in to our fears by sacrificing to any degree our liberties for the illusion of security. (Roger Nash Baldwin Papers, Box 23, Folder 9, Seeley G. Mudd Manuscript Library, Princeton, N.J., statement on the Fifth Amendment in the discussion with Professor Sidney Hook at the Bridgeport Community Forum, February 13, 1958.)

ABUSE OF POLICE AUTHORITY (1959)

One of the commonest violations of civil rights is the practice of what is known as the Third Degree to extract confessions. The police commonly do not notify persons arrested that anything they say may be used against them, nor does the average citizen know he is not required to make confessions to the police or to sign any statements they may prepare as a result of questioning. The police do not commonly permit persons arrested to have immediate access to counsel or take prisoners at once before a city magistrate. Frequently the period permitted for detention without a judge's orders is prolonged beyond the maximum period by fixed law.

Another common abuse of police authority is evident in the very large number of cases dismissed by magistrates for lack of proof of an offense. Many of these cases so dismissed may be due to a system of rating of the police according to the number of arrests made. Many arrests in many places are made without proper warrants. The cases of false arrests must be very numerous, yet citizens are reluctant to take action because of the time and expense involved as well as the general belief that the police are generally protected by their superiors.

In the case of many arrests, the police do not permit persons arrested to telephone at once to counsel, friends and family in order to arrange for bail. It is the practice in many police departments to procure arrests through officers posing as citizens to get evidence, which the police sometimes themselves induce. This is reported as fairly common in relation to sex offenses. In relation to political activities, particularly of Communists, the police in many jurisdictions keep an eye on meetings, even taking photographs and the license numbers of automobiles. Police frequently harass ex-criminals not under parole restrictions and

Courts only partially influence our liberties; they fix law and standards, moral and philosophical. I have always regarded the ACLU's main reliance on the courts, but our main foundation must be in public belief. The secret of liberty is courage.

make it difficult for them to hold jobs or to lead normal lives. Discrimination against minority people is common, and most police forces do not have sufficient representatives of minority people in their personnel.

The disciplinary action taken by police departments against officers charged with unlawful conduct in violation of a citizens' right is commonly in the hands of the higher police officers themselves without review in the court or the scrutiny of any independent agency. (Roger Nash Baldwin Papers, Seeley G. Mudd Manuscript Library, Princeton, N.J., Box 19, Folder 12, "Letter to Dean Russell D. Niles," New York University Law School, November 30, 1959.)

PROSPECTS FOR AMERICAN FREEDOMS (1961)

In light of the record, where do our rights and freedoms stand today and what is their promise for the future? To put the darker side first, we may well be disturbed by the excessive preoccupation with security at the expense of freedom which ignores what ought to be accepted—that our best security lies in our liberties. They are compromised, as President Eisenhower pointed out, by the power of the military-business alliance in both domestic and foreign policy, by the resistance of large parts of the South to equality of Negroes before the law, by the conformities of mass communications. But the chief threats lie in those pressures arising from the Cold War, the menace of the arms race and an unsettled and divided world which promotes conformity based on fear, penalizing dissent and curbing controversy. It may no longer be true, but only a few years ago the present chief justice of the United States Supreme Court was worried enough to doubt in print whether the Bill of Rights could be ratified by the Congress as at present constituted.

But the favorable tendencies have grown stronger. The national temper appears more mature in facing the perils of a dangerous and uncertain world. Open violations of freedom of speech, press and association have been greatly reduced; guarantees in law rest on firmer foundations. The forces of protest are sufficiently strong to combat inroads on freedom and to be heard. Labor relations cause no great disturbance of public order. Despite the resistance of the South, the Negro slowly gains in equality now that the courts stand firmly by the historic decision that rights cannot be separate and equal. Counted among the assets of freedom are those attributes of a welfare state toward which all governments seem to move, which add to our political freedoms the economic rights of social security, minimum wages, maximum hours and other protections.

Another decade should see the end of second-class citizenship, the most stubborn obstacle to the fulfillment of our democratic professions. The relations of church and state, particularly in education, will continue to bedevil public policy. Censorship, both by public and private guardians of morals and security, will continue to challenge the rights to see, read and hear without previous restraints. Familiar old problems of civil liberties will long be with us—police abuses of citizens' rights, fair trials, academic freedom in schools and colleges, discrimination against aliens.

But most unpredictable for our liberties will be the Cold War issues of national security, so involved in the global struggle that their resolution is inseparable from the whole course of democracy in the non-Communist world. The greater the growth of liberties abroad, the more secure are our own; just as the growth of our liberties contributes to strengthening the influence abroad of the world's strongest democracy. (Roger Nash Baldwin Papers, Seeley G. Mudd Manuscript Library, Box 23, Folder 9, Princeton University, N.J., extract of speech, May 12, 1961, Wayne State University.)

PROGRESS IN CIVIL RIGHTS (1963)

I have read with some very considerable reservations, Justice [William O.] Douglas's recent writings and speeches in regard to the low state of our civil liberties and the spirit of conformity of the American people, the lack of interest in civil rights and civil liberties, a general downgrading of what I would regard as a situation, an effort, an attitude which to my mind is much more hopeful. I think you could add up column-by-column, one column against the other, the advances and the defeats and the retrogression and come out with on the whole a plus conclusion.

But this is a matter of opinion, I agree. And while I have specialized most of my life in looking at the darker side of our liberties, concerned, as I always have been of course with the violations, I feel encouraged by what has happened. And what has happened has been that our courts on the whole have vindicated the principles; and while Congress and executive offices—governors and mayors and the like—all over the country haven't been particularly faithful in following the principles laid down by the Supreme Court, nevertheless I don't think the country in the last ten or twelve years declined in its application of the principles of civil liberties.

I know it's easy to say that we are a country of conformity and fear, and that the Cold War has produced an atmosphere in which it is easy to suppress anything by invoking the bogey of Communism, but that's not the whole picture. And when you come to consider the variety of expressions of American life in the many centers of power and influence we have—the press, a division of governmental powers, organized citizenry—it does not seem to me anyhow that we have lost much in the way of a resistance to inroads upon our rights.

Of course, in the field of civil rights so-called—that is, the equality of people before the law, the racial issue primarily—we've made very striking advances of course against a great resistance, and a resistance that doubtless will continue for a long time. But nevertheless the amount of hope and purposefulness which the Negro community particularly shows and which other racial minorities reflect, too, is a pretty good indication that we're moving ahead. (Columbia University, Oral History Research Office Collection, "A Conversation with Roger Baldwin with Thomas F. Hogan," April 11, 1963, pp. 65–66.)

The Bill of Rights (1968)

There has been an amazing revolution of recent years in the liberties of all Americans. The central element of this revolution is the fact that issues which before were the exclusive concerns of the States now are the concern of the federal government. Practically all constitutional rights have been nationalized; from the Pacific to the Atlantic, the Lakes to the Gulf, every American is guaranteed precisely the same rights by decisions of the ultimate umpire, the U.S. Supreme Court.

This remarkable shift in powers to the federal government has accompanied the growth of the welfare state and consequent responsibility of the national government not only for equal civil rights, but also for those economic and social rights which mark the modern state. The Supreme Court, Congress, the states and effective public opinion have reflected the demands for racial equality, freedom of conscience, belief, association and communication, justice in the courts, the protection of minority rights and higher standards of living and work.

The pace of advance does not lessen. The Civil Liberties Union has more cases on appeal involving new problems of civil liberties than it has ever had at one time, and the prospects are for no fewer in the complexities of a changing democracy. As the powers of government grow, so does the need to challenge their abuses. Whether that need is met depends on the courage of citizens exerted on courts and legislatures. The result has been to extend liberty and to restrict power. Government itself has even given birth to many agencies to protect the liberties won.

I like to recollect an observation of Justice [Louis] Brandeis long ago that the basic liberty of all is "the right to be let alone." Even if it is not entirely practical in a complex society, it breathes the spirit of what most people feel should be their private freedoms beyond the reach of officials or neighbors. The Bill of Rights was conceived in that intent. (Harold V. Knight, *With Liberty and Justice For All*, introduction by Roger Baldwin [New York: Oceana Publications, 1968], x–xiii.)

ON JUVENILE COURT REFORM (1974)

Q. Because you were involved in reform in St. Louis and with so many people who were in the juvenile court reform movement, do you think that today there are similar people who are doing good work with children and can be looked to for reform of the system?

A. Oh, yes, I think so. The Association of Juvenile Court Judges and, of course, the National Association on Crime and Delinquency here in New York is the expert agency here on it now. They're trying to find the answers. I don't know if there are any answers or not. It's very difficult to say how you should treat children aside from their schooling and their homes. What do you do? Foster parents? Institutions? Jail?

Q. I wonder whether back in 1910 in St. Louis you thought that there were some answers.

A. Well, of course, I did think there were; being in the probation business, that was the best answer. That if you could get enough people interested in the kids, the courts would befriend them and follow them and advise them and keep an eye on them, that you'd get the best answers there were because I knew institutions were no good. I knew that then. I knew they were just *de mieux*. Well, I adopted two kids, so I was demonstrating myself what I believed in. (Columbia University, CUOHROC, "A Conversation with Roger Baldwin with Alan F. Westin," editor, *Civil Liberties Review*, and professor of Public Law, Columbia University, December 18, 1974, pp. 45–46.)

CIVIL LIBERTIES "INSTITUTIONALIZED" (1974)

Q. What's changed in law and the courts?

A. Something has changed. I argue this point with some of my friends in the ACLU office and they tell me it's old stuff. That getting a distinguished lawyer doesn't help any. We used to go after them deliberately. We used to go after those law firms and get them to put a man on the job and then they would often get a partner to go ahead and do the job. It may be that pioneering has ceased. It may be that so many of the important issues have already been settled, that the litigation's over—and it's true that the Bill of Rights has expanded enormously by interpretation in the last twenty to twenty-five years—and that the great dramatic cases are finished. Obscenity. Race. Labor. All settled. There are no great cases in those fields. I think that that has something to do with it. I would think, if I would put it in just a very brief form, that civil liberties, as we understand them, have been institutionalized. And once a thing is institutionalized, and its pioneering quality has gone out of it, it becomes a part of the establishment. And in a sense, the Civil Liberties Union has become part of the establishment. A very bad boy. He's still a bad boy, but he's in the same school with the rest of them.

Q. In other words, if somebody wants to change society, in a real sense, you're saying he or she shouldn't join up with the ACLU because it's now involved in managing the civil liberties of the system. If you want to change society, you've got to find some other movement?

A. Oh, the Civil Liberties Union has been a handmaiden of the existing order, it just tries to make it work better, but it never tried to upset it. It has given aid and counsel and comfort to people who wanted to upset it, but only in terms of the preservation of order. (Columbia University, Oral History Research Office, "A Conversation with Roger Baldwin with Alan F. Westin," editor, *Civil Liberties Review*, and professor of Public Law, Columbia University, December 18, 1974, pp. 85–95.)

"TRAVELING HOPEFULLY" (1979)

We had one decision after the other that solidified the principles of the Bill of Rights. These are the mutual rights of our personalities and when we assume the exercise of these rights we will become a civilized society. We go into the Supreme Court where the doctrine of equality, the doctrine of equal rights, is tested. The fight for liberty never stays won. We will have to keep winning it over and over again, we will have to amass our forces and resist. Justice Learned Hand once said, "When liberty dies in the hearts of men and women, no Constitution, no court and no law can restore it."

And we know that there is a new spirit in America that has grown in these last fifty years which makes it possible to say that our democracy has gained in its spiritual and moral sense as well as in law. I think it is a real contribution that the Civil Liberties Union makes, its contribution to the spirit of liberty, to its spirit of existence, to the spirit of determination, its courage, which, as Justice Brandeis said, is the secret of liberty.

Robert Louis Stevenson once wrote: "To travel hopefully is better than to arrive, and the true reward is to labor." Well, I have been traveling hopefully with you all these years. And I am still traveling hopefully and so is the ACLU, and someday, sometime when the goal is clear and the road is hard and progress painful, when the hour approaches, we are beginning to approach, a tolerable world of peace, order and justice. (From "Traveling Hopefully," videotape produced in 1980 by the ACLU for the ninety-fifth birthday dinner for Roger N. Baldwin, July 13, 1979, courtesy of the American Civil Liberties Union.)

THE ISSUE OF GUN CONTROL (1981)

I don't understand people who want to keep guns. But apparently there is a passion among people in their middle class to keep them handy. They have no constitutional right. They keep saying that they have with the Second Amendment, but they haven't the right to carry guns. And the question is always the control and licensing of the hand weapons. None of this interferes with hunters and their rifles and shotguns. It's only these little handguns that people want to keep in their pockets or their homes. And these people resist any kind of regulation. There is no such thing as the liberty to defend yourself with a handgun. And there shouldn't be. The courts have made it quite clear that the right to carry arms was to state militia and any, in events of common interest. The Constitution is very specific about this. You can't maintain a militia with a handgun. (Roger N. Baldwin, *Rolling Stone* [October 15, 1981], 5.)

REFLECTIONS ON THE SKOKIE CASE (1978)

Ever since the ACLU was founded in 1920, its clearest obligation has been to defend equally the rights of all people without partisanship or favoritism. The free speech case in Skokie, Illinois, is yet another example of that duty in action, and the passions such a policy can arouse. For me Skokie's only surprise was that so many members, Jews and many non-Jews, resigned in protest over an extreme but traditional test of principle. Previous confrontations—even with the Nazis—had not in the ACLU's long history brought such a flood of resignations.

[*Author's Note:* The principle of defending free speech for everyone was illustrated in the case of neo-Nazis, whose right to march in Skokie, Illinois, in 1979 was successfully defended by the ACLU. At the time, then ACLU executive director Aryeh Neier, whose relatives died in Hitler's concentration camps during World War II, commented: "Keeping a few Nazis off the streets of Skokie will serve Jews poorly if it means that the freedoms to speak, publish or assemble any place in the United States are thereby weakened."]

The ACLU has defended all sorts of unpopular and hated people. Few members rejected or resigned over free speech cases involving anarchists, Communists, fascists, Nazis, Klansmen, religious bigots, or purveyors of smut—you name them, we defended their right to free speech. The American Jewish community especially has been put to the test often over these decades, and they've always stuck with us. None of the national Jewish organizations opposed ACLU defense of the rights of Fritz Kuhn and the German-American Bund before World

War II, nor of George Lincoln Rockwell and his storm troopers on the streets of New York in the post-1945 decades. Tolerance of what we hate is a daring doctrine and a hard lesson to learn. In Skokie, the ACLU followed its long-established policy and turned to the courts to protect the right of free speech—for a parade is clearly symbolic speech—and to oppose threats to stifle it. The Illinois ACLU, backed up by the national organization, stood firm on Voltaire's famous dictum: "I may detest what you say but I will defend to the death your right to say it."

Our natural instincts may tell us to suppress such dangerous threats to freedom as Nazis. However, the problem has always been, who decides? Benjamin Franklin once observed, "Of course the abuses of free speech should be suppressed but to whom dare we entrust the power to do so?" The ACLU has long accepted that warning, along with Jefferson's wise advice that, "It is time enough for the rightful purposes of government to intervene when words break out into overt acts against peace and order."

I often marvel that the ACLU has survived for fifty-eight years, but marvel more and with profound satisfaction that we have kept intact our original pledge to defend the rights of all equally without partisanship or favoritism. In the face of that, it matters little that some policies arouse dissent; I, too, disagree now and then, but privately. It has been a record of principle unmoved by the pressures of one of the most revolutionary periods in world history. But it remains an uneasy struggle, confronting constantly shifting challenges. As Emerson observed, "Living in a democracy is like living on a raft. It never sinks, but your feet are always wet." Skokie proved that for us again. (Roger Nash Baldwin Papers, Seeley G. Mudd Manuscript Library, Box 20, File 9, Princeton, 1978.)

ON BEING A "RADICAL" (1978)

I'm a radical in defense of the Bill of Rights. It is radical. I'm certainly radical—always been a man of peace and opposed to violation and coercion because it's regarded as radical because it doesn't belong with some of the coercive measures of government. We were under suspicion but we were really not defendants of everybody's rights. We were seen as being partial to the unions. It wasn't true. If they happened to be our clients, it was because they came to us for help. Nobody else would help them. Somebody had to hire lawyers to defend them. We were a general organization that held out its services to everybody whose rights were denied. The general concept—people have rights against the government—if the First Amendment would serve—is a very old one. If people have these rights as human beings and the government has merely assumed them in some kind of document or constitution, then the people are governed by their very nature of the right to speak and to associate. (From "Traveling Hopefully," videotape produced in 1980 by the ACLU for the ninety-fifth birthday dinner for Roger N. Baldwin, courtesy of the American Civil Liberties Union. The tape was recorded at a National Convocation on Free Speech, a dinner honoring Roger Baldwin, New York Hilton, Tuesday, June 13, 1978, sponsored by the ACLU.)

NOTES

1. Oliver Jensen, "The Persuasive Roger Baldwin," *Harper's* (September 1951): 55.

2. Columbia University, Oral History Research Office, "A Conversation with Roger Baldwin with Alan F. Westin," editor, *Civil Liberties Review*, and professor of Public Law, Columbia University, December 18, 1974, 1–15.

COMMENTARY
Baldwin: The Guardian of Free Speech
EDWARD M. KENNEDY

In 1980, [I attended a dinner in New York] celebrating Roger Baldwin, the guardian of freedom of speech. In Boston a week before, one of my constituents came up to me and said, " I hear you are going to give a speech to the ACLU and I hear those people go around defending Communists." I said, "Oh no, you've got it wrong. They defend Communists, and socialists, fascists, atheists, racists, segregationists, and members of the Ku Klux Klan." And the fellow said, "Well, that sounds like a mighty nice organization."[1]

Baldwin: Fought Long and Hard
EDWARD M. KENNEDY

Clearly, as we continue to work to bring terrorists to justice and enhance our security, we must also act to preserve and protect our

Constitution and those civil liberties for which so many people—especially civil libertarian Roger N. Baldwin—have fought so long and so hard. His writings in this chapter clearly reflect the importance of civil liberties during a time of war.

I strongly support giving law enforcement and intelligence officials the powers they need to investigate and prevent terrorism. However, the Bush administration bears the burden of proving why the particular measures it is seeking are needed. All too often, this administration has sought to undermine the checks and balances established by the Constitution, by bypassing the courts and stripping judges of their authority to make appropriate decisions in criminal cases. Before the independence of our judiciary is further undermined, the administration must show why our current laws on subpoenas and bail are inadequate.

As for the death penalty, the Justice Department should put its own house in order first. This administration has lost almost every death penalty case it has brought, in part because of the attorney general's unwillingness to follow the recommendation of local prosecutors.[2]

Senator Edward M. Kennedy (D-MA) has fought for decades for civil liberties, civil rights, and social welfare reform in the Congress of the United States. He was first elected to the Senate in 1962.

NOTES

1. Based on "Traveling Hopefully," a videotape produced in 1980 by the ACLU for the ninety-fifth birthday dinner for Roger N. Baldwin, courtesy of the American Civil liberties Union. The tape was recorded at a National Convocation on Free Speech, a dinner honoring Roger Baldwin, at the New York Hilton, Tuesday, June 13, 1978, sponsored by the ACLU. Norman Dorsen was national chairman of the ACLU at the time. Cochairs of the dinner were Morris Abram, partner, Paul, Weiss, Rifkind, Wharton & Garrison; John Cowles Jr., chairman, Minneapolis Star and Tribune Company; Winthrop Knowlton, president, Harper & Row, Inc.; Eleanor Holmes Norton, Equal Employment Opportunity Commission in Washington, D.C.; and Arthur Ochs Sulzberger, chairman, New York Times Company. Speakers included Congresswoman Elizabeth Holtzman, Sen. Edward M. Kennedy, and Sen. Jacob K. Javits. The award was presented by Professor Norman Dorsen, national chairperson, ACLU.

2. Statement for this book from Jim Manley, press secretary to Sen. Edward M. Kennedy, March 13, 2004.

COMMENTARY
No Favorites in Defense of Rights for All
Norman Dorsen

It is well known that Roger Baldwin and a small group of farsighted men and women founded the ACLU in January 1920. Post–World War I euphoria was then giving way to "normalcy" and nativism, culminating in the lawless Palmer raids against aliens and radicals. The Supreme Court had yet to uphold a single claim of free speech; criminal trials were often shams; racial minorities, women, and other disadvantaged groups found almost no judicial protection; workers were unable to organize labor unions legally; sexual privacy as a constitutional right was forty-five years away; and violations by state governments were subject to little if any constitutional control.

But when Roger retired as ACLU executive director in 1950, the modern foundations of the Bill of Rights were in place. The courts had taken huge steps to establish equal justice: They discredited anti-evolutionists in the Scopes "monkey trial" of 1925;[1] they vitalized the First Amendment by, among other things, protecting a freewheeling press, reversing the censorship of James Joyce's *Ulysses* and protecting the speech rights of Communists and Jehovah's Witnesses; they supported the Scottsboro boys' right to due process against a trumped-up rape charge; and they began the process to establish racial justice.

There were further gains for civil liberties over the next thirty years, including *Brown v. Board of Education*,[2] which declared state-supported racial discrimination to be unconstitutional; the protection of women's rights under the Fourteenth Amendment and the establishment of abortion rights; and many advances in criminal due process, free speech, and separation of church and state. Yet when the Supreme Court did not go as far as the ACLU wanted, when some earlier civil liberties gains were cut back, and, near the end of Roger's life, when a conservative movement took hold that persists to this day, Roger was not downhearted. He pointedly reminded his younger colleagues, such as myself, of the constitutional wasteland that existed when the ACLU was founded, and he exhorted us to redouble our efforts without becoming discouraged. Despite great provocation to be pessimistic, he would, I think, be saying the same today.

Roger Baldwin was not a lawyer, but through his leadership and acute eye for talent he harnessed the energies of many leading volunteer lawyers for the ACLU, including Clarence Darrow, Arthur Garfield Hays, Osmond Fraenkel, Harriet Pilpel, and Edward Ennis, and later he received counsel from lawyers of my generation, including Ralph Brown, Ruth Bader Ginsburg, and Marvin Karpatkin.

Despite many victories in the courts, Roger's first instinct was to seek political solutions. Thus he initially opposed a courtroom strategy to end racial segregation, he was most comfortable when rights were established legislatively, as in the case of labor unions, and (perhaps because of his social work background) he never fully accepted courts as arbiters of juvenile delinquency.

Roger's distrust of courts stemmed in part from the disastrous Supreme Court decisions in the *Dred Scott*[3] and *Lochner*[4] cases, in part because he always viewed himself as a "political reformer" (as well as a manager), and in part because of his faith in ordinary people. As he often said, he "traveled hopefully."

But Roger's skepticism about courts did not extend to his view of law. He regarded law as the means by which the aspirations of Americans—and people all over the world—for a freer and more just society would be achieved. And he recognized that only through the courageous efforts of "dissenters, heretics, and nonconformists" could unjust laws be challenged and repression overcome.

The principles Roger relied on long antedated the founding of the ACLU and even the ratification of the Constitution and Bill of Rights. They have their roots in the English charters of liberty, in the philosophy of the Enlightenment, in the words of the wise Athenians who first gave them coherent expression, and, although Roger was not a religious man, in the Sermon on the Mount. At the center of these principles is an idea, stark in its simplicity, but almost universally ignored throughout human history: the idea of consistency in the protection of human rights. Near the end of his life Roger wrote:

> The test of the loyalty of the ACLU to its principles lies in the impartiality with which they are applied—there can be no favorites in defense of rights for all. This is a hard test to impose against natural sympathies and prejudices; [it is] even harder to defend "the thought we hate."

Although Roger was an optimist, he understood with Albert Camus that justice is often a fugitive from the winning camp, and that energies must be focused on the latest outrage, the most recent affront, and not on past failures or successes. He was fond of pointing out that "no right stays won," a truth pertinent today as we struggle against new restrictions on writers, on sophisticated invasions of privacy, on attempts to undermine the right to abortion, and on fundamentalist attacks through "creationism" and biblical "literalism" on scientific knowledge. Similarly, we must continue to oppose discriminatory treatment of racial minorities, immigrants, women, the physically disabled, and gay men and lesbians. Roger often fought these battles under different names, but they all have their roots in the same timeless goal of equal justice under law, to which he subscribed throughout his life.

––––––––

Norman Dorsen is Stokes Professor of Law and Counselor to the President of New York University. He served as President, American Civil Liberties Union, 1976–91.

NOTES

1. *Scopes v. State, 154 Tenn. 105* (1927) (conviction of public school teacher for teaching Darwinism affirmed, but the decision met with widespread ridicule throughout the world).

2. *347 U.S. 483 (1954)* (segregation in public schools invalidated).

3. *Dred Scott v. Sandford, 60 U.S. 393* (1857) (the decision, that "a man of African descent, whether a slave or not, was not and could not be a citizen of a State or of the United States," inflamed the slavery issue and helped ignite the Civil War).

4. *Lochner v. New York, 298 45* (1905) (a state maximum hours of work law designed to protect the health of employees was held unconstitutional, leading to the invalidation of much early social welfare legislation).

Introduction to Chapter 5

*We are committed to democracy. We are committed to the right
of all peoples to live under governments of their own choosing.*
—Roger N. Baldwin, 1961

The ACLU's court victories in behalf of labor and other minorities of
the 1920s and 1930s came at a price. The federal government investigated possible movements or individuals who might be viewed as
"unpatriotic." A number of organizations affiliated with the ACLU,
including the Fellowship of Reconciliation, the International Committee for Political Prisoners, the League Against Imperialism, the
League for Peace and Democracy, and the Friends of the Soviet Union,
were seen by government officials as left-wing if not Communistic. In
point of fact, Baldwin had joined an organization in the Soviet Union
and helped raise money to send farm machinery to Russia. His 1927
trip to Russia, however, left him feeling uncertain and confused about
the grand goals of the Communists, because he discovered that the
Soviet government had jailed protesters on minor charges and Baldwin was refused a request to interview them. Thus, while some observers may have thought Baldwin was a "fellow traveler," as the
saying went, he had repeatedly said as a matter of public record over
the years that he was never a Communist Party member.

In fact, on August 23, 1939, Hitler and Stalin signed a nonaggression
pact, which so shook Baldwin's previous sympathies for the Soviets
that he immediately resigned from any organization that had anything
to do with the Communist Party, saying: "I became a consistent opponent of the Soviet dictatorship, of Communism, of all cooperation
with Communism," and as a result, the House Un-American Activities

Committee—which had been investigating Communists in America—completely cleared the ACLU and Baldwin of all "Communist connections." His misguided sympathy for those in labor who had sided with the Soviets evaporated. Moreover, the ACLU passed a resolution—causing a split in the ACLU's executive ranks—that stated, "It is inappropriate for a member of any organization which supports totalitarian dictatorship" to hold a high position in the Union. He said at the time: "We decided that we couldn't have Communists and civil libertarians together. Obviously the loyalty of the Communists was to the Soviet Politburo, as the dictatorship. This disqualified them for civil liberties. Despite that resolution or, perhaps as a result of it, civil libertarians to this day are not united on the action the ACLU took in 1939.

Nonetheless, as the New Deal's momentum increased under Franklin Delano Roosevelt, so too did the ACLU's. Members of the ACLU board had access to many of Roosevelt's cabinet members, if not the president himself. Of Roosevelt, Baldwin said: "I voted for Roosevelt four times. The advances made under his administrations in law, court decisions and administrative practice were the greatest in any period of our work. For the first time we had friends in almost every office, and while I would not exaggerate our influence, it certainly dovetailed with their own purposes, and therefore counted. We, like they, were the victims of international forces, fears and events which played on American life, and of our reactionaries at home, but the years from 1932 up to the war were for most of us—and for me especially with my tendencies to optimism—years both of hope and achievement."[1] Subsequent administrations in Washington were either supportive of the ACLU or, at worst, indifferent, except during Eisenhower's presidency. Of Harry S. Truman's administration, Baldwin said that the report of the President's [Truman's] Committee on Civil Rights in the fall of 1947 "was heralded throughout the country as showing how far the United States had gone toward realizing its professions of equality before the law and how far it had to go." He was more circumspect about Eisenhower: "I met him when he was president of Columbia and after he was president, never in Washington. We had little contact with him in the ACLU, and no issues I recollect," said Baldwin, who expressed unhappiness with the fact that Eisenhower, as president, failed to speak out against Sen. Joseph R. McCarthy when the Wisconsin Republican was at the height of his power in his anti-Communism witch-hunt in Congress. But he admired John F. Kennedy and his administration, stating: "Jack Kennedy was really one of us in spirit. I had met him in the Senate, and in public meetings. Once he invited me to the White House to a lunch for Tito, where I met the assorted big shots, shook the proper hands, including Jack's and Tito's. The Kennedy men always seemed fairly familiar through Bill vanden Heuvel, who worked for Robert and Ted.

"Johnson I met only when he was a senator, but the ACLU had access to him and used it. I don't know who induced him to send me so fulsome a letter of congratulations on my eightieth birthday, but it was a surprise. I never met Nixon after he became president, nor wanted to. I had met him as a congressman when somebody arranged a debate between us when he was on the Un-American Activities Committee. It was in Washington before a small audience, and so amicable that we went out and had coffee afterwards."

—W. K.

NOTE

1. Columbia University, Oral History Research Office, "The Reminiscences of Roger Nash Baldwin," interviews held by Dr. Harlan B. Phillips during the months of November and December 1953, and January 1954, pp. 201–20.

CHAPTER 5

THE GOVERNMENT
AND CIVIL LIBERTIES

*Just so long as we have enough people in this country willing to
fight for their rights, we'll be called a democracy.*
—Roger N. Baldwin, 1978

Author's Note: Roger Baldwin, always on guard against government intrusion on individual liberties, nonetheless put his faith in government as having the potential to offer solutions to the enormous wrongdoing he saw all around him—discrimination against minorities, labor, women, and especially immigrants. But, arguably, the most important lesson that he tried to teach his detractors was stated quite simply: "To defend a man's rights," said Baldwin, "is not to subscribe to his views." And Baldwin often pointed out that this maxim applied across the board—whether in politics, religion, education, or dissent against government, and especially in the freedom to express oneself publicly on any topic. Baldwin was a great believer in the First Amendment and of all the amendments in the Bill of Rights; he spent most of his time accepting and seeking cases involving that particular amendment. As some scholars have said, Baldwin did not invent the Bill of Rights, but he did invent an organization to make certain that it was used, indeed, protected in the case of every individual in America. His interest in the law was only in that it should be used to guarantee every individual the right to be left alone. Baldwin was obviously satisfied with the federal government under the stewardship of Franklin Delano Roosevelt and Harry S. Truman. "I suppose that all of us in the Civil Liberties Union recognized the New and Fair Deals as our allies, whatever our politics," he said in 1954. Although always a maverick and an antiestablishment figure, Baldwin defended the democratic form of government in the United States, no matter its faults. He put it this way: "Living in democracy is like living on a raft. It never sinks but your feet are always wet. Well, our feet are always wet and we continue to struggle and we will continue that way as far as we can see." Following are some of his observations on government and civil liberties.

—W. K.

In Baldwin's Words

DEPORTATION OF ALIENS (1931)

To defend a man's rights is not to subscribe to his views. And it would be impossible for us to share all the warring views of the assorted lot whose rights we champion. It should be axiomatic in any professed democracy that freedom of expression is essential to orderly progress. Without it, all the forces concerned with a given conflict cannot be appraised. Suppression of any opinion, however violent or revolutionary, encourages violence by invoking the violence of authority. It gives one party to a conflict an arbitrary and unfair advantage; any interference with the expression of views, however extreme, violates the sound principle long boasted as inherent American institutions. To stifle by force criticism of existing institutions evidences at once fear of their stability. It is a confession of weakness, of intellectual inability to examine and defend the established order.

Holding these views, I am opposed to deporting any alien for his opinions, whatever those opinions may be. I am equally opposed to refusing admission to any alien because of his views. And I am opposed to prosecuting or interfering with any aliens or citizens for expressing their views, conducting their propaganda, organizing political or industrial movements, and protesting against what they regard as the injustices of our system. Short of an overt act or an attempted act, I would interfere with nobody. Freedom to agitate promotes peaceful solutions. Suppression breeds violence.

The sole question before us is, how shall we deal with a minority movement professing a revolutionary program? How shall we protect American institutions, our government and our property system, from the menace of some 12,000 Communists armed with mimeographs and the printing press? What are the practical choices before us? How best may our institutions be preserved?

There are three ways open: suppression, tolerance—with whatever changes it may bring—and active reform of the evils on which

Communism grows. The policy to which the United States is already committed and which I have indicated, is the way of suppression. We refuse admission not to alien Communists as such, but to persons who advocate what Communists are presumed to believe. Since there is usually no evidence before the immigration authorities save the statements of the aliens themselves, it is not surprising that few Communists or anarchists are excluded. The law does not succeed in excluding them. It succeeds only in making them liars. The same is true of our deportation law. Communists as such are not deportable; but those Communists who are found advocating doctrines or distributing literature construed to advocate the violent overthrow of government, are deportable.

Is our government so weak, is our capitalistic system so tottering, our American schools and churches and homes such easy prey to Communist propaganda, that we must protect ourselves by outlawing it? I trust our institutions to stand as long as they serve the interests of our people. (Roger N. Baldwin, "Should Alien Communists Be Deported for Their Opinions?" Excerpts from a speech before the Boston Foreign Policy Association, March 14, 1931, pp. 2–12.)

THE NEW DEAL (1934)

A summary of liberty under the New Deal in its first year can be thus interpreted from the record:

First, we have had no wholesale suppression because there is as yet no significant opposition to suppress. The government is too well supported to fear criticism either from the extreme right or the extreme left.

Second, the central struggle involving civil liberties, that between capital and labor, has been greatly affected by the New Deal—first by encouraging the formation of trade unions, and second, by not vigorously backing up that encouragement in practice. The government has not intervened to stop employers' interference with union activities. It has not outlawed company unions. It has tended to restrict the right to strike. It has discriminated against left-wing and independent trade unions. It has not given labor representation in the code authorities. The present tendencies are to take labor into camp as part of the government industrial machine and thereby to lull opposition to sleep by making the workers believe the government will look after their interests.

Third, in those great channels of communication—radio, movies and the press—the New Deal has not moved contrary to the charges of its criticism to restrict radio, to censor the movies nor to gag the press. The power to do it is there, but it has not yet been misused. Yet unless that power is changed, the danger is always present.

Fourth, the encouraging aspects of the New Deal in relation to rights and liberties are the more tolerant policies toward aliens, toward Indians, the president's amnesty on Christmas restoring civil rights to those convicted under the Espionage Act during the war, and the treatment, for example, of the bonus army in Washington last summer, in contrast to its treatment under the Hoover administration. (Roger N. Baldwin, "Liberty Under the New Deal," *The Record of 1933–34*, American Civil Liberties Union, New York City [June 1934], p. 9.)

OUR COMMITMENT TO DEMOCRACY (1961)

We are all committed to the same rights for all people everywhere to live in freedom and decency. We are committed to democracy. We are committed to the right of all peoples to live under governments of their own choosing. We are committed to the United Nations and its human rights efforts. As Americans we are committed to freedom under our Bill of Rights, to the equality of all citizens and to the welfare of each.

These human rights are the strongest moving force in the conflict and struggles of our times. Never before have they had so wide an acceptance, such vigorous championship. I am an optimist regarding their continuing progress. When I look at my own experience of fifty years with civil liberties at home, I see an almost startling advance, despite the most adverse world events. National protection of rights never before recognized by courts or legislatures brought equality in law to blacks, to women, to organized labor. Social Security, welfare programs and the efforts to combat poverty created a new welfare state. The Civil Liberties Union won most of its cases in the Supreme Court, the Warren court, putting the Bill of Rights in a new perspective. The Warren court went beyond any previous court in bold interpretations of constitutional rights. We faced threats to these advances by the retreat of the Nixon administration from Johnson's Great Society and Warren's Supreme Court. They do not disturb me. I have too often seen the country thrown off balance by fear and abuse of power, and I have seen it always recover. (Roger R. Baldwin Collection, 1961 memo.)

RIGHTS: ASSERT OR LOSE (1970)

The phrase civil liberties has a long history in English and American political usage, but it was the American Civil Liberties Union that first adopted it in an organization's title and so brought it into a wider public vocabulary. Civil liberties have always described the freedoms of the people in a democracy to speak, publish and organize.

There are what many schools of political thought call natural rights, the inherent desires of people to express themselves and associate with their fellows. If strictly defined, they would, I think, come out thus: Civil liberties, asserted as a principle, become legal rights when they are embodied in enforceable law, as they are in the Bill of Rights. The Bill of Rights covers all the protections of citizens against government power abuses of the liberty of the people. It includes all the elements of fairness in the area of criminal justice, embodied in the phrase due process.

All rights of the people are restraints of government or guarantees to the people by government. They are individual, personal or collective, as the right of association. They find their political sanction in the supremacy of a sovereign people over their governments in a democracy. They find their judicial sanction in the protection of minority and personal rights against the majority. They find their philosophical sanction in the natural right of every individual to the fullest opportunity to develop his capacities. This purpose led Justice Louis Brandeis once to observe "the fundamental right is the right to be left alone."

Obviously the application of these general principles raised constant and highly controversial questions: conflict of rights, the precedence of one right over another, the proper powers of government, the social limits of personal freedoms—to name a few.

Democracy is choice; freedom of choice demands dissent, diversity, difference, all the contradictory counsels through which a majority arrives at a decision through public debate by press, radio, television and meetings of parties and organizations. This is the assumption underlying the ACLU activities for political freedom.

Without courage to assert rights, they weaken. The test of progress in American liberties is to be found in the determination of organized citizens to get and hold the rights they are presumed to have. Every minority won such rights as it has only by struggle, by organization, by insistence that its claims be recognized. "When liberty dies in the hearts of people," wrote Judge Learned Hand, "no constitutions and no laws will save it." (Roger N. Baldwin, "Rights: Assert or Lose," *The New York Times*, August 31, 1981, p. A17, published five days after he died. Excerpted from the introduction to the collected ACLU Annual Reports, published in 1970. See chapter 2.)

SPREAD OF DEMOCRACY (1973)

I am convinced democracy is the best form of government because, as Churchill once said, it is the least evil. Some forms of it are working well; I think, in local governments fairly well, in some aspect of the United Nations, for example, where all the states are equal whether they are little or whether they are big, weak or powerful. That's a form of democracy where each one has a single vote, and while their recommendations and decisions don't carry great weight, nevertheless it's a form of democracy and that's the only way, the only kind you could have that would suit the needs of all nations, these different peoples; democracy works in some relations and it doesn't work in others. (Roger N. Baldwin, from a speech at the American Jewish Committee dinner on Human Rights in the U.S.A and the United Nations, at which he received an award, May 17, 1973.)

ACLU'S RELATIONS WITH GOVERNMENT (1975)

The ACLU's relations with government officials have depended both on the personalities of men and on the political temper of the times. Always professional critics of government, we have never been received as colleagues, despite our own conception of our duties as supporting the very principles that officials are presumed to uphold. But the conflict over application of principles, always the crucial test, has commonly put them on the other side from us.

[Among all the administrations] the "New Deal" was our deal. The entire atmosphere changed in Washington with the advent of Franklin Delano Roosevelt and his Cabinet. They were civil liberty–minded; they were for the most part our friends, many of them former or present members of the Union. Access to the president was simple; his secretaries of our persuasion. A small organization like the ACLU, influential mainly by force of its disinterested purpose and prominent personnel with their many contacts, worked best in the New and Fair Deal era through sympathetic public officials, or, if unsympathetic, those who would rather yield than be involved in public attacks in a pro–civil liberty atmosphere. The New Deal gave us at once a host of sympathetic friends in Washington, and reforms long delayed began to come to life. I went to Washington much oftener [*sic*], with a dozen projects on my calendar, pushing our friends toward our goals.

The New Deal, which by necessity undertook such sweeping reforms as to create almost overnight new federal powers in a welfare state, was of course the response to the economic collapse of the inflated system of speculative profit of the 1920s. Its concepts of welfare brought also concepts of rights; for the ACLU it was an ally and friend. The Supreme Court in one decision brought under federal protection all of the Bill of Rights as applied to the states, making uniform the rights of all throughout the country for the first time in our history. The Court in a whole series of decisions paralleling the years of activities of the ACLU, but related only in the spirit of the times, defined and refined the content of one right or another.

Government became less the agent of restriction of rights, more the protector through law and administration as well as the courts. No greater period of expansion of rights marked the years until the civil rights revolution of the 1960s, led in the first instance by the Reverend Dr. Martin Luther King and the black masses, later by a whole array of forces committed to equality in law and practice. With industrial warfare turned peaceful and racial warfare so greatly reduced, political and public violence has almost gone from American life. I would put that at the head of the list of advances for civil liberties in the broad sense during all these fifty-odd years.

> *It is the business of government to see that no one interest suppresses another, that all get their chance to carry on their propaganda and activities. This is what the Bill of Rights is for. That is what democracy means.*

Today the Bill of Rights is far stronger in law and practice than when I started out fifty-odd years ago because of forces both within and outside the country. The world has come to a concept of human rights not only through the United Nations, which formulated them in a historic document, but through the rise to power of the former colonial states and worldwide acclaim of freedom and liberty. I count the Third World the key to world order. In the United States, minorities long silent are backed by press and citizen agencies; our democracy is more virile. Not all is right or current; nor can it be in a democracy ever facing new adjustments as it grows and changes. But the ACLU can claim on its record what I think the greatest good of all: to testify by deed to the enduring goal of mankind's search for the equal rights of all to live out their lives in peace and freedom. (Roger R. Baldwin Collection, Roger N. Baldwin memorandum to Alan F. Weston, editor, *Civil Liberties Review*, May 2, 1975, draft.)

"NO FIGHT FOR CIVIL LIBERTIES EVER STAYS WON" (1976)

Reform brought a number of test cases in the courts, some of which we handled, and which resulted in so liberalizing the concepts of morality that few challenges were made in later years by the Customs Bureau. Sensibly, it appointed as adviser a distinguished liberal, a cultivated gentleman, Huntington Cairns, of Baltimore, who decided in the first instance whether a book, pamphlet, work of art et cetera should be banned. He banned very few. Every appeal I made to him was promptly and favorably decided. Judges and juries in tolerant New York, center of most test cases, were uniformly favorable in the cases of the *United States vs. Married Love*—of all titles!—*Ulysses* et cetera. Birth control, nudity, even four-letter words became permissible.

Morris Ernst was our mainstay in these cases as adviser and contact man with the official, and developed through his work for us and others, coupled with his own predisposition to sex as a constitutional freedom, into probably the leading legal practitioner in the country in that field. Not only was the censorship of the Customs Bureau cleaned up; that of the Post Office, with far more of a contest, followed. The two had to work together; what the Customs Bureau banned from importing, the Post Office refused to admit to the U.S. mails in U.S. editions. The list was enormous—a thousand titles. The Post Office solicitors, usually Catholics, or under a Catholic postmaster general, responded readily to the pleasure of the Legion of Decency or the Catholic Organization for Decent Literature, with bishops at their heads. They would not more than listen to our libertarian views, though we labored over the years in endless conferences.

Only the courts finally checked them. In a series of cases taken to the U.S. Supreme Court on the initiative of our Council on Freedom from Censorship, of which Elmer Rice, the playwright, was the vigorous and uncompromising leader from its inception, the Post Office censorship was changed from a bureaucracy to suicidal decisions. The *Police Gazette* and *Esquire* cases nailed down the principle that only the courts could determine the question of access to the mails. The Post Office Department didn't give up without a fight in Congress, where it tried to change the law to permit prosecutions at the place of receipt rather than of sending, to get away from those New York juries into some favorable illiterate spot like Mississippi.

The struggle was one of my major preoccupations for several years, since it represented bureaucratic censorship at its most dangerous point—the reading matter of the whole country. The fight cannot be said to be wholly won; no fight for civil liberties ever stays won. The road ran uphill for us, and the going got hard. But Truman himself, even more than Roosevelt, became a civil rights president, manfully standing by the recommendation of his commission on civil rights despite the disaffection of the South. We had nothing to do with the appointment of that commission, inspired, I think, largely by the NAACP, but Morris Ernst, our general counsel, was one of its members, and all of them were friends. (From Roger R. Baldwin Collection of Papers, draft by Roger N. Baldwin, 1976.)

BALDWIN AND J. EDGAR HOOVER (1977)

Author's Note: Following are excerpts from an interview with Roger Baldwin conducted by Alan F. Westin, editor of the *Civil Liberties Review*. Baldwin was then ninety-three years old. The ACLU had just obtained through the Freedom of Information Act ten thousand pages of reports that the FBI had compiled about the ACLU in a half century.

Westin: From these papers can we pinpoint when the FBI first started compiling dossiers on ACLU leaders and activities?
Baldwin: Right from the start. A "radical confidential" report was sent by agent "836" to J. Edgar Hoover, a young assistant in the Bureau of Investigation, then headed by the professional private detective, William J. Burns. This report contained the shocking news—to the FBI—that we were supporting "free speech, free press, etcetera" for everyone, "no matter whether they be anarchists, IWW, Communists

or whatever." And even if they want to "speak and write . . . against this government." The report also said we had "unlimited financial backing," unfortunately untrue.

What disturbs me on reading these reports is not so much the distortion of our public activities, but the covert intelligence information about U.S. senators, AFL officials, and others that the FBI collected and recorded.

Agent 836 told Mr. Hoover that "Justice Brandeis of the United States Supreme Court" is helping the ACLU and "has advised these people to sue Attorney General Palmer for the [antiradical] raids which have been conducted by this Department . . ."

Westin: Did you know at the time that the FBI was compiling such reports?
Baldwin: We knew that the intelligence agencies were compiling dossiers on everything they considered radical, including what they called "extreme liberals" who supported the Bill of Rights for radicals, unionists, and the like.

Westin: Did you ever protest this to the Justice Department?
Baldwin: Indeed, we did. Our protests were directed at the FBI's overall system of political espionage and harassment. As early as May of 1924, the ACLU sent a detailed memorandum to the attorney general challenging the FBI's use of wiretapping, planted agents, opening letters, seizing publications, recruiting organizational informers, conducting raids on meetings and headquarters to seize literature and records, and similar teahouse. We said these were creating "a secret police system actively interfering with the civil rights of citizens." Our memo also condemned the FBI's collection and dissemination of "grossly inaccurate and obviously colored" information about the so-called "Red menace," as well as the FBI's maintaining a master list of "several hundred thousand" people branded as "supporters" of radical activities.

Westin: I see from these records that J. Edgar Hoover, by 1924, the acting director of the FBI, wrote a detailed "refutation" of those charges to the attorney general.
Baldwin: Yes, he evidently took us quite seriously. He denied a few of our charges, said others were hearsay, defended many, and explained that some of the practices had been abandoned. That last was true—Hoover was far better than his superior, William J. Burns, who had been fired by the attorney general. In fact, when I called on Hoover in the summer of 1924 to discuss our charges, he declared that the FBI would observe the rights of all citizens "scrupulously."

We had high hopes for Hoover and the bureau under Attorney General Harlan Stone's guidance. And even issued press releases commending a "new" FBI. Hoover wrote me a letter of thanks that said, "If I can leave a desk each day with the knowledge that I have in no way intruded on the rights of the citizens of this country ... then I will be satisfied.

Westin: How long did the FBI reforms last?
Baldwin: Well, most violations of civil liberties in the late 1920s and '30s came from local and state governments, not the FBI, so we had only a few occasions to challenge FBI actions in that period. After World War II, when the FBI stepped up its political surveillance, we often condemned its role in attacking the political opinions of citizens and its extensive role in wiretapping and unlawful spying. We now know from the FBI documents that Hoover never stopped his surveillance of the ACLU, even to authorizing "confidentially" an FBI membership in the ACLU.

Westin: How did you react to the disclosure that in the 1950s, after you retired as director, an ACLU staff member [Irving Ferman, head of the Washington office] gave information to the FBI about suspected left-wingers in the ACLU?
Baldwin: That was a shocking experience, to find an ACLU official using the FBI to check up on his own colleagues. None of us knew anything about it. It was a secret contact, which as not affected the integrity and good faith that the ACLU established over all these years.

Westin: What is your strongest conclusion after looking over these heretofore-secret FBI papers?
Baldwin: That the FBI should not be concerned at all with the political opinions and activities of citizens. We condemned that as early as 1924 and recently in the Watergate period. It should be clear that a democracy and a political police cannot live comfortably together. (Roger N. Baldwin, "J. Edgar," *The New York Times*, excerpted from Op Ed, August 26, 1977, p. 25.)

DEMOCRACY DEFINED (1978)

Living in a democracy is like living on a raft. It never sinks but your feet are always wet. Well, our feet are always wet and we continue to struggle and we will continue that way as far as we can see. So long as we have enough people in this country willing to fight for their rights, we'll be called a democracy. (Baldwin statement in 1978, from "Traveling Hopefully," videotape produced by the ACLU for the ninety-fifth birthday dinner for Roger N. Baldwin at the New York Hilton, Tuesday, June 13, 1978.)

COMMENTARY
Baldwin and the U.S. Government's War on Terrorism
JOHN SHATTUCK

In March 1981, I received a letter from Roger Baldwin. Roger was then ninety-six, and I had invited him to speak at an ACLU conference on the threat to civil liberties posed by the new Reagan administration and right-wing leaders like Sen. Jesse Helms (R-NC) who had taken over the Senate. The entire civil liberties agenda seemed to be on the line—from the separation of church and state to the gains of the civil rights movement, to the defense of free speech and the right to privacy. Citing reasons of infirmity, Roger declined my invitation, but his letter exhorted "a new generation of ACLU leaders to defend freedom in this most dangerous time for civil liberties that I've seen." He ended his letter on a characteristically upbeat note, repeating his famous advice that one must always "travel hopefully" in the battle for human rights.

Roger's observation that the Reagan era promised to be the "most dangerous time for civil liberties that I've seen" was riveting but also surprising. After all, he'd witnessed the Palmer raids, the internment of Japanese-Americans during World War II, the anti-Communist witch hunts of the McCarthy era, Watergate and Nixon's intelligence agency abuses, and plenty of other treacherous times for the Bill of Rights in twentieth-century America. Against this perilous history, I took Roger's dire assessment of Washington in 1981 to be a statement of his belief that no battle for liberty is ever finally won, and every danger seems greater than the last until it is confronted. He was urging us to confront the radical right as it grasped for the levers of power in the 1980s.

If he were with us today, I believe Roger Baldwin would make the same assessment about the "war on terrorism," and he would exhort us once again to confront the danger it poses to human rights. At the height of the Vietnam War, in 1970, Roger reminded us that the defense of liberty is most urgent in times of crisis. He wrote: "Those of us who insist on maintenance of the Bill of Rights in wartime are constantly confronted by the argument that we should suspend our liberties until victory is won. But we deny that any such sacrifice is necessary. On the contrary, we affirm that a war for democracy cannot be won if we sacrifice the very liberties we not only profess to at home but extend to all the world.... We concede the necessary controls of military information, of enemy aliens, and of activities presenting a clear obstruction of the war, but we do not accept controls of opinion, nor of debate and dissent on the critical issues."

To honor these words, let us extend their logic to the situation today. Here, then, is what Roger Baldwin might have said about the war on terrorism.

The savage terrorist attacks on the World Trade Center, the Pentagon, the Spanish Railways, the London Underground, and other places around the world have shattered our expectation of security and driven us to consider new security measures that would sharply reduce our freedom. But as we defend our open society against terrorism, we should remind ourselves why freedom is worth defending. Indeed, the very freedom that makes us vulnerable to acts of terror is also our greatest weapon against terrorism because it binds us together as a people and rallies our defenders around the world.

What security measures can our government adopt without destroying our liberties? At the heart of our freedom are four rights enshrined in the Constitution: the right to speak freely; the right to be free from discrimination because of one's race, religion, or national origin; the right to privacy; and the right to due process of law.

Freedom of expression is what promotes the flow of information and ideas through an open society, restrains government, and provides space for the beliefs and practices of minorities. Freedom of expression should rarely be curtailed, but it is not unlimited. Some forms of expression are not protected, such as speech in furtherance of an act of terrorism, which can be investigated and prosecuted. Spending money is not a pure form of expression, and the government's authority to trace and block sources of funding for terrorist crimes can be strengthened without damaging core liberties. But free speech in general is more essential than ever to a nation in crisis, and its restriction will only serve to undermine, not promote, national security.

The right to be free from discrimination on the basis of race, religion, or national origin is what keeps our diverse immigrant society dynamic, and helps it avoid the ethnic and religious conflicts that are threatening to engulf the world today. As waves of intolerance against Muslims sweep over Western societies, it is clear that no time is more important to hold the line against group discrimination than a time of stress after a terrorist attack, when the temptation is great to find scapegoats.

If screening systems are put into effect to identify suspected terrorists, they must avoid the use of racial or ethnic profiling because that will only fuel the climate of discrimination and hate. Not only is our freedom at stake in the way we deal with discrimination; our security will be further threatened if we appear to respond to terrorism by putting the blame on ethnic or religious groups such as Arabs or Muslims. The roundup of thousands of Arab or Muslim men in the United States in the weeks following the September 11 attacks came dangerously close to ethnic or religious profiling.

The right to privacy is what protects individuals against an overbearing government and preserves their freedom to live their lives as they choose. With the benefits of electronic communication, we have come to accept the costs that some information about us will become broadly available to others and that our lives will no longer be so private.

But there is a limit to how low we should allow our expectation of privacy to go if we are to preserve our most basic freedoms. It has been proposed that one way to stop terrorism is to require people to carry computerized "smart cards" that track their movements and contain their personal histories. This is beyond the limit of our privacy expectation because it would move us toward controlled automatons, just as broad government authority to conduct unlimited electronic surveillance would turn us into talking records. The enactment in the fall of 2001 of the so-called "USA Patriot Act" was a big step backward for the right to privacy.

Due process of law is what distinguishes our society from authoritarianism and anarchy. It is the heart of the justice system in a democracy. To be sure, there is no single formula for what constitutes due process, and the Constitution would allow some aspects of the justice system to be expedited or briefly delayed in processing terrorism cases. But the right to be released unless charged with a crime, and to a fair trial when accused, cannot be compromised without sacrificing basic freedom. The well-documented abuse of foreign prisoners by the American military in Iraq, Afghanistan, and Guantánamo was a wholesale assault on the principles of due process under both domestic and international law.

In the end, the gravest threat to an open society is not the risk of terrorism, it is the risk of overreaction to terrorism that dangerously restricts freedom.

Fifty-eight years ago the international human rights movement was launched when the Universal Declaration of Human Rights was signed at the United Nations. The Universal Declaration was patterned after our own Bill of Rights. In order to live up to our role in drafting that historic document, and in response to terrorism, we should make the protection of human rights a central feature of American domestic and foreign policy. Reasserting a commitment to freedom—especially in times of crisis—is the best way to protect our security.

———

John Shattuck, CEO of the John F. Kennedy Library Foundation, served as National Counsel and Washington Director of the ACLU from 1971 to 1984; Assistant Secretary of State for Democracy, Human Rights and Labor from 1993 to 1998; and U.S. Ambassador to the Czech Republic from 1998 to 2001. He is the author of *Freedom on Fire: Human Rights Wars and America's Response.*

At the height of his career as founder of the American Civil Liberties Union, in his office in New York, circa 1950.
—*Courtesy of the Roger R. Baldwin Collection*

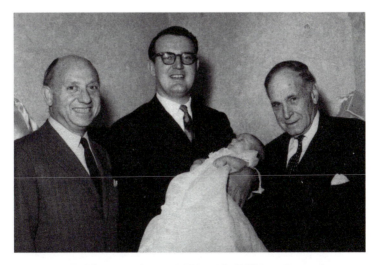

Roger N. Baldwin, right, in 1958 with William J. vanden Heuvel, center, holding his infant daughter, Katrina [now editor of *The Nation* magazine], and Sen. Jacob J. Javits (R-NY). Vanden Heuvel, a protégé of Baldwin, worked closely with him at the ACLU and in establishing the International League for Human Rights.
—*Photo by Friedman-Abeles*

Roger N. Baldwin talking with Sen. Edward M. Kennedy
(D-MA), at a dinner in 1964, in Baldwin's honor on his 80th
birthday in New York.
—*Courtesy of the International League for Human Rights*

Roger N. Baldwin, right, with his oldest son, Roger
R. Baldwin, in front of the Baldwin home, Windy
Gates, in Chilmark, on Martha's Vineyard,
Massachusetts, in 1948.
—*Courtesy of the Roger R. Baldwin Collection*

Roger N. Baldwin, right, with his son, Roger R. Baldwin, and his daughters-in-law, far left, Mary Ellen Baldwin, wife of Carl R. Baldwin, and Pat Baldwin, Roger R. Baldwin's wife, circa 1960s.
—*Courtesy of Roger R. Baldwin Collection*

Roger N. Baldwin, left, with his close friend, Gov. Luis Munoz Marin, the first governor of the Commonwealth of Puerto Rico, inside *La Fortaleza*, the governor's mansion in 1957. Baldwin regularly taught a course in constitutional justice at the University of Puerto Rico Law School.
—*Photo by El Mundo*

Roger N. Baldwin, right, talks with India's Vengalil Krishnan Menon, in 1958, during a meeting in New York City. He was a member of India's Parliament and one of the most influential men in India as the principal aide to Prime Minister Jawaharlal Nehru in foreign policy.
—*Photo by Leo Rosenthal*

An avid outdoorsman and bird-watcher, Baldwin is seen here in 1956 in the woods and with his canoe in the Ramapo River near the Baldwin home in Oakland, New Jersey.
—*Courtesy of Roger R. Baldwin Collection*

Roger Baldwin with his wife, Evelyn Preston Baldwin, in Haiti in the 1950s.
—*Courtesy of the National Tourist and Industry Services*

Roger N. Baldwin speaking at the Sheraton Baldwin Palace Hotel in 1956, with an ACLU attorney, Ernest Besig, looking on.
—*Roger R. Baldwin Collection*

By the 1960s, Baldwin had built the ACLU into a formidable nationwide civil liberties organization. He then went on to found the International League for the Rights of Man, which worked closely with the United Nations.
—*Courtesy of the Roger R. Baldwin Collection*

Roger N. Baldwin on his 95th birthday on
August 2, 1979, receiving a birthday cake from
Norman Dorsen, New York University professor
of law, and, far right, Kurt Vonnegut.
—*Courtesy of Norman Dorsen*

William vanden Heuvel, Deputy Ambassador to the United
Nations, left, presents the Presidential Medal of Freedom,
on behalf of President Jimmy Carter, to Roger Nash Baldwin,
right, seated in a hospital in New Jersey. Baldwin was too
ill to join other recipients of the medal who received it
from President Carter in a ceremony in Washington, D.C. at
the same time—3 p.m. on January 16, 1981.
—*Photo by Lawrence Frankel*

The test of progress lies in increasing freedom for the enrichment of individual life. Democracy and civil liberty are a means to that end. So, too, is the organization of labor.

—Roger N. Baldwin, 1938

Labor unions have not always been a part of the American mosaic. The early labor organizations established in the late eighteenth and early nineteenth centuries were an enigma to businessmen, most of whom considered the concept of "worker's rights" alien to the profitable flow of profit from industrial enterprises. Nonetheless, "business unionism" came to be accepted by management as the economy expanded and the entrepreneurs of business soon realized that they needed to pay workers more in order to have them purchase the goods made and sold by business. In the 1920s, with the formation of the American Civil Liberties Union, there was an increase in labor unrest as government set the rules for labor and management, basically inhibiting unions from organizing and denying their right to indulge in collective bargaining.

But not for long. When Roger Baldwin put together the first board of directors for the American Civil Liberties Union in 1920, he made a point of securing the involvement of five unions: the Teacher's Union of New York, the Amalgamated Textile Workers, the Amalgamated Clothing Workers, the Telephone Operators Union, and the Illinois Federation of Labor. Baldwin wanted his board to have the cache of respectability, so he successfully persuaded Felix Frankfurter of Harvard and James Weldon Johnson of the NAACP to be among the members, the majority of whom had pro-labor backgrounds. At a time when unions were losing membership because of intimidation by management and government, Baldwin asked the ACLU to step up to the challenge. It went to bat for the United Mine Workers to organize a free speech campaign that wound up with the company's owners evicting workers from their company-owned dwellings, resulting in the outbreak of violence. Two dozen miners were arrested for inciting violence, but they were acquitted—thus giving Baldwin and the ACLU a start on its reputation as "a friend of the working man."[1]

Baldwin would later look back on this initial progress, and subsequent court victories, and write: "Very few people today can appreciate the bitterness and the defeat of this struggle between the employers and employees all over the United States. How many people died in that struggle, how many people were jailed in that struggle of the strikebreakers. We were effective because of our principles, not because of our size. We were not influential from the point of view of members, but we were quite influential when we went to court with a lawyer and insisted that the Bill of Rights should be enforced. And the courts paid attention. The trade union movement had to wait until the Supreme Court upheld the National Labor Relations Act. It ended practically all of the violent labor strikes and for the first time the public authorities had to enforce the Bill of Rights in the industrial field."[2]

Baldwin himself became an active participant in strike protests, beginning in 1924 when he joined eight thousand silk workers who went out on strike in Paterson, New Jersey. When the police closed down the public hall in which the strikers had intended to meet, Baldwin left his office and went to Paterson, where he held a "public meeting" on the steps of city hall. "We'll get a lot of American flags and we'll have a parade down to city hall. We'll show them that this is the Bill of Rights that we're defending," he said at the time. When some of the thirty protesters were arrested and Baldwin was not, he marched down to police headquarters and asked to be arrested with the others. The police obliged, charging him with "rout, riot, and unlawful assembly." He would be acquitted by the Supreme Court of New Jersey in a unanimous opinion.[3]

In 1973, Baldwin received an award from the American Jewish Committee for his fight for labor's human rights. In his acceptance remarks, he made it clear how important progress in labor had been both to him and to the ACLU and the nation: "When I look at my own experience of fifty years with civil liberties at home, I see an almost startling advance, despite the most adverse world events. National protection of rights never before recognized by courts or legislatures brought equality in law to blacks, to women, and to organized labor," he said.[4]

The challenge for labor in the twenty-first century, of course, is no longer a just a matter of civil liberties. It is maintaining its political muscle as the AFL-CIO itself begins to split apart, with a number of large unions—such as the Teamsters Union—breaking away from the parent organizations. One of the contributing factors to the spinoffs, experts say, is the fact that in the past fifty years labor has been reduced in its membership from about one-third of all workers in America to approximately 13 percent today. That in itself poses a new and staggering hurdle for the labor movement in general.

—W. K.

Notes

1. Diane Garey, *Defending Everybody: A History of the American Civil Liberties Union* (New York: TV Books, 1998), pp. 71–72.

2. Memo to file on the president, 1975, from Collection of Roger R. Baldwin.

3. *Defending Everybody*, 74.

4. Roger N. Baldwin, from a speech at the American Jewish Committee dinner on Human Rights in the United States, May 17, 1973, at which he received an award.

CHAPTER 6

LABOR AND CIVIL LIBERTIES

The employers of the United States have on the whole accepted, though reluctantly, the new era of labor organization and collective bargaining.

—Roger N. Baldwin, 1938

Author's Note: Labor was the cradle in which Roger Baldwin launched the movement to preserve and protect individual liberties under the Bill of Rights. At first, he saw labor as the victim of callous business barons who cared not a bit for the people whom they hired. He was profoundly dedicated to resisting management's taking advantage of all men and women in the work force. He saw the situation in stark terms. "It is still local fascism—that is, the rule of property interests by lawless violence directed against the working class," he wrote in 1935. Even when labor began to gain a foothold in the mid-1930s, Baldwin still believed that the New Deal at first did not move quickly enough. He saw Franklin Delano Roosevelt and his administration as "timid and vacillating." In 1937, Baldwin hailed the U.S. Supreme Court's decision upholding the National Labor Relations Act "a turning point not only in the history of labor but in the history of constitutional rights." By 1938, however, Baldwin wrote with great satisfaction, "The unions developed a growth and a self-assurance. It is a reasonable prophecy that with these tendencies the United States may well be headed for a vast strengthening of the democratic principle by the curtailment of industrial autocracy." His most significant pronouncement on the issue of labor unions and civil liberties came at the close of 1938 when he wrote: "The total force of articulate public opinion, reflecting their attitudes to economic conflict, shows evidence of shift, in the direction of labor." Indeed, Baldwin looked upon the struggle for labor's rights as having succeeded even before World War II. "It is a fair conclusion from the record that 75 to 80 percent of the employers in industries where labor organizes abide by the law without resistance," he said even as America began to gird for a war it did not want—but, ironically, would open the labor market at home to tens of thousands of jobs for union members, including women for the first time because most of the men were in the service. Following World War II, of course, labor gained a firm foothold in American business and industry. Eventually the unions grew powerful enough so that they no longer needed to turn to the ACLU. Accordingly, Baldwin moved on to other challenges. Arguably, the ACLU did as much—or more—to put labor on the front burner as a national issue during those early years of the Great Depression than any other group in America. Following is Baldwin's overview of those years when the ACLU was deeply involved in the labor movement.

—W. K.

In Baldwin's Words

ORGANIZED LABOR WINS RECOGNITION (1938)

Many defenders of civil rights on principle are content to accept them without defining progress. I am not. My frame of reference requires a concept of progress. In general terms, it is the extension of the control of social institutions by progressively larger classes, until human society ultimately abolishes the violence of class conflict. The test of that progress lies in increasing freedom for the enrichment of individual life. Democracy and civil liberty are means to that end. So, too, is the organization of labor.

A society of class interests like ours is beset by conflicts of liberties. Employers claim the right to hire and fire at will as a necessary condition of efficient business. Workers claim the liberty to organize and bargain collectively. Other workers claim the right not to organize and to bargain individually. The public claims the right to be free of disorder and to uninterrupted public services.

We are confronted today not by a temporary industrial struggle in our national life, but by a long and historic struggle throughout the world. For the issue of civil liberty in industrial conflict underlies the phenomena of fascism, socialism, and the preservation of political democracy. It lies at the heart of those forces that today make for both civil and international war. Our appraisal of contemporary industrial conflict in the United States almost inevitably colors our judgment of those vaster world conflicts determining the survival and extension of the liberties which civilization has, with compromise and limitation, achieved.

It seems to me inescapable that a student of history must accept the conclusion that political and economic change depends largely upon the development of power residing in the self-interest of one class or another. The classes whose self-interests are in conflict today are those controlling private property and the means of production, and those employed by them. Between the clear alignment of opposing interests, between those who hire and those who are hired, stands in every country a larger or smaller middle class of small propertied and professional people. They identify their welfare ordinarily with the larger propertied classes. The vast changes we are witnessing today throughout the world are largely dependent upon the political direction this middle class takes. The overwhelming popular support in the 1936 election of the present administration, in a country dominated by its middle classes, was a clear indication that the controllers of business, Mr. Roosevelt's "economic royalists," had lost popular support, forfeited by the collapse of "rugged individualism" in 1929 to 1933. However confused and indefinite their purposes, both the working and middle classes at least are unwilling to return to a system of comparatively unregulated industry. They are definitely embarked on a program of public control by democratic means of the organization of our national economic life.

Quite as significant as this popular political revolt have been the changes through which democracy as a principle of organization has expanded in industrial relations to collective bargaining by labor, protected and encouraged by law. Significant, too, is the advance of the democratic principle through public ownership and operation of industries affected, as the lawyers say, by a public interest. It is evident in the Tennessee Valley Authority, in municipal ownership of public utilities, and in the widespread drift to public ownership of the railroads and of the electric power industry. Whatever one's view of the merits of public ownership, it is plainly a form of democracy in which the whole public as consumers becomes the owners of community services. It is this extension of the democratic principle to industry and public ownership that the autocrats of private business fear, and which in every land they resist. It is this resistance that creates the conflict between our political civil liberties, used for these ends, and the repressive and anti-democratic tactics of the masters of industry, determined to retain their established positions and power.

A reasonably objective view of the means for strengthening democracy must look to the most significant popular force in politics over the last fifty years—the rise of the organized power of the producers of wealth, the wage-workers and farmers. These economic movements with their political parties have, in all industrialized countries except our own, come to represent either the opposition or the government. The rise in power of labor, everywhere supporting the instruments of political democracy, is met by the determined opposition of the defenders of property—the employers of labor. In that struggle the employing class become the opponents of that democracy by which the working class seeks to rise.

The long history of the suppression of labor's civil liberties in the United States has until recent years reflected the domination of law by employers. One hundred years ago the early trade union movement was regarded in law as a conspiracy against property rights. Combinations of workingmen were treated as crimes both here and in England. From that early outlawry the law progressed to a halting recognition of rights made necessary to meet the insistent demands of men for collective action. But the long road of their organization is marked by bloody repression unparalleled in any other industrial country in the world; for the American employer, product of a pioneering and violent civilization, has demanded his unrestrained right to do business as he pleases. He has resisted interference by government on the one hand, by organized workers on the other. Every device he could contrive to prevent organization he has used. The law responded to his demands in the injunctive mandates of courts, in the statutes, and in the use of troops to suppress industrial "disorder."

That American strikes, like strikes elsewhere, have been marked by occasional damage to property and by violence against strikebreakers, is a matter of common knowledge. Attacks on strikebreakers are an almost instinctive response by workers against those who it seems to them are stealing their jobs. But that characteristic violence in strikes has not justified the wholesale measures of military policing taken by federal and state governments. So responsive are governors to employers' demands for the protection of property and so unrestricted is a governor's power in calling out the militia, that this use of the state's ultimate power is tragically easy. It requires no imagination nor indeed any sense of partisanship to understand that where troops come in, civil liberties go. As there are virtually no civil liberties in wartime, so there are no civil liberties under military rule.

Judging the complex record of suppression, the evidence is plain that the most powerful weapons against civil liberties in industrial conflict are troops and injunctions. Our industrial history shows that where one has not been invoked, the other has, and with equally disastrous effects upon labor's rights. But it would be unfair to the record to charge the agencies of government under pressure, acting through these powerful weapons, with the larger responsibility for suppressing labor's legal rights to organize and strike. Constitutional rights have been far more often violated by the lawlessness of employers' agents than by the public authorities, acting lawfully or lawlessly.

Happily, the long record of legal opposition or indifference to labor's right to organize has undergone an almost revolutionary transformation in the past few years. The passage by Congress in 1935 of the National Labor Relations Act under the influence of a liberal administration and pressure by stronger organization of labor has succeeded in putting labor's rights upon a firm legal foundation. From the point of view of the Bill of Rights, no more profound change has taken place in our history. The decision of the United States Supreme Court in April 1937 upholding that act is a turning point not only in the history of labor but in the history of constitutional rights.

With the encouragement of the trade union movement by the New Deal administration, the unions developed a growth and a self-assurance, which aroused the employers. A warfare unprecedented in extent and character, conducted by private and official violence and the mushroom counter-growth of the company-controlled union, combined to check the new power of labor. The year 1934, climax of resistance by employers to a rising labor movement, showed a longer record of industrial conflict than any year since the world war. The National Labor Relations Act of 1935 was in part the answer both of the government and the trade unions to the unparalleled warfare on labor's rights to organize.

In the year which has passed since the Supreme Court upheld the National Labor Relations Act, its salutary effects have become evident to all who can view it without prejudice. It still runs a gauntlet of conservative criticism as one-sided, partisan to

> *Employers have come to accept collective bargaining under the pressure of the unions and of the law.*

labor, and unfair in administration. The theory on which it is based is manifestly one-sided, but it is all on the side of civil liberty. It assures to labor its rights to organize free of coercion by employers. It abolishes the company-controlled union. It prohibits discharge for union membership. It restrains employers from coercing their employees in their choice of the agencies for collective bargaining. It requires them to bargain collectively in good faith.

The employers of the United States have on the whole accepted, though reluctantly, the new era of labor organization and collective bargaining. It is a fair conclusion from the record that 75 to 80 percent of the employers in industries where labor organizes abide by the law without resistance. The average employer does not of course welcome trade unions. He would prefer no unions. When that happy day went, he chose company-controlled unions. Since the law now denies him these, he prefers the A. F. of L. When he cannot get the A. F. of L. he will, with some difficulty, accept the CIO—or resist. But resistance is constantly growing less. When the greatest steel corporation in the country accepts a contract with a CIO union without a fight and renews it a year later, when the greatest automobile producers sign a contract with a CIO union and renew it a year later, it is fair to assume that the major industrial interests have come to recognize that the price of industrial peace is cheaper than the price of industrial warfare.

As the National Labor Relations Act has become more generally accepted, the sit-down strike has pretty nearly disappeared. It can be reasonably prophesied that this emergency method of combat will be completely abandoned wherever the legal machinery for adjustment of industrial strife works. Resistance by the bitter-enders among the employers may provoke a few more such demonstrations. One other aspect of alleged lawlessness charged against both the A. F. of L. and CIO unions concerns the rapid development in recent years of picketing in large numbers, so-called mass picketing. The right to picket, which is a form of free speech, advertising grievances to the public and workers, has been established in law. It is still subject to restraints based upon the superior rights of the public to the use of streets and sidewalks, upon the control of violence and disorder, and upon the use of fraudulent or libelous signs. The courts have generally come around to the common-sense view that at one location a single picket may violate one or another of these rights, while at another location a thousand men may not. Mere numbers are no justification for restraint. Yet an incessant propaganda is directed against mass picket lines in every major strike on the grounds that they intimidate loyal workers who want to work. They commonly run a gauntlet of jeers or of placards in the hands of strikers. But not even mass picketing in large numbers has succeeded, save in rare instances, in preventing the access of workers or officials to their plants. Those rare instances have been overdramatized, not only because they are dramatic in themselves, but because of the anti-labor bias of the press. In every such instance the picket lines have been almost immediately broken by police action.

We are engaged in a transitional economy that carries the support of one section of the population and arouses the opposition of another. But the substitution of law for industrial warfare is one of the more stable phases of transition. The gains won by the labor injunction laws, the federal and state labor relations acts, and the court decisions extending labor's rights are in substance secure. The exposures of employer violence and espionage by the Senate Committee on Civil Liberties have already gone far to disarm the professional strikebreakers and to put the industrial detectives out of the unions. The unions, though divided, are growing. The great mass-production industries are well on the road to complete industrial organization. The percentage of workers organized, though still less than 20 percent of the total, has doubled in three years. The conviction among workers that they will remain in the working class and that protection of their rights lies only in powerful organization has replaced the indifference and individualism of the more fluid years before the Depression. Employers have come to accept collective bargaining under the pressure of the unions and of the law. (Roger N. Baldwin, and Clarence B. Randall, "Organized Labor and Political Democracy," in *Civil Liberties and Industrial Conflict* [Cambridge, MA: Harvard University Press, © 1938 by the President and Fellows of Harvard College], pp. 3–48.)

COMMENTARY
Defense of Labor's Rights: A Central Theme of Baldwin's
ARYEH NEIER

The early reports by Roger Baldwin on the work of the organization of which he was the principal founder focus on the battles the ACLU fought over the great issues of the day. Many of these battles involved the ACLU's defense of labor's right to organize, a central theme of Baldwin's own efforts for many years. As he pointed out in the annual report for 1921: "We are not concerned to promote any radical program or the cause of any class. But the circumstances of industrial conflict today force us chiefly to champion the rights of labor to organize, strike, meet and picket, because labor is the class whose rights are most attacked." Another struggle that preoccupied the ACLU in its founding years was its attempt to secure freedom for hundreds of critics of America's engagement in World War I, including socialist presidential candidate Eugene V. Debs, still serving federal prison sentences in the early 1920s for their peaceful protests. Yet Baldwin also made it the ACLU's business from the start to demonstrate that the organization's concern with free expression applied to all. In the same report in which he emphasized the primacy of the battle to defend labor's rights, he also made clear that the ACLU would uphold the rights of the enemies of most of its other clients. He wrote that: "Efforts of the New York City police to break up meetings of the Ku Klux Klan and to handle Klan activities in the same lawless manner as they often handle radicals met with a vigorous protest from the Union. Although we are, of course, uncompromisingly opposed to the principles and activities of the Klan, nevertheless we have demanded for them as for everyone else the free exercise of their civil rights without official interference."

Roger not only committed the ACLU from the beginning to defend the liberties of even the enemies of liberty; equally significant, he forged our belief in the universality of rights. They must be defended for all. In an essay he published in 1970 in conjunction with the organization's fiftieth anniversary, Roger set forth what I believe is the distinctive organizing principle of the institution he founded. He said that, "The task of the ACLU is to . . . proclaim that the rights of all depend on the rights of each, not to suffer without action the slightest invasion of liberties in the conviction that to tolerate one is dangerous to all."

There have been other individuals and institutions that have defended liberty but, to my knowledge, the ACLU is unique in its commitment to carry out that principle. Because it believes in that principle, with which Roger imbued the organization, the ACLU has not limited itself to defending freedom in what seem to be important cases, or cases on behalf of clients who seem notable or attractive. It has also devoted itself to defending freedom in matters that may appear trivial in their own right or that may involve the most repugnant clients. The principled commitment to the view that the rights of all depend on the rights of each is the basis for the development of the ACLU's nationwide, decentralized structure. It does not suffice, for those committed to that principle, that there should be a team of top lawyers in New York or Washington prepared to take on significant violations of civil liberties. It is also essential that the ACLU should be on the scene in Arizona, Wisconsin, Tennessee, and every place else in the United States to defend the liberties of anyone—librarian, soldier, criminal defendant, high school student, or member of a racial or religious or minority—whenever their liberties are threatened.

Probably the most controversial case that I was involved in during my tenure as Roger Baldwin's successor twice removed as executive director of the American Civil Liberties Union was the defense in 1977 and 1978 of free speech for a group of American Nazis who wished to hold a demonstration in Skokie, Illinois. Among the many hundreds of letters I received from ACLU members and others about the case were a lot that did not quarrel with our contention that even the Nazis had a right to express their hateful views. Rather, they excoriated our decision to devote some part of our resources to the defense of the Nazis. What they were asking was that the ACLU should repudiate its history and its reason for being.

I recall that while the Skokie case was under way, I met Roger for one of our periodic lunches in which we would talk about the state of the world and in which Roger would give me advice on one or another issue of current concern to the ACLU. On this occasion, Roger was uncharacteristically a few minutes late. He apologized profusely, blaming his lateness on the fact that, because he had emphysema and his physician had told him not to climb stairs, he had taken a taxi rather than the reliable subway (at the time, he was ninety-three or ninety-four). I brushed aside his apology, telling him that my schedule had been more hectic than usual because of Skokie. Therefore, I had relished the few quiet moments while waiting for him to show up. Roger did not commiserate with me. Instead, he said, "You're having fun, aren't you?" I acknowledged that, indeed, I was having fun.

It was another lesson I learned from him. He was a happy warrior, at his most zestful when doing battle for a cause in which he believed. Though not blessed with his temperament, watching Roger and talking to Roger taught me a lot about how to enjoy a good fight, especially a fight over principle.   ˙

Aryeh Neier, a former National Director of the American Civil Liberties Union and Executive Director of Human Rights Watch, is President of the Open Society Institute in New York.

Introduction to Chapter 7

The net result of the drive of entrenched religious forces has been to intrude religion into the schools, to establish Christianity as a state religion so far as the schools are concerned, and to discourage dissent by those who oppose such a concept of education.
—Roger N. Baldwin, 1944

Education in the public schools is now being permeated with talk of religion. Across the country, right-wing organizations are working to infuse religious dogma into public education. In Congress, there has been a resurgence of a movement to revive the so-called "school prayer" amendment. There is also a movement afoot to take the science out of science in the classrooms of the public schools. Since the famous 1925 Scopes "monkey trial," in which the ACLU defended a Tennessee teacher convicted of teaching evolution, the ACLU has fought off attempts by opponents of the scientific theory of evolution to forbid, limit, or otherwise undermine the teaching of biological evolution in public schools. Instead, the new mantra is called "intelligent design," a theory that an intelligent supernatural entity has intervened in the history of man on earth.

"The backlash from a nation fed up with the ACLU kicking crèches out of municipal Christmas displays has created a new balance," is the way that one veteran journalist puts it. "State-supported universities may subsidize the activities of student religious groups. Monuments inscribed with the Ten Commandments are permitted on government grounds. The Federal Government is engaged in a major antipoverty initiative that gives money to churches. Religion is back out of the closet."[1]

Not only does the threat of religion in the classroom endanger the constitutional provisions of separation of church and state (see chapter 10), but the federal government is permitting taxpayers' dollars to be funneled into private, parochial schools in the form of "vouchers," as well as to other religious institutions. Many professional educators—particularly those who have long supported the public school system of education in the United States—fear that by siphoning off funds from the public schools they will, inevitably, wind up with a shortage of funds, thus hurting the very students that government is committed to help.

In this environment, is it any wonder that teachers and school administrators alike are up in arms about the "No Child Left Behind Act," which calls for every public school in America to meet certain standards or be categorized as "failing"? Is it any wonder that more and more teachers find themselves in the uncomfortable position of being forced to "teach the test" rather than bringing their own innovative techniques of teaching into the classroom?

This is the educational battle line for civil liberties today. The question will be: How can the quality of our public school teachers and students be raised while, at the same time, shortchanging the school system by not funding it to carry out the strict provisions of the so-called "No Child Left Behind Act"? The ingredient that the federal government has left behind is the money with which to fund the programs that are intended, admirably, to raise the level of education of schoolchildren of all ages in America.

It should also be mentioned that the issue of academic freedom has come back into play, indirectly as a result of 9/11. For example, on the Columbia University campus, students claimed they had been intimidated by "advocacy" teaching, in this case Jewish students who felt threatened academically because of expressing a pro-Israel point of view in a class taught by professors of Middle Eastern origin, who denied the charges. The president of Columbia, Lee Bollinger—one of the country's preeminent scholars on the First Amendment—appointed an ad hoc faculty committee to look into the complaint, but the committee's report in the spring of 2005 said it found no evidence of any statements made by faculty that could reasonably be construed as anti-Semitic. Nonetheless, the Columbia incident was one of several conflicts concerning Middle East studies programs on other campuses, which began with the passage by Congress of a bill in 2003 that mandated that area studies programs that receive federal funds under Title VI of the Higher Education Act must "foster debate on American foreign policy from diverse perspectives." Although the bill languished in the Senate, it sent a chill through many Middle East scholars because it was an intrusion by the government into teaching in the nation's university classrooms. The issue continues to be unresolved as America's academicians try to find an appropriate balance—but without government intervention.

—W. K.

NOTE

1. Charles Krauthammer, "Essay," *Newsweek* (August 8, 2005): 78.

CHAPTER 7

EDUCATION: KEY TO PROTECTING LIBERTY

The issues of academic freedom which have broken out into overt action in the legislatures and courts are trifling compared with the underlying causes of the restraints on the liberties of teachers and students.

—Roger N. Baldwin, 1944

Author's Note: Of all the issues that Roger Baldwin spent his life tackling, one of the most important to him was academic freedom—the right for teachers and students to make full use of their First Amendment rights to speak, write, and be heard in the marketplace of ideas in our primary and secondary schools and institutions of higher learning. In 1924, only four years after he founded the ACLU, he said about the U.S. educational system: "A servile attitude has been created throughout the public school system. A healthy, critical attitude has gone. In this atmosphere no real training for citizenship in the sense of getting children to do their own thinking is possible." He warned in 1927 that education was, in general, "for the status quo," and he expressed his concern about academic freedom as well. Sadly, in many of America's public schools today, Baldwin's words still apply. His lifelong battle for the young people of America to use their minds to explore all kinds of theories—political or otherwise—has resulted in some progress, but in too many classrooms of America today, students and even teachers feel compelled to "toe the line" when it comes to the teaching of civics, history, political theory, economics, sociology, psychology, and the whole range of fields young minds want to tap into. Yet even as he deplored any constraints on free expression of opinion by teachers or students, he derived some satisfaction as a result of the student movement of the 1960s—the mass demonstrations, the civil rights movement, and the widespread antidraft protests. "I think," he said in an interview in 1974, "that the student movement for participatory democracy, as they called it, had a lot of merit to it. In some schools students have votes on faculty matters." He expressed his attitude toward affirmative action in that same interview when asked how he felt about quotas: "I hope I see it always, all of these devices in which sex or color, even religion, are recognized as steps on the way toward a—what the Marxists call—a classless society." That said, Baldwin worked within the democratic system to bring about change; he enjoyed being perceived as an old "radical," but in truth he found his way easily in the corridors of power in government, in private industry, in the labor unions, and in the professions—especially teaching, a field in which he participated at the University of Puerto Rico, where he taught a course in government. Academic freedom continues to be an issue on campuses in the United States. Baldwin's writings on education were clear and uncompromising.

—W. K.

In Baldwin's Words

EDUCATION FOR THE STATUS QUO (1927)

If the schools are to help build a new social order, freedom of opinion among schoolteachers is indispensable.[1] Anyone concerned with the cause of free speech, as I have been in the years since the war [WWI], must feel dismay in calculating the unprecedented inroads on the freedom of teachers and students alike.

By law and by pressure of self-appointed guardians of patriotism and religion, the schools and colleges have been put under such restraints of critical dissent as never before existed. More laws have been passed by the states interfering with teaching by imposing prescribed rites and subjects than [at any time] in American history. More teachers and students have been disciplined for unpopular views in the years since the war than in any previous period. What was a mere tendency before the war to discourage independence has since been buttressed by law or dictated by interested minorities.

On the whole, it may be said without question that the public schools have been handed over to the keeping of the militant defenders of the status quo—the Daughters of the American Revolution, the American Legion, the Fundamentalists, the Ku Klux Klan and the War Department. Look at the twelve-year record! Compulsory patriotic rites and flag-saluting by law in most states; compulsory reading of the Protestant Bible in eighteen states, contrary to the provision for the separation of church and state; compulsory teaching of the Constitution by prescribed routine; making a crime of the teaching of evolution in three states; special oaths of loyalty for teachers not required of other public servants in ten states; loyalty oaths required of students as a condition of graduation in many cities; history textbooks revised under pressure to conform to prejudice; restriction or ban on teachers' unions affiliated with the labor movement; laws protecting tenure beaten or emasculated; compulsory military training in both colleges and high schools, with inevitable pressure on students and teachers by the military mind.

The school system has in these years since the war been bound by the controls of the dominant interests of the country. Teachers who challenge the status quo have been intimidated or removed. A servile attitude has been created throughout the public school system. A healthy, critical attitude has gone. In this atmosphere no real training for citizenship in the sense of getting children to do their own thinking is possible. No task is more difficult than to wean the educational function, created and maintained by the public, from the control of those minority interests who dominate the public by playing on majority prejudice.

From a long experience with a multitude of cases coming to the Civil Liberties Union from schools and colleges, I can prophesy only that the road to that goal will be increasingly difficult, and that those who dare in the interests of freedom even to discuss a new social order, will, however patriotic, bear the burdens of all pioneers. (Roger N. Baldwin, paper submitted in 1927 by ACLU for guidance to a special Committee on Academic Freedom, which it created.)

BOLSTERING ACADEMIC FREEDOM (1944)

For over twenty years a standing committee of the American Civil Liberties Union has been tackling problems of what is inadequately termed "academic freedom," fighting out the issues in the legislatures and the courts, and organizing pressures on school and college administrations. No other national agency has undertaken such a task on so wide a front, and no other has conceived freedom in schools and colleges as identical with the liberties of all citizens. The narrow concept of academic freedom as applied only to teaching in the classroom, to a teacher's liberty of opinion and action outside it, and to uncontrolled research and publication, fundamental as they are, covers only a fraction of the obligations that these chaotic years have imposed on the defenders of liberty in education.

The struggle for that liberty has involved such varied issues as the attempts to deny by law the right to teach the doctrine of evolution; to exclude from the schools children who refuse on religious grounds to salute the flag; to use public monies for private schools; to take public school time for private religious instruction; to deny public education to students conscientiously opposed to taking military training; to prohibit teachers from joining a union affiliated with organized labor; to prohibit students from inviting outside speakers to address them without administrative approval; to censor student papers and associations; to impose loyalty oaths on teachers alone among public servants; and to regulate the textbooks selected by the educators.

—————

While our schools and colleges have manifestly not achieved that independence that should characterize the educational process, and while teachers are still under too many arbitrary administrative controls, the past twenty years have marked up sharp advances in resisting outside pressures. Educational freedom is on much more solid foundations, despite autocratic systems and a still too easy conformity with majority dogmas. Those advances are to be noted in the failure of the campaign to outlaw the teaching of evolution, now effective only in small regions of the "Bible Belt," in the Supreme Court decision permitting children to attend public schools without participating in flag-saluting; in the removal of almost all restrictions on the freedom of teachers to join an association affiliated with organized labor; in the virtual nullification of the teachers' loyalty oath laws; in the disappearance of the furor over Communism in the schools; in the greater liberty of college students, as a result of their own insistence, to form associations, publish papers and invite outside speakers; and in the decline of the movement to use public money or time for religious purposes.

These achievements add up to the defeat of the forces attempting to impose on the schools and colleges their own brands of patriotism and religion. Their power in our national life has also declined as democratic forces have expanded. Professional patriots like the DAR and the Legion have abandoned their intolerant crusades against "subversive" elements; the Fundamentalists have withdrawn from the educational front, licked, while the Klan and a host of little quasi-fascist patriotic societies have been liquidated. More liberal forces command public office; the courts have vindicated civil liberties in one decision after another; and the power of labor, tending toward greater democracy despite many inner anti-democratic practices, has cheeked our autocratic industrialism.

The issues of academic freedom that have broken out into overt action in the legislatures and courts are trifling compared with the underlying causes of the restraints on the liberties of teachers and students. In the Civil Liberties Union we have dealt only with the effects, too late usually to undo the damage, or too superficially to accomplish much more than neutralize some of the most arrogant pressures on the schools. The real job lies with the teaching profession itself, organized, independent, courageous—as it is only slowly getting to be—leading boards, trustees, alumni, donors, and legislative committees to a recognition that only unrestricted freedom in the hands jointly of teachers and the taught can build character, citizenship, and universal democracy on the ruins of the greatest Holocaust in history. For the task confronting educators after the war is not the salvation of American democracy alone, but its integration with the struggle for larger democratic liberties throughout the world. Our own will be secure only as liberty everywhere is secure. Our children will be prepared for citizenship in America only as they are prepared for citizenship in the world. (Roger Nash Baldwin Papers, Box 22, Folder 6, *American Federation of Teachers* magazine, 1944, Princeton University, N.J.)

> *Freedom in presenting and studying all of the facts, freedom of teachers to believe as they see fit and to express their beliefs like other citizens obviously cannot be achieved without organization. The present pattern of control from on top down must be replaced by control from the bottom up.*

THE VOICE OF THE STUDENTS (1974)

Author's Note: The following interview was conducted in 1974 at Columbia University.

Q. In the student movement of the 1960s, you have written mostly about the mass demonstrations and the civil rights movement. You refer to antiwar and antidraft expressions. What do you think of the need for reforming universities and colleges?

A. I think that the student movement for participatory democracy, as they called it, had a lot of merit to it. In some schools students have votes on faculty matters.

Q. *So you think that there has been some student voice incorporated into the faculty's decision-making process?*
A. Yes, yes. University administration is still open to so many reforms.

Q. *Given all the years that you spent trying to win free speech rights at the university, what was your reaction when the students shouted down professors in the classroom and then refused to allow people to come on the campus who were controversial speakers?*
A. They had a big incident up at Harvard where they wouldn't allow anybody that was opposed to the students' interest to talk. Shocking affair. Shocking! The students never learned the lesson that the rule must be applied to everyone equally, and what's good for the other fellow is good for you: that one man's right is another man's right. They don't learn that. They still believe what the average citizen believes: that your enemies don't have the same rights as you have.

Q. *Since you have seen so many decades of this, when you say they never learn, are you saying that each group comes up either claiming its own rights or believing it has the answer to society's problems?*
A. You have to teach them over and over again, that this is the only way they get along. And it's a hard lesson.

Q. *Do they learn?*
A. I suppose they learn in those circumstances because somehow or other they're stopped from putting into effect their prejudices. And that's one of the reasons, it seems to me, that the law has the right to coerce people into not interfering with other people's rights. I would use any kind of coercion to assert rights, yes, to establish them. But I wouldn't approve of coercion in general. I'm against it in principle. But it has good uses, very dangerous ones, too.

Q. *Do you see any cumulative generational carryover, though, or does each generation of students have to start from scratch?*
A. Well, I wouldn't say each generation, but I would say the instincts of most everybody is to repress the things they hate and fear, and you have to teach them that that isn't the way things ought to be done.

Q. Does your experience lead you to be uncomfortable with quotas, either quotas for women or quotas for blacks in terms of affirmative action programs [in college admissions], or do you see some need for this as a transitional device from a kind of crystallized discrimination into something more equal?

A. I hope I see it always, all of these devices in which sex or color, even religion, are recognized as steps on the way toward a classless society. It is a society without distinctions as to what your origins are, or your race or your beliefs. I hope so. (Columbia University Oral History Research Office Collection, "A Conversation with Roger N. Baldwin with Alan F. Westin," editor, *Civil Liberties Review,* and professor of Public Law, December 18, 1974, pp. 25–45.)

NOTE

1. As executive director of the ACLU, Roger Baldwin dealt with scores of cases involving freedom of speech or press for students and teachers. So numerous were the issues that in 1924, the ACLU created a special Committee on Academic Freedom, headed by Professor William H. Kirkpatrick of Teachers College, Columbia University, to deal with the major conflicts these cases presented.

COMMENTARY
How Much Do People Know about the Bill of Rights?
Did Roger Baldwin Make a Difference?
SAMUEL WALKER

It is a standard exercise that always produces much hand-wringing. A public opinion survey reveals that Americans are woefully ignorant about the Bill of Rights. A 2004 survey of one thousand adults, for example, found that only 15 percent know that the First Amendment protects freedom of the press, and only 17 percent know that it protects freedom of religion. True, 58 percent know that it protects freedom of speech, but we still might reasonably ask, *only* 58 percent?

This game has been played for decades, with little change in the results. The earliest poll that I am aware of was done in 1939. The fact of the matter is that, Fourth of July rhetoric aside, Americans are incredibly illiterate with respect to the history of this country, the specific details of how our government functions, and the fundamental principles expressed in the Constitution and the Bill of Rights.

The persistent ignorance of most Americans about the Bill of Rights raises an intriguing question. Does civil liberties advocacy make any difference? The ACLU and other rights advocacy groups have always engaged in active public education programs. Do these efforts succeed in improving public knowledge about the Bill of Rights?

We can approach this question through the career of Roger Baldwin. As the founder and thirty-year director of the American Civil Liberties Union (ACLU), Baldwin was a tireless advocate of civil liberties. In my history of the ACLU, I argue that Baldwin's primary role was as an advocate. He was not a lawyer and fashioned no new legal doctrine, and was not an intellectual. But he was a tireless spokesperson, giving innumerable speeches and writing numerous magazine articles on particular issues. From the 1920s through the early 1950s he was widely regarded as "Mr. Civil Liberties." Did his efforts actually enhance public understanding of the Bill of Rights?

There is no way to answer this question scientifically. We cannot go back and survey people from the 1920s and 1930s. But there are other indicators that we can use, and they suggest that, while people are weak on the specific legal details, they do have a strong, gut-level sense of their rights and that this awareness has grown.

We first need to distinguish between different categories of Americans. There is no question that among members of the elite, awareness of civil liberties has grown enormously. Judges, attorneys, law professors, law students, and other intellectuals are, quite obviously, deeply immersed in and knowledgeable about civil liberties. It is what they do. Equally obviously, all such people are far more aware of civil rights protections today than their counterparts were in 1950. They are also more aware of privacy rights than were their counterparts in the 1960s.

Baldwin played a significant role in this long-term process. When the Supreme Court embarked on the protection of individual rights in the late 1930s, it enunciated in formal legal terms ideas that Baldwin had advocated in layperson's terms for almost two decades. The lawyers who argued the early cases and the justices who adopted civil liberties principles got these ideas from somewhere—Baldwin, the ACLU, and a handful of others were principal sources.

Among ordinary Americans, the issue is a lot more complicated. In my opinion most Americans have a strong sense of a right to free speech and a right to privacy, even if they are weak on the exact legal basis. The words "I have a right to...," and "They can't make me...," fall easily from peoples' lips. Week in, week out there are stories about ordinary people who raise a First Amendment claim: the person who challenges an employer's ban on wearing overtly religious symbols or clothing; the high school student who insists on a right to wear a T-shirt with an offensive slogan, or the claim that a government official has no right to ask questions. A sense of one's "rights" is now a deeply embedded aspect of American popular culture.

True, people are often quick to deny the same right to someone they don't like, but they at least have some sense of what their rights are, and this is an aspect of American culture that was not true in earlier decades. Much of what ordinary people know comes from the work of the elite. They have heard about free speech, privacy rights, and perhaps most famously the right to remain silent from celebrated cases. Thus, the long-term process is intellectual change that begins with a few lonely advocates (mainly Baldwin, in this case), to a broader elite, to elite institutions and new law (the Supreme Court), and finally to the general populace.

Are Americans well versed in the details of the Bill of Rights and civil liberties? No. Do they have a sense of entitlement to certain rights? Absolutely. Has that sense grown over the decades? Of course.

Did Roger Baldwin play an important role in that development? Yes.

Samuel Walker is Isaacson Professor of Criminal Justice at the University of Nebraska at Omaha, where he has taught since 1974. He is the author of eleven books on policing, criminal justice history and policy, and civil liberties, including *In Defense of American Liberties: A History of the ACLU*, 2d ed. (Southern Illinois University Press, 1999).

Introduction to Chapter 8

The historic function of liberalism is to interpret the new to the old; to defend it against persecution; to act as a shock-absorber in class strife; to attack injustices; to destroy faith in privilege and to establish the moral bases of equality and liberty.

—Roger N. Baldwin, 1941

Born out of the labor movement and rooted in urban centers, the term "liberal" was at the turn of the last century used to describe labor leaders who came under severe attack by the courts. In *Loewe v. Lawlor* (1908), the United States Supreme Court found a labor boycott by the hatter's union for potential customers not to patronize an anti-union company—such a radical move that it was deemed a "conspiracy in restraint of trade" under the Sherman Antitrust Act. In a 1906 "bill of grievances," the American Federation of Labor demanded—unsuccessfully—that Congress give labor unions immunity from the onslaught against its members.

Nonetheless, Roger Baldwin's early support of the unions helped "organize" labor and, by the time the ACLU in was founded in 1920, it was perfectly acceptable for its members to be called "liberals." The United States lagged badly behind Europe in its protection of workers and, to make matters worse, the battle to support labor became inextricably entwined with the increasing attacks on immigrants. "In many ways," writes one historian, "certainly in the Great Depression, ethno-cultural issues provided a stronger basis for urban liberal politics than did economics. And because the Democrats cultivated the immigrant vote, they became destined to be the majority party once a second generation came of age. The shift from Republican domination, although not complete until the 1930s, began during the Progressive Era."[1]

By the late 1920s, "urban liberalism," as it was called, began to become a tangible movement, in New York in particular, when Gov. Al Smith promoted legislation backing public health programs, workmen's compensation, and conservation programs. Still, American liberals' hope for an improved life at home were put on hold after World War I and it was seen as a temporary setback. However, by the 1930s liberalism began to spread in the form of a progressive political tradition that was embodied in the politics of the New Deal and symbolized by President Roosevelt. Liberal and left-wing activists persuaded Franklin Delano Roosevelt to announce a "court reorganization" that would permit the president to appoint six new Supreme Court judges that would give him a ten-to-five majority. The Roosevelt plan touched off a strong reaction and was labeled an "arrogant power grab" by conservatives. It failed, but the fundamental spark for reform and individual freedom that liberals promoted so passionately grew into a full-fledged movement across America.

Arguably one of the most influential people in the nation in the cause of liberalism was Arthur M. Schlesinger Jr. One academic, a professor of communications, described Schlesinger's contributions this way: "He has been influential in shaping our understanding of American political history and has written important treatises on the Jacksonian America, the New Deal, the Kennedy administration and the American presidency. Political commentators and historical scholars alike have long recognized the important role Schlesinger has played in shaping liberal political thought in America."[2]

Schlesinger, perhaps, is the best barometer with which to measure liberalism's progress. He has expounded on his theory—as others have, as well—that the tides of national politics explain political events, and that the pendulum swings back and forth over the decades. As he wrote in 1986, "Change is scary; uncharted change, demoralizing. If the law of accelerations is not to spin out of control, society must cherish its life-lines to the past. . . . So much of the past abides."[3]

Franklin Delano Roosevelt was Arthur Schlesinger's boyhood hero and, as such, set the standard for him on the topic of liberalism. That in itself shaped his view of liberalism for the rest of his life. In 1949, Schlesinger wrote:

> I heard Franklin Roosevelt's first inaugural address as a boy at school, fifteen years old. Since that March day in 1933, one has been able to feel that liberal

ideas had access to power in the United States, that liberal purposes, in general, were dominating our national policy. For one's own generation, then, American liberalism has had a positive and confident ring. It has stood for responsibility and achievement, not for frustration and sentimentalism; it has been the instrument of social change, not of private neurosis. During most of my political consciousness this has been a New Deal century. I expect that it will continue to be a New Deal century.[4]

As Roger Baldwin himself expressed his view of liberalism at the height of his career at the ACLU in 1948: "Despite the many and often distorted uses of liberalism, both in doctrine and as applied, it remains as an essential characterization of an attitude inherent in social progress in all areas of human relations."[5]

—W. K.

NOTES

1. James A. Henretta, David Brody, and Lynn Dumenil, *America: A Concise History* (New York: Bedford/St. Martin's, 1999), 565–67.

2. Stephen P. Depoe, *Arthur Schlesinger Jr. and the Ideological History of American Liberalism* (University of Alabama Press, 1994), ix.

3. Arthur M. Schlesinger Jr., *The Cycles of American History* (Boston: Houghton-Mifflin, 1986), 46.

4. Depoe, *Arthur Schlesinger Jr.*, p. 9.

5. Roger Nash Baldwin Papers, Box 20, Folder 8, Seeley G. Mudd Manuscript Library, Princeton, N.J., for Grolier Encyclopedia, April 1948.

CHAPTER 8

LIBERALISM AND POLITICAL CHANGE

Liberals see better than those who accept for the moment some higher goal that liberties once surrendered, even in a good cause, may be the authors of new tyrannies.

—Roger N. Baldwin, 1941

Author's Note: Roger Baldwin did not grow up thinking of himself as a "liberal." In fact, he thought he was part of the Harvard aristocracy, which kept an open mind on social issues and was imbued with the wish to "do good," but that was a far cry from what the word "liberal" came to mean in the passage of time. He abhorred political labels and, when pressed, would identify himself for the purpose of stirring up discussions as a "radical"—meaning he departed from the norm. However, his definition of "liberal" changed over time. In 1941 he wrote: "They [liberals] proceed on the assumption that liberty and democracy, their touchstones, are promoted mainly by the expanding power of new classes breaking the bonds of entrenched institutions." A few years later, in 1948, he offered this description of liberalism: "A philosophy of moderate and rational change in social institutions, characterizing an attitude between conservatism on the right and radicalism on the left, and therefore essentially a centrist position of reform." In fact, he rarely included the word liberal in his speaking vocabulary, though it did show up in some of his writings. Baldwin scholars say that is because he saw the term as meaning "reform," but not necessarily a strong enough term to describe the sense of immediacy that he always felt about undoing injustices when he found them. To Roger Baldwin, his journey was not in some great, overarching cause—but rather a series of starts and stops in the quest to make his quest to defend of the Bill of Rights. He knew that most Americans took the Bill of Rights for granted or did not know what they were. He eschewed any term such as "liberal" ascribed to him. His goal was simply to uphold a part of the foundation of the Republic to which he was so deeply committed.

—W. K.

In Baldwin's Words

LIBERALISM AND THE UNITED FRONT (1941)

Most great struggles for the extension of liberty have been marked by a union of some strong section of liberalism with the self-interest of a class fighting for its own advancement. An indispensable trend of these historic struggles is always the alliance of forces differing sharply in their ultimate goals, but agreeing on the accomplishment of immediate ends. These united fronts, formulated as a political tactic only in recent years, have marked great revolutionary crises and most struggles for freedom. They constitute the means by which new forces, feared and persecuted, bridge the chasm between the established order and their goals. They proceed on the assumption that liberty and democracy—their touchstones—are promoted mainly by the expanding power of new classes breaking the bonds of entrenched institutions.

The historic function of liberalism is to interpret the new to the old; to defend it against persecution; to act as a shock-absorber in class strife; to attack injustices; to destroy faith in privilege and to establish the moral bases of equality and liberty. The liberals prepared the moral and intellectual foundations for the French Revolution and they helped to lead what was, until the counter-revolution, a peaceful change from feudalism to new political and economic freedoms. They performed the same function in the Russian Revolution. In all lesser revolutions the liberal intellectuals have played their role of softening the old to make way for the new. That they have been often engulfed by the very forces they aided to power, when fresh consolidations succeeded the old, is an evidence not of their naïveté, but of the inability of men to avoid the temptations of power.

Yet, recognizing the risks of new tyrannies, the liberals have acted on the belief that social progress is achieved only by the organized and determined self-interest of larger and larger classes seeking for themselves the liberties which some form of autocratic control denied. They have championed the advance to political democracy and private capitalism from autocratic feudal rule as the basis of a power established not by divine right, birth or priestly privilege, but by the people themselves.

The fluidity of the liberal position, its lack of dogma and its preoccupation with immediate issues give it its force and its influence in a social community. The charge that liberals don't know where they are going but are on their way is, in fact, a compliment. The essence of social progress is to be on one's way. To know exactly where you are going, save in a general direction, is to subscribe to Utopian dogmas which explode under the pressure of events with the finality that has marked the end of a dozen Marxist sects. When liberals define a precise and ultimate goal, when they adopt a dogmatic body of tactics, they usually move over to another camp. Thousands of them have thus moved into Communist, socialist or anarchist sects, but they no longer function as liberals. Their influence as liberals demands freedom from any "isms," but also active participation in the struggles for freedom. That active participation is achieved most effectively in direct alliances. Liberals do not seek out alliances, but they are receptive to the appeals of various organizations and political wings who have an immediate, common purpose.

Of all the objectives which most readily unite the liberals, the fight for civil liberties takes first place. In every democracy, middle-class organizations of varying strength have united diverse elements on a common platform of the political rights necessary to keep open the highway for peaceful progress. And in every country these organizations of the middle class have been preoccupied with issues raised by repression of labor and of minority radical groups. Inevitably they have been characterized as pro-labor and pro-radical, however loudly they professed their disinterestedness. The personnel of all such organizations in all countries have been dominated by liberals sympathetic with the extension of the democratic principles, therefore hostile to established privilege.

To many liberals, the collapse of the united fronts is a matter of small concern, particularly in the United States where the parties of the left have made little progress and hold no substantial stake in the trade union or farmer movements. But in Europe, where organized labor has been long dominated on the political front by socialist or Communist leadership, they have had a vast significance. Among liberals the world over, seeking the dynamics of social advance in unity, they have created a belief in their strategy out of all proportion to their net influence on the more substantial movements of labor and farmers.

It is reasonable to conclude that the wave of the future will roll in on the tide of democratic advance after the war. Whether the transformation of our democracies is achieved by one means or the other, coercion or necessity, the problem of liberty is likely long to confront us. For the expansion of public powers in a state controlling so vast an area as our entire economy raises at once the questions of how those powers are in turn to be controlled, and to what degree the accustomed liberties of a democracy may be sacrificed in the process. It is in this critical function of social evolution that liberals may be counted upon to exert their major influence. For as the entire history of their participation in the greater movements of social progress indicates, their guiding passion is directed to preserving personal and civil liberties. No goal seems to them superior to those liberties by which men freely express their needs and desires, create their cultures, and associate together for their common interests. To them, the State, like all institutions, was made for men and their freedoms. They will not yield to any claim, however good, however temporary its sponsors allege it to be, which sacrifices to autocratic authority the practice of liberty.

Of all the objectives which most readily unite the liberals, the fight for civil liberties takes first place.

The preservation of the substance of democracy in Britain in wartime, its rapid growth in the United States from political to industrial and economic forms, its firm roots throughout the British Commonwealth and in the colonial world, all are encouraging evidences. And in all of these countries, as in others before the war, the striking fact to be noted is that the initiative and driving power for democratic advance arose from coalitions of labor, liberals and the left. Under the necessities of the economic crisis, and pushed by these advancing forces, governments have grown in power to a point where they, not private capital, are in a decisive position in the conduct of our economy. It is this combination of governmental controls and democratic support that promises a power sufficient to overcome reactionary resistance to change, and to avoid new autocracies. The degree to which change can be effected by peaceful means after the Holocaust, and the degree to which essential liberties can be sustained to guide it, will depend in large part on the vigor and influence of liberalism, and its capacity to impress its value at strategic points and moments on popular democratic forces. (Roger N. Baldwin, *Whose Revolution? A Study of the Future*

Course of Liberalism in the United States [New York: Howell, Soskin, 1941], 166–84.)

LIBERALISM DEFINED (1948)

A philosophy of moderate and rational change in social institutions, characterizing an attitude between conservatism on the right and radicalism on the left, is therefore essentially a centrist position of reform. Liberalism as a body of doctrine, derived from the use of the word "liberal," denotes a departure from the established institutions, standards and dogmas in an effort to change them for what is regarded as less authoritative and freer from tradition. Its central concept is that of individual rights, diversity of interests, decentralization of authority, freedom of conscience.

Liberalism describes bodies of doctrine in politics, religion, education and the arts. In politics it is used in the United States as synonymous with progressivism. In other countries it is identified with the institution of the "liberal arts" colleges and with the progressive educational principles of Professor John Dewey. In religion, it is identified with the revolt against Roman Catholicism and against Protestant fundamentalism. In art and literature various schools claim liberalism against the traditionalists.

The commonest use of the word is in politics, where liberalism achieved widespread currency in the later half of the nineteenth century in Europe. Its doctrines of revolt against feudalism, of laissez-faire in economics, of individual rights and freedom of conscience were embodied in political parties in many countries bearing the name "liberal." They regarded the state as an impartial arbiter between conflicting classes and opposed the extension of state power or its subordination to any class. With the development of trusts, protective tariffs and the rise of trade union power, liberalism declined, giving way to the dynamics of organized class power. The spirit of liberalism has, however, remained as a force in organized labor. In the United States liberalism is an essentially middle-class concept commonly expressed by its intellectual representatives, and adopted even by politicians. The New Deal of President Franklin Roosevelt embodied what was then regarded as the essence of liberalism, though its principles were far from its traditional political forms in Europe, requiring a great extension of state power, but in the interest of the "common man."

Typical of the editorial expressions of political liberalism in the United States are the periodicals, *The Nation* and *The New Republic*.

The principles of liberalism are philosophically bound up with the idea of equality. "Liberty, equality, fraternity," the slogan of the French Revolution, expressed the relationship between them, meaning more than equality before the law; rather equality of opportunity for all in all phases of life. Despite the many and often distorted uses of liberalism, both in doctrine and as applied, it remains as an essential character-ization of an attitude inherent in social progress in all areas of human relations. (Roger Nash Baldwin Papers, Box 20, Folder 8, Seeley G. Mudd Manuscript Library, Princeton, N.J., for Grolier Encyclopedia, April 1948.)

COMMENTARY
Pragmatic in His Liberalism as the Wiliest Pol
VICTOR NAVASKY

At various points in his amazing career Roger Baldwin offered his definition of liberalism:

- "The principles of liberalism are philosophically bound up with the ideal of equality."
- "Of all the objectives which most readily unite liberals the fight for civil liberties takes first place."
- "No goal seems to [liberals] superior to those liberties by which men freely express their needs and desires, create their cultures and associate together for the common interest."

Yet it was his deeds as much as his words that defined Baldwin's liberalism. In April 1948 he wrote the "Liberalism" entry for the Grolier Encyclopedia. It is fitting and proper that Baldwin, who began his career as a social worker and quickly saw the need for fundamental change, cited the New Deal idea that the "essence" of liberalism "re-quired a great extension of state power, but in the interest of the common man."

He also observed in his Grolier entry that, "Typical of the editorial expressions of political liberalism in the U.S. are the periodicals *The Nation* and *The New Republic*," for both of which he wrote. But the first time Baldwin's byline appeared in *The Nation* his piece was more radical than liberal and it was not an article written specifically for the magazine. It was a reprint of his address to the court on the occasion of his being sentenced for violation of the Selective Service Act, on October 30, 1918.

His words perfectly incarnate the tension between the radicals and the liberals. His stance was radical ("The compelling motive for refusing to comply with the Draft Act is my uncompromising opposition to the conscription of life by the State for any purpose whatever in time of war or peace"), but the ideas on which he based his act of conscience, the sentiment which informed it came out of the classic liberal playbook: "We have stood against hysteria, mob violence, unwarranted prosecution, the sinister use of patriotism to cover attacks on radical and labor movements, and for the unabridged right of a fair trial. . . ."

During the so-called McCarthy era, which began well before the senator arrived on the scene, liberals and liberalism came to be tainted by the equation which seemed to dominate those politically overwrought times: To be a liberal-was-to-be-a-fellow-traveler-was-to-be-a-Red-was-to-be-a-spy. At the same time so-called Cold War liberals were tarnished from the libertarian left as collaborators by those (like yours truly) who believed that the Red-hunters did more damage to democracy than the domestic Reds (whose liberties they were willing to curtail in the name of national security) ever did.

For all his idealism, when he felt he had to, Baldwin could be as pragmatic in his liberalism as the wiliest pol, even when or perhaps because, great issues of principle were at stake. Thus in 1940, when three preeminent ACLU Board members (including the boisterous Morris Ernst) demanded an ACLU statement denouncing Communism and the expulsion of Elizabeth Gurley Flynn, an open Communist, from the national board, Baldwin, fearing that these men might quit and establish a rival organization, perhaps fatally wounding the ACLU's chances for survival, acceded to their demands. Samuel Walker, author of *In Defense of American Liberties: A History of the ACLU*, reports "Although his accession was a deviation from ACLU principles, he rationalized it on the grounds that it would allow the ACLU to defend Communists with clean hands. If in his heart he knew it was a betrayal, he never said so publicly." On the other hand, when Freda Kirchwey's *Nation* issued a belligerent call to "curb the fascist press," Baldwin's ACLU refused to buckle under and Kirchwey resigned from the ACLU's National Committee in protest. Also, in 1976, when the ACLU posthumously reinstated Flynn to the Board, Baldwin confided to one of its officers that it did the right thing.

Over the years the term liberal seems to have been something of a political Rorschach test. In the sixties and seventies, militant New Leftists disdained liberals as wishy-washy moderates unwilling to take to the streets in the fight for racial justice and equality and against the Vietnam War. But ever since LBJ's Great Society lost its way in the Vietnam War, a shifting coalition of the radical right, evangelical Christians, neoconservatives, and plain vanilla Republicans has been so successful in demonizing the L word that mainstream Democrat candidates have been in perpetual flight from it; which in turn ironically seems to have rehabilitated liberal as a term that at least parts of the left are again willing to embrace.

Nevertheless, the same internal tension between radical, purist Baldwin and liberal, pragmatic Baldwin—the tension that led him to found the ACLU in the first place—endures. And Baldwin's legacy, his commitment to the struggle for civil rights, civil liberties, and human rights, his preference for nonmilitary solutions to political problems, his struggles on behalf of the dispossessed, and, the Elizabeth Gurley Flynn exception notwithstanding, his core belief that dissent is a form of patriotism, helps define liberalism's ultimate values.

Victor Navasky, former editor and publisher, now publisher-emeritus of *The Nation* magazine, is a prizewinning author and writer. His book *Naming Names* (2003) won the National Book Award. His latest book is *A Matter of Opinion* (2005).

Introduction to Chapter 9

The First Amendment has expanded in itself.... many things
have been added to it and I think in a complex society like ours
that you go on and keep finding new issues and new conflicts.
— Roger N. Baldwin, 1974

A United States Supreme Court decision in 1972 read, in part: "Above all else, the First Amendment means that government has no power to restrict expression because of its message, its subject matter, or its ideas or content."[1] That statement reinforced the First Amendment in the Bill of Rights dated December 15, 1791, stating: "Congress shall make no law respecting an establishment of religion, or prohibiting the free exercise thereof; or abridging the freedom of speech, or of the press...."

Throughout U.S. history, the press—a term that has been broadened to include the Internet and all of its information technologies—tries, with all of its flaws, to bring objective truth to the people. It sees itself as the independent watchdog of government and other institutions of power in a democratic society. That, of course, is not how it is perceived by the public. Journalism and reporters, in general, do not rank high on the public's scale of credibility, a notch above, perhaps, politicians and used car salesmen. That, in essence, is why it is so important to hold the media to some kind of uniform standards that today do not exist.

For all of its achievements in ferreting out corruption and crime in the corridors of the highest levels of government and corporate life, many observers believe the press has yet to put any noticeable restraints on itself. As one highly respected journalist-turned-author put it: "Journalism has become too important to be left to journalists. We went too far, and technology has come too far, and now we are in trouble, much of it our own making."[2]

Arguably the most important arena where the press has invoked the Freedom of Information (FOI) Act to force the government to share information with the public it represents is that of national security. And it is precisely in this controversial battleground that civil libertarians put the most emphasis—especially in times of war. There is precedent here. The framers undoubtedly were aware of the danger that the government would throw up such a roadblock—today we call it national security. They understood that the only way the press could be denied was if the information it sought would endanger the nation's security. As James Madison wrote in a letter to Thomas Jefferson, "Perhaps it is a universal truth that the loss of liberty at home is to be charged to provision against danger, real or pretended, from abroad."[3] Article 2, Section 3 of the Bill of Rights states: "Treason against the United States shall consist only in levying war against them, or in adhering to their enemies, giving them aid and comfort."

There is no question that during times of war (see chapter 3) that civil liberties have, frequently, taken a backseat to national security. The passage of the USA Patriot Act in 2001 contained enough provisions to tip the balance toward national security and, according to the ACLU, tipped it too far. Actions of Congress and the president during World War I and World War II, the Cold War, and even the Vietnam War and the war in Iraq have led both the executive and legislative branches of government to take actions that were construed as suspending constitutional rights in the interests of national defense. The courts upheld laws that prohibited citizens from speaking out against the draft in the First World War—certainly Baldwin was a prime example himself—and the internment of Japanese-American citizens was also upheld for quite some time before it was finally reversed.

One of the most important modern victories for civil liberties in the field of free speech occurred during the Nixon years with the much-heralded *Pentagon Papers* case. The Supreme Court's six-to-three decision permitted *The New York Times* to publish the top-secret record of the Vietnam War—a reaffirmation of the First Amendment. This was the first time in U.S. history that the court had been asked by the government to stop the publication of information it had obtained. During this era, the Watergate scandal broke. It led Congress to amend the Freedom of Information Act by calling for judicial review of the government's position that information was classified.[4]

After the Jimmy Carter administration came to office, it turned to the courts again, seeking injunction against *Progressive* magazine, which was about to publish an article on how to build an H-bomb, and the magazine had to hold up publication for a month. Only the publication of the same material in another magazine prevented the case from being heard by the high court. Subsequent administrations have also tried to limit the flow of "confidential" information to the public, but the media continues to press on with the use of the First Amendment. To this day, however, the aftershock of government's pressure on the media and the public has led to subtle but visible abuses of the First Amendment right of free speech. President George W. Bush's administration, for example, continues to draw wider and wider circles around the president and any dissenters wishing to peacefully gather at a site where he is speaking; the government has also screened out any individuals who do not agree with the administration from participating in the so-called "town hall" meetings Bush holds around the country. There is no doubt, civil libertarians say, that this erosion of the First Amendment is taking its toll on an individual's constitutionally guaranteed right to dissent. Further, the Bush administration has successfully managed to use the media when it describes protesters against the Iraq war as "unpatriotic" and "giving aid and comfort to the enemy." While Baldwin believed a great deal of progress had been made up until his death in 1981, political trends since then—and especially under the administration of George W. Bush—have alarmed civil libertarians who object to the administration's efforts to censor "whistleblowers" and other government officials who publicly criticize the government. The White House has also violated journalism ethics by "planting" and paying for stories about its favorite programs with specific members of the media.

Sadly, this does not appear to upset many of the high school youth of our country. According to a 2004 survey, "One in three U.S. high school students said the press ought to be more restricted, and even more say the government should approve newspaper stories before readers see them." One longtime civil liberties advocate explained the extraordinary attitude of the students this way: "Perhaps it should come as no surprise that more than a third of our high school students don't understand the Bill of Rights. Why, indeed, should they? Their government doesn't seem to understand either."[5]

—W. K.

NOTES

1. *Police Department of the City of Chicago v. Mosley*, 408 U.S. 92, 95 (1972).

2. Richard Reeves, *What the People Know: Freedom and the Press* (Cambridge, MA: Harvard University Press, 1998), p. 7.

3. Contained in a letter from James Madison to Thomas Jefferson, May 13, 1798. Referenced in *Our Endangered Rights*, chapter "National Security," by Morton H. Halperin, ed. Norman Dorsen (New York: Pantheon Books, 1984), pp. 281–82.

4. Public Law 93-502 (1974) 5 U.S.C. 551 (1976)

5. John J. Simon, immediate past president of the Connecticut Civil Liberties Union, a member of the board of directors of the Connecticut Center for First Amendment Rights, and a frequent spokesman for People for the American Way. From the *Westport News*, February 1, 2005, p. A37. The survey was commissioned by the John S. & James L. Knight Foundation and conducted by the University of Connecticut.

CHAPTER 9

LIBERTY AND THE MEDIA

If you can only say the things with which everyone agrees, you haven't free speech.

—Roger N. Baldwin, 1923

Author's Note: Roger Baldwin's ACLU took the position when it was formed in 1920 that free speech was not, in fact, being permitted in the United States. "The lid is on. There is no doubt about that. Everywhere in the United States the hysterical anti-Red campaign has clamped the lid on free speech and free assemblage," he wrote in the first year of the ACLU's existence. Over the years, however, as Baldwin became more and more effective as a free speech advocate, the government—and the public—began to awaken to the fact that our democracy was not what it should be. By the end of World War II, Baldwin would paint a more optimistic picture: "We are so accustomed to regard our freedom-loving country as setting the gauge for world democracy that we accept without question our forms of free communication as a pattern for all peoples," he wrote. By 1975, he looked back with satisfaction and, in an interview, he concluded: "Upholding the First Amendment was the New Deal's major achievement in the protection of civil liberties." Following, some excerpts of his thinking.

—W. K.

———◆———

In Baldwin's Words

FREEDOM OF OPINION (1920)

The lid is on. There is no doubt about that. Everywhere in the United States the hysterical anti-Red campaign has clamped the lid on free speech and free assemblage. In substance, it is an attack on the right of labor to organize, strike, and picket. Organized business is engaged in a colossal anti-labor campaign. The campaign is waged through two forces, law and direct action. The program of law for every state includes the prohibition of strikes through industrial courts, strike-breaking state constabularies, criminal syndicalism and sedition acts, and anti-picketing or injunctions.

The only places in the United States today with free press and free assemblage is where the workers or the farmers are strongly enough organized to take and hold these rights. For instance, North Dakota and Wisconsin alone among western states have none of the criminal syndicalism or sedition laws under which free opinion is gagged. Even in Montana, no convictions can be obtained under the criminal syndicalism law, because of the clean-cut issue between farmers and workers on the one side and the copper companies on the others. But the fiction that constitutional American rights can be maintained through law has been pretty well exploded. Everywhere the realization is growing that legal rights are hollow shams without the political and economic power to enforce them. The road to industrial freedom is the way to all freedom. (Roger N. Baldwin, "Freedom of Opinion," *Socialist Review* [August 1920]: 115.)

DEFINITION OF FREE SPEECH (1923)

Free speech is the right to say without interference things that are new and unpopular. If you can only say the things with which everyone agrees, you haven't free speech. If men who voice new ideals are sent to jail merely for utterances, plainly speech is not free. That is the condition we have in the United States today, despite our traditions and constitutional guarantees.

There are for instance still today in federal prisons fifty-three men convicted solely for their opinions during the war. There are over fifty in state prisons under criminal syndicalist acts, directed primarily at mere membership in the Industrial Workers of the World. This theory of guilt by mere membership has gone so far in California, where alone of all the states such prosecutions continue actively, that Miss Charlotte Anita Whitney of Oakland, well-known clubwoman and social worker, faces a long prison term merely because she joined the Socialist Party. Her local branch of the party became a local of the Communist Labor Party in 1919 and her membership automatically was transferred to it. Membership in that party was held to be a criminal offense under the syndicalist law, and Miss Whitney with others was sentenced. Her case is on appeal to the United States Supreme Court.

Why is it important to have free speech? The importance of freedom of opinion is that it is the only sure means of guaranteeing orderly progress. Repression of new ideas and forces over a long period of time inevitably results in disorder, violence and bloodshed. History is eloquent on the subject. In the industrial struggle in the United States today, where the rights of labor are restricted, violence follows. Violence is almost always used first by the employing class and public officials. Where labor can exercise freely its rights to organize, strike and picket, there is rarely violence *or* disorder.

Where should we draw the line? State laws, city police, federal deportation acts, are all out to punish certain ideas as such. The ideas aimed at by the law are "the overthrow of government by force and violence" and "the unlawful destruction of property." But the cases brought under those laws go far beyond any such ideas and show how impossible it is to administer fairly laws punishing opinion. Someone has to be judge, and that someone often lets prejudice and caprice guide him. The long record of political trials since the war proves that point beyond argument. Furthermore, it is true that only those persons are attacked who represent radical ideas and working-class movements. Those who stand for "things as they are" and who advocate force and violence against radicals are never prosecuted.

No one suggested prosecuting Secretary of State Langtry of Massachusetts when, in a public address, he said speaking of radicals:

> If I had my way I would take them out in the yard every morning and shoot them and the next day would have a trial to see whether they were guilty. (*New Republic*, January 21, 1920.)

Nor the mayor of Davenport, Iowa, when he said in an order to the Police Department:

> Load up the riot guns for immediate use and give them a reception with hot
> lead. We don't want any Reds here and we will go to the limit to keep them
> out. (*The New York Times*, January 9, 1919.)

These are just samples of reckless talk by men in and out of public
office who go much further than the radicals themselves, and always
without even a suggestion of prosecution. How can we get free
speech? Free speech never exists as an abstract right or as a guarantee
in the Constitution. It takes the determination and organized power of
men who want free speech for themselves or others, to get it. It was
James Russell who said: "They have rights who dare maintain them."
It is only in the unity of the organized workers' and farmers' movements, and in the help given them by liberal and religious bodies, that
the right of free speech can be made to live in reality. Tolerance of new
ideas and forces depends largely upon the unity and courage of those
forces themselves. The political unity of those forces in the election last
November won a greatly improved condition of civil liberty in a dozen
states where repression had been rampant. One of the most conspicuous
examples of the ability of men to get their rights against overwhelming
prejudice and odds is the history of the International Workers of the
World (IWW) free-speech fights, particularly on the Pacific Coast. Their
willingness to go to jail in large numbers for what they believed to be
their rights has almost always resulted in winning them. That was
equally true of the Woman's Party pickets in the suffrage campaign at
Washington.

What is the issue? All over the world today, there is a conflict between two ideas of property, the old system of private property for
profits, and a new system for property for use as expounded by
working-class and farmers' organizations. In that conflict, all over the
world civil rights are restricted; men and women are jailed for expressions of opinion, and in many cases, shot or hung. The course of
that conflict is marked by violence wherever the propertied classes use
violent methods of repression. It proceeds by orderly processes only
where civil rights are freely exercised.

How shall the inevitable industrial struggle be fought through in the
United States, by civil warfare, violence and bloodshed, or by the
unlimited exercise of civil and political rights on the field of political
and industrial conflict? (Roger N. Baldwin, "Have You Free Speech?"
Vital Questions Leaflet, Number Three, issued by the Methodist Federation
for Social Service, New York, 1923. Andover-Harvard Theological Library, Cambridge, MA.)

Danger of Suspending Free Speech (1931)

The Civil Liberties Union stands on the traditional principle of drawing the line between word and deed or attempted deed (and direct incitements of such deeds). We do not accept the recent decisions of the Supreme Court of the United States. We hold that the best way to avoid violence is to let people advocate any doctrine, however revolutionary, violent or radical their language may be. The essential basis of free speech is that it is a safety valve against explosions. Suppression, not free speech, makes for conspiracies and ultimate violence.

Nobody can tell what the effect of mere words will be. As Benjamin Franklin said: "Of course the abuses of free speech ought to be suppressed, but to whom dare we entrust the duty of doing it?" No man is able to exercise wisely the power of declaring what ideas are dangerous enough to be jailed and what are not. One man's opinion would differ from the next, and who is right? The opponents of free speech say the line should be drawn short of an overt act. They hold that even general language advocating violence will produce violence. All the facts of history are against them. Conditions, not words, produce violence. It should be clear from our statement of the facts and public policy that unlimited free speech is the best antidote to violence, and that the suppression of free speech by the violence of government or self-appointed "patriots" produces the very evils it purports to prevent. (Roger N. Baldwin, "The Right to Advocate Violence," American Civil Liberties Union, January 1931, p. 6.)

Free Speech for Nazis? (1933)

The controversy over permitting the United German Societies to hold a meeting in a city armory in New York aroused an amazing opposition to the almost routine sponsorship by the American Civil Liberties Union of the right of peaceful assemblage—even for Nazi speakers. The Societies proposed to put on their program an alleged Nazi agent, around whose activities the controversy raged. Although the American Civil Liberties Union as a defender of free speech has championed rights for all sorts of causes, even its friends bitterly protested its championship of the right of Nazis to speak. Defenders of free speech with records for a decade in behalf of unpopular minorities began to fall by the wayside with choleric diatribes against the right of this "murderous crew of assassins, Jew-baiters and tyrants" to raise their voices on American soil.

But two lawyers representing the Union, both Jews, Morris L. Ernst and Harry Weinberger, arose at the Mayor's meeting and championed the rights even of their bitter enemies to the same liberties which as lawyers and libertarians they have so long demanded for all without discrimination. At once they were assailed in the press and by letters, as well as by speakers at the meeting and from two sides. Conservatives attacked them on two grounds: first, that the meeting would certainly result in a riot; and second, that no representative of a government which persecutes Jews should be allowed to defend that government in New York. Communists attacked them on the grounds that free speech is to be regarded only as a weapon of class warfare, and it is the business, therefore, of radicals to oppose its use by reactionaries. They characterized the position of the Civil Liberties Union as that of "ivory-tower liberals expressing the ideas of a decrepit and bankrupt middle-class liberalism."

The Union's championship of the right of the Nazis to conduct their propaganda rests on precisely the same grounds as its championship in the past of the right of the Ku Klux Klan, Italian Fascists and other reactionary elements to have their say, whenever they were in a minority, as they were in many American communities. The Union takes the perfectly clear position that if a mayor or chief of police can ban one speaker today because he hates his doctrine, he can tomorrow ban any meeting or speaker against whom pressure is directed. Such a position leaves every mayor and chief of police the sole dictator of who may or may not speak in his town.

But it is on an even more significant ground than this that the ACLU bases its case, namely, that experience proves that propaganda like that of the Nazis is far better combated in the open than under suppression. Making martyrs out of them helps their cause. Their silly and arrogant doctrines of race superiority and their brutal persecutions once exposed to public ridicule and scorn, they will stand condemned and powerless. Nazis can't live long in the open in America.

The Jewish attorneys for the ACLU made another argument, and that in behalf of the Jews. They maintained that the Jews themselves were in no position to protest discriminations against their own race in America or elsewhere when they, too, take the same position as the Nazis in suppressing opponents' meetings. For the sake of the cause of the Jews, a minority people, they urged even for Nazis, that tolerance which the Jews are always demanding for themselves; and they did this not as a matter of principle but as a matter of strengthening the Jewish cause. The obligation of every champion of free speech is to oppose any and all suppression. (Roger N. Baldwin, "Free Speech for Nazis?" *The World Tomorrow* Fellowship Press, November 9, 1933: 613.)

Unions and Freedom of the Press (1938)

Public opinion as reflected by the daily press is increasingly attentive to organized labor. Despite the ready acceptance of employer propaganda against the new unions in the mass-production industries and the success of press campaigns in strikes for the right to work of non-union workers, the newspapers generally show a fairer, if not impartial, treatment of industrial strife. The news headlining of the operation of labor relations acts commonly displays fair reporting, accurate headlines, and adequate space. But editorially the larger and more influential newspapers tend to be biased, at least against the administration of the national act. This hostility doubtless flows in large part from the newspapers owners' resistance to collective bargaining with editorial employees.

Though the mechanical departments of the papers have been unionized for years, recognition of a union of reporters and editors is regarded as threatening unionization of the news and a menace to "freedom of the press." The American Newspaper Guild, now a CIO union, has waged an unceasing uphill fight against the united opposition of the American Newspaper Publishers Association.

In the vast area of public opinion influenced by the radio, labor's case fares more poorly. Far more than newspapers, radio stations are subject to pressure from their audience because the spoken word elicits a response which the printed word does not. Listeners are constantly urged, not only to buy, but to express themselves in regard to programs. But the program-makers are wary of industrial controversy. So fearful is radio of involvement that the three great networks, with a show of professed impartiality, prohibit the sale of time either to employers' organizations or labor unions.

The motion picture as a vehicle of public education is the most circumscribed of the three means of mass communication in its approach to industrial strife. The newsreel alone reflects it. Entertainment films do not. The editorial selection of newsreel subjects and the method of their treatment have a persuasive power in creating public attitudes. Newsreels of the larger strikes are common enough. But they tend to play up disorder or the implications of disorder by labor, since peaceful activities are not dramatic. Lawless violence against labor is rarely portrayed.

> *Free speech is the right to say without interference things that are new and unpopular.*

Most feature films, as everybody knows, deal with what are regarded by the producers as safe issues. They do not portray themes likely to undermine confidence in the existing economic system. Their unconscious bias supports the virtues of an acquisitive society—luxury, expensive leisure, competition, commercial success. Rarely do they depict the conditions of life of the underprivileged, the working class, or that lower third of our citizenship described by the president [Roosevelt] as "ill-housed, ill-clad and ill-fed." The dramatic material of life flowing from the colossal conflicts of our time, occupying the front pages daily, stirring universal emotions and loyalties, is only exceptionally pictured. The producers defend their apparent blindness to the issues by deference to the public's desire to be amused, not depressed by contemplation of struggle and injustice. Whatever merit there may be in that contention, it may be fairly assumed that the superior motive of the industry is, like that of radio-station owners, an inclination to remain safely on the side of the status quo. (Roger N. Baldwin, "Organized Labor and Political Democracy," in *Civil Liberties and Industrial Conflict* [Cambridge, MA: Harvard University Press, 1938], pp. 48–55.)

PROPAGANDA AND CENSORSHIP IN WARTIME (1941)

We will agree that our political democracy and the liberties essential to it should be maintained in war as in peace: A war for democracy makes no sense if we suspend democracy in conducting it. We will differ sharply as to the degree and character of certain restraints in wartime, but we cannot disagree on the democratic need of keeping open the channels of discussion, and, with it, of criticism and of dissent. We will agree that the government is justified in controlling the sources of military information. We will agree that enemy aliens are subject to reasonable restraints. We will agree that the government has the responsibility of dealing swiftly and firmly with any acts, committed or attempted, either against the government or the public peace.

But we will disagree as to the extent to which the government should censor or prosecute propaganda that may be construed to be hampering the war effort, to be undermining national unity, or to be interfering with industrial production. We will disagree as to government policy in relation to American movements reflecting the interests of totalitarian governments, both Communist and fascist.

For my part, I am concerned primarily with the freedom of us all to hear every side of public policy and to make up our minds in democratic fashion. That requires that no minority, whatever its character— democratic or antidemocratic—should be suppressed merely for its propaganda. The line should be drawn, as it has been traditionally, between words and deeds. We should not discriminate against the propaganda to the left and be blind to the propaganda of reaction. Democracy requires that the great agencies of communication—radio, the press, and the newsreels—should be free of government censorship.

If we are to accept these responsibilities in the peace to come, we can insure that peace only as we overcome the enemies of democracy within and without. They can be overcome, not by repression, but by the superior force of democratic morale, vigor, and purpose. Instruments of censorship and repression, once created, only too easily become weapons that can be turned against democracy itself. The road to freedom, my friends, lies not only in the Bill of Rights, but mainly in voluntary unity and voluntary restraints; the road to dictatorship lies in the outlawry of minorities, in prosecution of "dangerous thoughts," in censors, in secret political police, and in fear of free debate. Our choice is clear. (Roger Nash Baldwin Papers, Seeley G. Mudd Manuscript Library, Princeton, N.J., "Town Meeting" Bulletin of America's Town Meeting of the Air, Columbia University Press, vol. 7, no. 9, pp. 4–5, December 15, 1941.)

RADIO MUST AIR "FEARLESS DISCUSSION AND CRITICISM" (1942)

Effective use of radio in the war effort rests on the proposition that the public should be fully informed as to all the major policies of the government and with the right to hear critical discussion of their merits. Radio programs that reflect only the official views of the government might just as well be arranged by the government itself. The chief virtue in our system of private ownership of radio lies in the fact that our government does not control what is said on the air. This is not true in any other country. If we are to keep that system it can be justified only on the grounds of freedom to criticize government policies courageously. If radio does not permit that, it will lose public support and pave the way to government ownership. And nothing could be more disastrous to our democracy than to give sole control of the most influential means of communication and opinion to the government.

The tendencies now in wartime are to leave leadership to government agencies, and to go easy on criticism. Yet this is not the way to build national morale. Real unity comes from a free acceptance of policies arrived at by unrestricted public discussion. Discussion cannot be free unless minorities are heard. Radio should perform a service to morale-building as great as the newspapers. I venture to say that what the press prints by way of dissent and criticism cannot be paralleled in the radio forums, news commentators or the broadcast programs of public meetings. Timidity marks the selection of topics and speakers.

Radio has made advances in recent years. But radio still suffers from a lack of diversity in presenting varied viewpoints, and of courage in tolerating what program directors regard as unpopular views. Yet if the war is to be conducted on the basis of democracy, the necessary national unity and morale can be achieved only by the fullest possible debate of the conduct of the war, of the aims of the war and of the structure of the peace. Hundreds of publications raise issues on which radio is silent.

There is no easy prescription to cure timidity and bias. But it would help if all radio stations were required to report publicly their policies by filing records of what they refuse as well as what they take. It would help if monopoly practices that prevent local radio stations from presenting certain programs were abolished. But these remedies will only go a little way toward stiffening radio's independence.

A war for democratic ends can be won only by democratic practices. Democratic practices mean fearless discussion and criticism. Radio, in its own interest, can justify its independence only by its service to that end. (Roger Nash Baldwin Papers, Box 24, File 5, Seeley G. Mudd Manuscript Library, Princeton, N.J., "Is Radio Being Used Effectively in the War Effort?" Abstract of remarks at the Ohio State Institute of Education by Radio, May 3, 1942.)

LIBERTY AND ITS LIMITS IN A FREE COUNTRY (1942)

With the United States at war there is raised more sharply than ever the issue as to where a line should be drawn for interference with propaganda regarded as hostile to the national effort. We are always confronted with the difficult problem of limitations upon freedom of speech and the press. The best working principle is that the line should be drawn between language on the one hand and acts or incitements to acts on the other. That is the historic American position. We have always regarded it proper for the law to suppress all forms of the use of force and violence and all preparations for it.

While this has been the general rule, the Supreme Court of the United States laid down a somewhat different test under the pressure of the First World War. The Court at that time adopted the principle of "clear and present danger," which means in effect that language could be punished if it presented an immediate danger of inciting acts hostile to the conduct of the war or to the public peace. But when the Court attempted to apply this test it divided so sharply on what constituted a danger that in days of peace it has been pretty much ignored. During all the long years of Communist agitation only a comparatively few prosecutions were undertaken based upon that legal theory, and those chiefly under state laws.

The public policy which seems to be sound for a democracy is that no language should be punished in the absence of acts for three very good reasons—first, it is exceedingly difficult to discriminate between utterances dangerous to the public safety and those that are harmless; second, if successful, such prosecutions only drive such movements underground into secret conspirational channels; third, any limitations upon the rights of one minority are likely to be extended to cover others and thus create a general pattern of repression. We have developed the principle, with a fair degree of evidence to support it, that nobody's liberties are safe if anybody's liberties are denied.

Yet, the question of the increased dangers of wartime is insistent. We are urged to adopt different rules than in times of peace. Governments obviously will adopt different tests. If we fall back on the "clear and present danger" idea, we must hold that certain language that is harmless in peacetime becomes obstructive in wartime. But the tendency of an excited public is to characterize all sorts of unpopular doctrines as hostile to the conduct of a war. While the rules may be more rigidly applied, the need for criticism and debate in wartime is even greater than in time of peace, if governments are to keep in line with the people and public policies subjected to thorough examination. Any national security secured by any other means does not rest upon a democratic foundation. (Roger Nash Baldwin Papers, Seeley G. Mudd Manuscript Library, Box 22, Folder 2, May 22, 1942.)

ON OBSCENITY (1974)

Q. One new issue that has come up is the field of obscenity and what ought to be the law dealing with the publication of things.

A. Well, when the ACLU came to the conclusion that obscenity doesn't exist except in the mind of the beholder, I felt that perhaps they were right, but I also felt that the police have a right to stop certain things. And the certain things I'm not quite sure about, but I know there are some things which publicly are so shocking and so indecent that in public places something's going to happen. It's going to be stopped. They're either going to do it from the point of view of disorderly conduct or disturbing the peace, even if we have no definitions of obscenity. I sympathize with the necessity of control; at the same time I sympathize with the fact that there are very few things that need to be controlled. I think X-rated films, which I've never seen, put them in a class by themselves and I suppose it's all right as long as people are warned that they would see something that is regarded as indecent or obscene. You can't protect people that way from publications. I couldn't have the censors. I think the kind of self-restraint such as the radio people and the TV and the film people in part exercise is necessary in the field of publications, too. But I don't know how you can impose it, except by pressure upon the people who are responsible for the media. We have come to a pretty low state when almost all the media are geared to what you call the lowest common denominator of taste and the kind of things that go over big are the things that appeal to the crudest emotions and I don't like it. I think American life has been somewhat corrupted by this necessity of making an awful lot of money out of very low taste.

Q. The great dilemma is to wonder whether censorship would help that situation.

A. No, I don't think so.

Q. Our culture really invites people who will make large amounts of money to go and exploit it. Is that something temporary?

A. We have another tendency in the United States, too, fortunately, although it's an elitist tendency, and that is to cater to the best as well as to the lowest, and so every community wants its symphony orchestra and they all want to have their elegant Channel 13 movies and they all want foreign films and they all want the good things. (Columbia University, Oral History Research Office, "A Conversation with Roger Baldwin with Alan F. Westin," editor, *Civil Liberties Review*, and professor of public law, Columbia University, December 18, 1974, pp. 60–62.)

COMMENTARY
The Insistent Living Legend of Roger Baldwin
NAT HENTOFF

I met Roger Baldwin toward the end of his life, and was pleased when he said he'd read some of my writings on civil liberties; but then— solemnly and urgently—he told me: "Don't ever forget—no civil liberties battle is ever won, permanently!"

Remembering the Alien and Sedition Acts of 1798, Lincoln's suspension of habeas corpus during the Civil War, the Palmer raids and the rise of J. Edgar Hoover following Woodrow Wilson's near abolition of the First Amendment during the First World War, and Joe McCarthy's shadow over the land, Roger Baldwin's warning has never left me—as a journalist and a citizen.

In his important book *Civil Liberties in America*, Samuel Walker— previously a valuable historian of the ACLU—says that, "Baldwin's most important contribution to civil liberties lay in his charismatic leadership. He inspired many people to commit themselves to the cause of civil liberties."

That was true then; but Baldwin's vital contribution was to actually create the ACLU in 1920, and like the living document that is the Constitution, his legacy continues to exemplify—in protecting our liberties—what Louis Brandeis said: "Sunlight is the best disinfectant."

From the first inclination that John Ashcroft would ram the USA Patriot Act through Congress, the ACLU staff—through its detailed analysis of the bill and all the later legislation and executive orders— has enabled the national press and more and more of the citizenry to resist this administration's unprecedented overreach of executive authority in reckless violation of the separation of powers.

For one of many examples of its nurturing of Roger Baldwin's legacy, it was an ACLU lawsuit and subsequent federal district court decision that alerted at least some of the media and the public to one of the most dangerous sections of the USA Patriot Act.

Section 205 greatly expanded the government's use of National Security Letters that allow the FBI to obtain personal information about anyone connected to telephone companies and Internet service providers—without obtaining any judicial approval. Like the general writs of assistance—which helped precipitate the American Revolution when British customs officers searched the colonists and their homes and offices at will—National Security Letters allow the FBI to write their own search warrants.

In striking down this part of the USA Patriot Act (the government has appealed), U.S. District Court Judge Victor Marrero in New York noted that with these letters the FBI could use a National Security letter to discern the identity of someone whose anonymous weblog, or blog, is critical of the government.

If Samuel Adams were alive now, that prolific writer of causes for revolution against British tyranny would be a busy, often anonymous blogger—and could be found out by the FBI.

Also, because of the nationwide organizing of the Bill of Rights Defense Committee (BORDC) in Northampton, Massachusetts, soon joined by the ACLU and all its affiliates around the country, hundreds of towns and cities and four state legislatures—Alaska, Hawaii, Vermont, and Maine—have passed Bill of Rights defense resolutions requiring their members of Congress to change sections of the Patriot Act and other legislation and executive orders to conform to the Constitution. These grassroots latter-day disciples of Roger Baldwin have been heard by a growing number of liberal Democrats and conservative libertarians in Congress, who are filing bills to end the administration's raids on the Bill of Rights.

Another telling illustration of Roger Baldwin's legacy in full drive has been the stark illumination of our government's abuses of detainees in Iraq, Afghanistan, Guantánamo, and elsewhere—some of these abuses encompassing actual torture.

Because of a Freedom of Information Act lawsuit, the ACLU—joined by a number of human rights organizations—has forced the government to release thousands of pages—with many more to come—of internal memoranda and e-mails by FBI personnel and navy and counterintelligence agents in those countries that disclose appalling mistreatment of prisoners by army officers and Marines and special forces operatives.

In a detailed lead editorial on December 23, 2004, "War Crimes," the *Washington Post's* first sentence began: "Thanks to a lawsuit by the American Civil Liberties Union and other human rights groups... government documents have confirmed some of the painful truths about the abuse of foreign detainees by the U.S. military and the CIA—truths the Bush administration implacably has refused to acknowledge."

In this tribute, which essentially was also directed to founder Roger Baldwin, the editorial continued that "the new documents establish beyond any doubt that every part of [the administration's continuing] cover story is false." And with the anger of a Roger Baldwin, the *Washington Post* concluded:

"The record... indicates that the administration will neither hold any senior official accountable nor change the policies that have produced this shameful record. Congress, too, has abdicated its responsibility under its Republican leadership." (I would add that the Democratic Party leadership has also largely abdicated its responsibility.)

Thomas Jefferson said: "The spirit or resistance to government is so valuable on certain occasions, that I wish it to be always kept alive.... The People are the only sure reliance for the preservation of our liberty."

But the People have to be informed on the dangers to their liberties; and through the legacy of Baldwin's American Civil Liberties Union, they are continually not only being made aware of diminishing liberties, but also, as the Quakers say, of how to speak truth to power.

On January 9, 2003, the American Civil Liberties Union charted what has to be done for us to preserve our liberties:

"Many of the new security measures proposed by our government in the name of fighting the 'war on terror' are not temporary. They are permanent dangers to our laws. Even the measures that, on the surface, appear to have been adopted only as long as the terror lasts, could be with us indefinitely... because... terrorism is a permanent condition."

Without the ACLU and other watch guards of the Bill of Rights, in this war without a discernable end, a new generation can grow up conditioned to increasing government restrictions on speech, privacy, and the press. Roger Baldwin was keenly aware of the fragility of our liberties unless they are constantly protected.

As Justice William O. Douglas emphasized: "The Constitution and the Bill of Rights were designed to get Government off the backs of the people—all the people. Those great documents . . . guarantee for us all the rights to personal and spiritual self-fulfillment. But the guarantee is not self-executing.

"As nightfall does not come all at once, neither does oppression. In both instances, there is a twilight when everything remains seemingly unchanged. And it is in such twilight that we all must be most aware of changes in the air—however slight—lest we become unwitting victims of the darkness."

There are more and more distinct chilling changes in the air; and because of what Roger Baldwin brought into being, there is also increasing light to keep back the darkness.

———

Nat Hentoff, a nationally known award-winning journalist, is a longtime civil liberties commentator. His column is published weekly in *The Village Voice* and a different column is syndicated by United Media and appears in 250 newspapers, including the *Washington Times*. His book, *The War on The Bill of Rights and the Gathering Resistance*, focuses on the increasing resistance across America to the incursions of government on the Bill of Rights in the post-9/11 era.

Introduction to Chapter 10

Religion is a concept that no one understands, but each has its own.

—Roger N. Baldwin, 1961

The preamble to the Constitution of the United States makes no mention of God. It reads, simply: "We the people of the United States, in Order to form a more perfect union, establish Justice, insure domestic Tranquility, provide for the common defence (cq), promote the general Welfare, and secure the Blessing of liberty to ourselves and our Posterity, do ordain and establish this constitution for the United States of America."

The men who drafted the Constitution in 1787 were undoubtedly men of religious conviction who believed in God, and they were well aware of what they were doing when they purposely left any reference to God out of the document. The phrase, "separation of church and state," does not appear in any of the founding American documents. It is, rather, drawn from the First Amendment, which reads: "Congress shall make no law respecting an establishment of religion, or prohibiting the free exercise thereof...." Ironically, in those early days of the Republic, it was the churches that ran the local governments in the new towns of America, the churches that provided the education, levied taxes, and ensured a keen sense of morality in all of the towns founded in New England. Yet the concept of a secular rather than a religious state was fundamental to the basic foundation of the Constitution. "The source of the colonists' oppression, England, was also the source of the intellectual arsenal Americans used against her in the Revolutionary War," wrote two contemporary scholars.[1]

The concept of inserting a "religious tests" clause to the Constitution was rejected repeatedly, echoing Thomas Jefferson's words that "the insertion was rejected by a great majority, proof that they meant to comprehend within the mantle of its protection, the Jew and the Gentile, the Christian and the Mohometan, the Hindoo (cq), and the infidel of every denomination."[2] Jefferson is credited with the phrase "wall of separation"[3] between church and state, but it followed a decade after approval of the First Amendment in 1791, which has often been cited as the cornerstone for the constitutional prohibition against merging church and state affairs.

In 1863 the framers' concept was somewhat modified when the phrase "In God We Trust" was stamped on U.S. currency; it was further modified by insertion of the phrase "under God" in the Pledge of Allegiance in 1954. Since then, scores of individuals and organizations have tried to bring religion into the courtroom, in public squares, and in virtually all walks of life having to do with the political process. The courts have, in fact, dealt with specific cases involving the Mormons, the Jehovah's Witnesses, the Sabbath, conscientious objectors, the Amish, and many other religious sects.

The phrase "wall between church and state" was reinforced in the body politic again in 1947 when Supreme Court justice Hugo Black wrote in *Everson v. Board of Education*, 330 U.S. 1, that "the First Amendment has erected a wall between church and state. That wall must be kept high and impregnable. We should not approve the slightest breach." Most of the U.S. Supreme Court's decisions since then have been based on the Everson case.

The presidential election of 2000 arguably saw the wall of separation begin to crumble. As one leading magazine editor put it: "George W. Bush set the tone by raising the likelihood of his candidacy after a prayer breakfast and later declaring that his favorite philosopher was 'Christ because he changed my heart.' Not to be outdone, [then vice president] Al Gore boasted that he decided important questions using the religious shorthand, 'W.W.J.D.'—for a saying,' he explained, 'that's popular now in my faith, "What would Jesus do?"'"[4]

Looking at other presidents, Jimmy Carter was seen as, arguably, the most religious of presidents before Bush because of his constant references to his faith in public speeches. Ronald Reagan, however, did not use his religion in politics, although his Armageddon-like commentaries about Russia as "the evil empire" could be seen as semireligious, and his wife Nancy's tendency to turn to astrology as a form of religious prophecy was also a semireligious issue. Bill Clinton took full advantage of his thorough knowledge of the Bible and his own religious upbringing, especially when he was in black churches with black clergymen ("Clinton was the first black president," is a familiar refrain), but it was not until George W. Bush emerged, combining his New England Yankee Episcopalian background with a full-blown Christian "crusade," a word he used as an outgrowth of his strong backing from the Christian Coalition before the outset of the war against Iraq and to serve him politically. It was dropped from his speeches after his speechwriters realized it was being interpreted as inflammatory by Muslims. The so-called "religious vote" has increasingly become evangelical, which accounted for Presidents Ford, Carter, Reagan, and George W. Bush to declare themselves "born again" Christians.

The movement against a so-called "godless Constitution" actually began in the 1980s when a religious leader, the Reverend Pat Robertson, became a candidate for the Republican nomination for president in 1988. The Christian Coalition which he created has gained increasing influence in the body politic to the point where Bush was elected in 2000, in large part by publicly embracing God as one of the fundamental building blocks in his political campaign.

On December 13, 1999, at a primary debate in Des Moines before the Iowa caucus, the anchor of the local WHO-TV station, John Bachman, appearing on the program with longtime NBC anchor Tom Brokaw, asked the opening question: "What political philosopher do you most identify with and why?" When he called upon then-governor George Bush, of Texas, Bush replied without hesitation: "Jesus Christ." He went on to explain: "When you turn your heart and your life over to Christ, when you accept Christ as the Savior, it changes your heart. It changes your life. And that's what happened to me." Bush also stated after that when asked if he consulted with his father, George Herbert Walker Bush, that he consulted with "a higher authority."

In the third presidential debate, on October 13, 2004, in Tempe, Arizona, Bush was asked about his religious convictions by moderator Bob Schieffer, who asked specifically about what Bush meant when he said that he had not consulted with his father about the Iraq invasion but with a "higher authority." Bush explained: "When I was answering that question, what I was really saying to the person was that I pray a lot. And I do. And my faith is very—it's very personal. I pray for strength. I pray for wisdom. I pray for our troops in harm's way. I pray for my family. I pray for my little girls. But I'm mindful in a free society that people can worship if they want to or not. You're equally an American if you choose to worship an Almighty and if you chose not."

In his January 2003 State of the Union address to Congress, during which he made a strong case for the Iraqi war, Bush made what one academic called an "explicit appeal to God, divine will and Providence to justify the sacrifice of American lives; for they will be dying not just for the American people, but for freedom which is 'God's gift to humanity.'"[5] Following his election victory, supported in droves by the evangelical far right, Bush's beliefs in spiritual matters were reinforced by a statement he made in a news conference on April 13, 2004, when he offered his justification for his Iraq policy: "I have this...strong belief that freedom is not this country's gift to the world. Freedom is the Almighty's gift to every man and woman in this world. And as the greatest power on the face of the Earth, we have an obligation to help the spread of freedom."

Shortly thereafter, appearing on CNN's TV program *Larry King Live*, journalist Bob Woodward, the author of *Plan of Attack*, told King how Bush responded when he [Woodward] questioned him about consulting his father on the war. "When I asked about his father, he said, 'In terms of finding strength, I appeal to a higher father,' meaning God," Woodward said. "And when he ordered war, he prayed. And he prayed that he be a good messenger of God's will."

The Bush administration has promoted the so-called "culture of life" philosophy to oppose a woman's right to choose to have an abortion, and it has also catered to the religious right in numerous actions, including efforts to post the Ten Commandments in schools, occasional attempts to make recitation of the Pledge of Allegiance in the schools mandatory, and by accusing anyone who is opposed to its ideology "unpatriotic." It has been a successful strategy politically, but it has also raised serious concerns among American scholars, civil libertarians, lawyers, and the academic community about limiting freedom of speech as well as protecting the fundamental principle of separation of church and state.

There is further evidence endangering the long-held belief of church and state. The vouchers program—which would allow students to use goverment money to attend religious schools—is yet another example. It should be noted that for a brief period from the early 1970s to the late 1980s strict separationsists had the support of the majority of the Supreme Court justices. During this period, even after-school prayer disappeared from the public schools. Today the court is on the verge of replacing the principle of strict separation with a very different constitutional principle that demands equal treatment for religion. The wall between the two began to tumble in the 1980s and 1990s because government was failing to provide the social services that nonprofit, "faith-based" organizations, such as churches, could offer on a grass-roots level.

Finally, in 2005, the latest battle over the teaching of evolution in public schools in Kansas provides, said a *New York Times* editorial, "striking evidence that evolution is occurring right before our eyes. Every time the critics of Darwinism lose a battle over reshaping the teaching of biology, they evolve into a new form, armed with arguments that sound progressively more benign, while remaining as dangerous as ever."[6] Charles Darwin unveiled his theory of evolution more than 150 years ago in *The Origin of the Species* and the U.S. Supreme Court has in recent years held that teaching "creationism"—another term for God's handiwork—violated the First Amendment's separation of church and state.

Nonetheless, difficult as it may be to believe, the 1925 Scopes trial in Tennessee, in which a teacher was tried in the famous "monkey trial"—pitting evolution versus creationism as a central concept of the development of mankind—is being revisited with Darwinian critics in Dover, Pennsylvania, and Lawrence, Kansas, where the school boards have argued that students be taught a new theory—known as "intelligent design"[7]—that fails to mention God but says life is too complicated to be explained simply by evolution; and thus, there must be an intelligent designer at work. The two debates have led to an outbreak of bitter fights over this controversial issue in at least two dozen states, and they are expected to continue.

In a question-and-answer session with reporters from Texas newspapers in August 2005, Bush offered his views on the issue: "Both sides ought to be properly taught," he said, "so people can understand what the debate is about. . . . I think that part of education is to expose people to different schools of thought." *Time* magazine opined in its August 15, 2005, cover story, "The Evolution Wars," that: "It is a subtler way of finding God's fingerprints in nature than traditionalism." This proposition sounded reasonable enough to many observers, but as *Time* pointed out, "To biologists, it smacks of faith-based science. And that is provocative because it rekindles a turf battle all the way back to the Middle Ages."[8]

Darwinists now believe the door could be opened to teaching in the public schools that reverts to the Genesis account of God as the creator of the universe—a phrase still used among many faiths, including

Judaism, to this day. The "issue," claim Darwin supporters, is a made-up subject since the intelligent design proponents have no scientific evidence whatsoever to support their theory. Nonetheless, the debate mushroomed into a full-blown controversy last year when the media—newsmagazines, newspapers, television, and the Internet bloggers—all escalated it in the news and opinion outlets. In fact, *The New York Times* published a series of page one stories, "A Debate over Darwin," which gave the topic legitimate standing. So, too, the public has climbed aboard the seemingly runaway topic and has flooded the airwaves and the press with letters, op-ed pieces, and even discussions at houses of worship of all denominations. Most veteran political observers see the controversy continuing well into the future, depending, of course, on who becomes president in the election of 2008.

—W. K.

NOTES

1. Isaac Kramnick, and B. Laurence Moore, *The Godless Constitution: The Case against Religious Correctness* (New York: W. W. Norton, 1996), p. 67.

2. Ibid., 93.

3. Jefferson used this phrase in a letter to the Baptist Association of Danbury, Connecticut, written on New Year's Day, 1802, when he stated: "I contemplate with sovereign reverence that act of the whole American people which declared that their legislature should 'make no law respecting an establishment of religion, or prohibiting the free exercise thereof,' thus building a wall of separation between church and State." *Writings of Thomas Jefferson*, Albert E. Bergh, ed., Washington, D.C., 1904–1905, vol. XVI, pp. 281–82.

4. Jeffrey Rosen, "Is Nothing Secular," *New York Times Magazine* (January 30, 2000), p. 40.

5. Hugh Urban, "Bush, the Neocons, and Evangelical Christian Fiction," May 27, 2005, p. 4. Jeisoft Enterprises, Ltd.

6. *The New York Times* (May 17, 2005), p. A20.

7. President Bush said on August 1, 2005, that he believes schools should discuss "intelligent design" alongside evolution when teaching students about the creation of life. "I think that part of education is to expose people to different schools of thought," Bush said. "You're asking me whether or not people ought to be exposed to different ideas, the answer is yes." The theory of "intelligent design" says life on earth is too complex to have developed through evolution, implying that a higher power must have had a hand in creation. Christian conservatives—a substantial part of Bush's voting base—have been pushing for the teaching of

intelligent design in public schools. Scientists have rejected the theory as an attempt to force religion into science education. During a roundtable interview with reporters from five Texas newspapers, Bush declined to go into detail on his personal views of the origin of life. But he said students should learn about both theories, Knight Ridder Newspapers reported.

8. *Time* (August 15, 2005), pp. 28–29.

CHAPTER 10

SEPARATION OF CHURCH AND STATE

Religion is a subject that must be separated from government. It is, in fact, in the Bill of Rights.

—Roger N. Baldwin, 1936

Author's Note: Born in 1884 and reared in the Boston suburb of Wellesley Hills, Roger Baldwin was raised in a patriarchal household, where his parents considered themselves "agnostic Unitarians." Baldwin always considered himself a nonconformist—in his social life, his politics, his professional career, and in his spiritual beliefs. In his early years Baldwin supported labor's ties with religious leaders in the class struggle against the barons of business, and he maintained a philosophy that the practice of human rights—"the rights of man"—mark all religions. Baldwin started his career as a dissenter by refusing to report for induction into the army and thus set into motion the entire conscientious objector movement for decades and wars to come. In what Baldwin himself called the most high-profile case in which the ACLU ever participated—the "monkey trial" in Tennessee— Baldwin was instrumental in getting the most eminent attorney of the time, Clarence Darrow, to defend John Thomas Scopes, the schoolteacher who taught evolution against state law. While the trial found Scopes guilty, it was reversed by a higher court and, Baldwin thought, that would be the last of the issue. Baldwin would have been astounded, it is fair to say, had he been able to look into a crystal ball and discover that once again at the start the twenty-first century the issue has been reopened over the teaching of evolution in the public schools in many states where forces who oppose the long-accepted theory of Darwin's evolution are fighting once again to eliminate any mention of evolution from the classrooms of America.

Following, some of his most incisive thoughts about the topic, remarkably, back in the news.

—W. K.

━━•✦•━━

In Baldwin's Words

RELIGION AND THE CONSTITUTION (1936)

The same pressures for conformity to the notions of the American Legion and the Daughters of the American Revolution which demand the outlawry of subversive doctrines also insist on affirmative rituals of patriotism. The teachers' oath laws, which catch not only the disloyal but the conscientious objectors on religious grounds, represent their spirit. They are buttressed by compulsory flag-saluting on the part of children, made by statute or rule. This enforced patriotism, highly questionable from the viewpoint of promoting loyalty, has resulted only in punishing children from families of religious sects opposed to recognizing symbols of earthly power. Chief victims are members of Jehovah's Witnesses, widely scattered over the country, who recognize no power but Jehovah's and rest their refusal to salute on biblical authority. The invasion of their liberty of conscience has caused the expulsion of schoolchildren in six states, where the ancient issue of religious freedom is again in the courts.

But the United States Supreme Court, protector presumably of individual liberty, offers little encouragement for the affirmation of the principle that loyalty to God transcends loyalty to the state. The state in these totalitarian days is the supreme authority. God gets off second best. That was the issue in the case of the admission to citizenship of one religious objector to war; it was the issue in the refusal on religious grounds of two Methodist college boys to take military training. In both cases the Supreme Court laid down the rule that the citizen is the servant of the state, unprotected by the claims of religious loyalties in a refusal to obey any command the state may make. Personal liberty as achieved in the old struggle for the right to worship God as one will, even against the state's demands, has been vanquished.

Only in one major case has the Supreme Court upheld the personal liberties of citizens as against the state. In Oregon, when the Ku Klux Klan was a powerful political force some ten years ago, it succeeded in submitting to the people by initiative petition, and in getting passed by a great majority, a law compelling all children to attend the public schools, thus in effect abolishing all private schools. This was a blow at private conscience, religious and personal, unprecedented in American history. It was to be the forerunner of a hundred percent American education for children all over the country. But the private schools which contested it won in the Supreme Court on the principle that parents have some rights as against the state to determine their children's education. (Roger N. Baldwin, "The Constitution in the Twentieth Century," May 1936 issue of *The Annals*, of the American Academy of Political and Social Science, summarized June 2, 1936, over a nationwide network of NBC in "You and Your Government" Series XIII, Lecture No. 18, "Personal Liberty.")

RELIGION AND LABOR (1938)

A profession with growing evidence of concern for the cause of labor is the clergy. The church, the conservatives insist, should confine itself to spiritual matters and not pontificate on such temporal affairs as class struggle or the ethics of our economy. While organized religion tends to uphold the property system which supports it and to ignore the interests of labor, yet so large a section of the clergy as to be conspicuous has taken a vigorous position in support of labor. Noteworthy for this activity in Protestantism is the Federal Council of Churches of Christ in America, whose industrial department has a long and consistent record of sympathetic interpretation of strikes, and support of labor legislation and trade union organizations. Frequently attacked for its forthright sympathies as Communist and subversive, it maintains in uncompromising support of democracy applied to industry. Together with other religious leaders, its officers were largely responsible for the campaign that resulted in the appointment of the invaluable Senate Committee on Civil Liberties.

Less conspicuous because representing a smaller constituency, liberal religious organizations among the Jews voice the same social creed. The section of the Roman Catholic Church represented by the National Catholic Welfare Conference likewise champions the rights of labor. All three agencies, Protestant, Catholic, and Jewish, have frequently joined in common efforts to resolve strikes in favor of union recognition. In every movement for the defense of civil rights for the industrial democracy these liberal clergymen stand as conspicuous and courageous leaders with increasing influence. (Roger N. Baldwin and Clarence B. Randall, "Organized Labor and Political Democracy," in *Civil Liberties and Industrial Conflict* [Cambridge, MA: Harvard University Press, © 1938 by the President and Fellows of Harvard College], p. 58.)

THE SCOPES TRIAL (1961)

How did the Union get involved in the Tennessee evolution case? The origin of the most publicized trial we ever handled was quite casual. It was my routine to check up daily on items in the press reporting violations of civil liberties and along in 1924 I began to note dispatches from Tennessee about a wholly novel bill before the legislature which made a crime of the teaching in public schools evolution as contrary to the Bible story of man's origin. We had not been aware of the strength and drive of the religious fundamentalists in the South who in the turmoil of the postwar era determined to buttress their faith by law. When it was reported that the legislature had passed the bill, I sent a press release to all Tennessee newspapers offering to back the defense of any teacher who challenged the law. It was so clear a case of making crimes out of ideas alone that I did not even consult our board. But I could not have imagined the consequences of what at the time appeared as a mere routine.

Only a few days after the Tennessee papers published our offer I was called on the long-distance phone by a man in Dayton, Tennessee, who said: "I'm a businessman. Do you really mean what you offered in the papers? Would you furnish lawyers and costs if a teacher is willing to risk his job and livelihood? If you do, I have one, a young biology teacher in the high school here named [John Thomas] Scopes."

I answered, "Of course we mean it. Have him send us his name and a request for help and we'll tell him what to do." I consulted our lawyer, Arthur Garfield Hays, who advised that he visit the district attorney, tell him that he was violating the law, and submit to arrest and prosecution. He did and the district attorney obliged. I sent out a story to the press in the hope it might attract attention, but I was not prepared for the immediate national coverage it got. We had evidently hit on what newspapermen at once sense as a great drama, the conflict between science and religion. The drama got top billing when William Jennings Bryan jumped into the defense of this law, offering his services to the State of Tennessee. I had calculated we would get the services of some local Tennessee lawyers, but this was too big stuff for them. I consulted Hays.

"Should you be interested," I asked, "to go into the case yourself?" "Would I?" he replied. "Of course, and I'd like to have Clarence Darrow in on it with me. I'll phone him." Darrow was not only a great trial lawyer but a great agnostic. Darrow agreed at once to drop everything else and volunteer his services. When I asked him after the trial why he had made such a sacrifice of his other obligations, he said: "I've always wanted to put Bryan in his place and this was too good a chance to miss."

The trial was set for the summer of 1925. Hays organized the legal defense with Darrow, his former partner Dudley Field Malone, and a couple of Tennessee lawyers. I organized the finances. Nobody had to organize the publicity; it was a public relations man's dream. When Scopes came to New York before the trial on my invitation to meet his backers, he was fairly mobbed by the press. An attractive, unassuming young man, he regarded himself only as an instrument in the cause of freedom to teach, and modestly resisted exploiting his personal views.

Getting the money to finance the defense was easy. I figured that all scientists would chip in and so circularized the membership of the American Association for the Advancement of Science for ten dollars each. The response was immediate and more than met the costs.

Legally we were up against a tough case, simple as it looked on its face. Did not the legislature which created the public schools have the right to prescribe their conduct? Could not the majority, as represented by the legislature, determine what subjects might and might not be taught? Did freedom to teach mean teaching heresy to dominant religious views?

We had to rely on a doctrine which so often in civil liberties conflicts and court decisions is the only practicable test, what is "reasonable." Was the Tennessee law a reasonable application of an undoubted power? It was not difficult to foresee what kind of battle on that issue would be waged between Bryan, defender of the literal words of the Bible, and Darrow, apostle of science and freedom of thought, and inquiry.

The story of that trial is too well known from play and movie to be repeated. The lawyers, of course, made the usual motions to quash the indictment on the ground that the law was unconstitutional for indefiniteness, for establishing a religion, for unreasonableness, and for destroying freedom of thought and speech. Scopes pleaded not guilty on the grounds that the law was unconstitutional, although he admitted teaching the banned subject. But his defense was a matter of law, not fact, so he never testified. The students he taught, however, testified to what he so readily admitted teaching. The trial, lasting ten days in the Rhea County courthouse, turned on the clash of the two protagonists—Bryan and Darrow. The legal issues faded into obscurity against the vivid advocacies of unquestioning faith and of a rational and probing common sense. Bryan threw his challenge to the defense lawyers, stating, "These gentlemen . . . did not come here to try this case. They came here to try revealed religion. I am here to defend it. . . . I am simply trying to protect the Word of God against the greatest atheist or agnostic in the United States." And Darrow replied to him, "We have the purpose of preventing bigots and ignoramuses from controlling the education of the United States and you know it, and that is all."[1]

I did not attend the trial; I stayed in New York and handled the voluminous office work it entailed. The facts are too well known to need retelling; how Darrow "made a monkey out of Bryan," how Bryan died of a stroke just after the trial, how Scopes was convicted and the conviction was reversed on a technicality by the Tennessee Supreme Court, which avoided the constitutional question and so prevented an appeal to the U.S. Supreme Court.

The concept and the principles and, to less degree, the practice of what we call human rights—the rights of man—mark all religions, the struggles of history, and the aspirations of men and women all over the world today.

But the case put an end to the crusade to write Genesis into law. A few other Southern states made similar gestures, but the practical effect was to leave the public schools free to decide for themselves what to teach. Many of course yielded to fundamentalist pressure. Even textbook publishers in the North modified biology books to fit Southern customers.

But in time the pressure let up and in all the years since no cases have arisen in teaching to put the cause of revealed religious dogma against science. The "monkey trial," a victory in defeat, ended them. (Roger Nash Baldwin Papers, Box 21, Folder 1, Seeley G. Mudd Manuscript Library, 1961, Princeton, N.J.)

SUPPORTING CONSCIENTIOUS OBJECTORS (1976)

Freedom of religion early on came under severe attack in the case of a religious sect, the Jehovah's Witnesses, whose conscientious objection to saluting the flag and to accepting military service provoked widespread hostility and interference. The Union has been the chief organization to defend their rights, associated with dozens of court cases throughout the country, two of them now pending in the Supreme Court.

In the cases of conscientious objectors, the Union has assisted the legal efforts of many claiming unjust classifications, has sought the release of imprisoned men on parole to the Civilian Public Service Camps, and has urged a wider system of civilian service in hospitals and agriculture. (Roger Nash Baldwin Papers, Box 2, File 2, "Origins of the ACLU," January 25, 1976, Seeley G. Mudd Manuscript Library, Princeton, N.J.)

A Sense of Right and Wrong (1976)

Religion is a subject that must be separated from government. It is, in fact, in the Constitution. Religion is a concept that no one understands, but each has its own. One God instead of many Gods, well, I don't know. I think most of us tend to live by catchphrases, anyhow. People really do have quite a number of Gods. That is, things they are loyal to, things that are the best description of God in a sense of right and wrong—a conscience, if you like, that is bigger than we are in relation to our fellow man. You obviously have a certain set of personal standards, personal guidelines or ethics. I think conscience, this sense of right and wrong—that's a good a word as any—that is the guide and if you try to define what is right and what is wrong you'd have to change that quite often. What I thought was right at one time is probably wrong now, and vice versa. And people change, they used to think that nudity was wrong and now you look at some of the costumes, most everybody thinks it's right, women didn't expose their breasts and now they do, the kinds of clothes people wear, the attitudes they have, those are superficial to be sure, but even the basic concepts of right and wrong are quite different in our society. You are supposed to have only one wife but in a Muslim society you can get four. Which is right and which is wrong? (From an interview with this writer, 1976.)

Note

1. Quotes from the official transcript of the Scopes trial, seventh day, page 743.

COMMENTARY
Roger Baldwin and the Separation of Church and State
REV. WILLIAM SLOANE COFFIN JR.

Emile Zola, the ever-provocative French writer, once claimed that he had been born "to live out loud." Many of us felt much the same way about Roger Baldwin. He was a giant of a man, a Boston patrician, the underdog's best friend, America's best-known champion of the First Amendment, and a determined believer in a more democratic and egalitarian future for all Americans—all reflected in his writings.

Convinced that doing good was twice as important as being good, he indulged himself in a certain churlishness that actually rather became him. When I told him that Yale's president, Kingman Brewster, thought the world of him, he growled back, "He ought to, I taught him everything he knows." When the treasurer of a not-for-profit organization hard-pressed for funds announced proudly at a board meeting that the organization was in the black, Baldwin countered, "That's unacceptable. Were we doing the things we should be doing we would be in the red."

These days when the American Civil Liberties Union feels pushed around by Republican conservatives and especially by the Christian Right, it's worth remembering that in 1920 when the ACLU was formed, religious leaders were on hand to help. Baldwin was appointed the Union's first and longtime director (1920–50). His religious colleagues, like him, believed in the separation of church and state. They understood that neutrality is the very meaning of secularism in a democratic state. But the separation was an organizational one, decidedly not designed to separate religious believers from their politics. The believers wanted religious freedom to fulfill biblical mandates such as truth-telling, confronting injustice, and the pursuit of peace. Jews and Christians alike, they viewed the biblical prophets in their criticism of the monarchy as distant precursors of the legal rights guarantee in the First Amendment—freedom of the press and free speech as well as freedom of religion.

Likewise, and again for religious reasons, many in the religious community have joined the ACLU in opposition to prayers in the public school. Not only are school prayers offensive to nonbelievers, and quite contrary to Jesus' injunction to pray in secret, such prayers cheapen the costly commitment of genuine religious faith. Mandatory school prayers are rarely heartfelt, and lip service to God weakens, it doesn't strengthen religious faith.

Today, leaders of the Christian Right want to dismantle what Thomas Jefferson called "the wall" separating church and state. They view it as once did Joshua at the walls of ancient Jericho: If enough people shout long and hard enough, walls "come tumblin' down." So they cheer loudly President Bush's determination to channel federal dollars to faith-based charities. The ACLU is opposed and again with religious allies. Clearly the president is not only fudging the separation of church and state, he is reneging on his constitutional responsibility "to promote the general welfare." He is putting charity in the way of justice when what the poor need is wholesale justice, not piecemeal charity.

All Americans should recognize that while charity seeks to alleviate the ill effects of injustice, justice seeks to eliminate the causes. Charity preserves the status quo, justice demands what Baldwin wanted—a more democratic and egalitarian society.

Further, religious institutions receiving federal dollars would be reluctant to criticize other government policies and practices with the result that churches, temples, and mosques would increasingly serve the state merely as an auxiliary kind of ambulance service. Finally, it is important to note that the legal rights of the First Amendment are presently endangered by the Bush administration's response to the threat of terrorism. Alexander Hamilton warned that "to be more *safe*, the nations at length become willing to run the risk of being less free." The ranks of the ACLU are today swelling with Americans who fear that our country may become more concerned with defense than with having things worth defending.

James Luther Adams, a stellar Christian theologian, once suggested that every American clergy person be actively and persistently engaged in at least one secular organization promoting peace and justice against the forces of hatred and greed. Joining a library board, he said, wouldn't qualify unless the librarian was being called a Communist.

I recommend the ACLU. When I joined, it was out of religious conviction and from a deep desire to further the highest hopes of Roger Baldwin.

Dr. William Sloane Coffin Jr. is a clergyman and a longtime peace activist. He served as Chaplain at Yale from 1958 until 1975, during which time he preached civil disobedience, played a prominent role in the "freedom rides" in the South challenging segregation and the oppression of blacks. He also was one of the foremost leaders of the anti–Vietnam War peace movement in the 1960s and the movement against nuclear weapons. He later served as Senior Minister at the Riverside Church in New York City.

*Too often American generosity, even where it is completely dis-
interested, is resented as the benefactions of a rich Uncle Sam who
is not loved any more than other rich uncles among poor relatives.*
—Roger N. Baldwin, 1960

The United Nations, which celebrated its sixtieth anniversary in 2005,
was a product of the victorious nations in World War II whose leaders
agreed, in principle, that a world organization should be set up to
avoid a World War III. It was intended to be stronger and more lasting
than its predecessor organization, the League of Nations established in
1919 and embraced by, among others, U.S. president Woodrow Wilson, at the Paris Peace Conference as part of the Treaty of Versailles.
The League of Nations' goals of addressing world issues such as international cooperation on armament control, a World Court, and
action against aggressor states were noble but carried little weight
with the majority of nations who were—and still are—nationalistic,
even in a global economy. Although it proved to be ineffective, the
League of Nations did not officially close its doors until after the
United Nations was created.

The actual name "United Nations" is attributed to President Franklin Delano Roosevelt and was officially accepted on January 1, 1942,
when officials from twenty-six nations[1] signed a U.N. declaration at a
meeting in Washington, D.C. The signing of an Inter-Allied Declaration on June 12, 1941, in London, had preceded it. The charter for the
fledgling world organization was unanimously approved at a conference of fifty-one original members of the United Nations in San
Francisco on October 15, 1945, in the name of Eleanor Roosevelt, who

had died a month before the meeting after working diligently in the hope of seeing the United Nations born. The charter, which included an important reference to "human rights,"[2] went into effect on October 24 after the permanent members of the Security Council—the United States, the United Kingdom, China, France, and the Soviet Union— ratified the charter. In 1947 the General Assembly officially designated October 24 as "United Nations Day."

Parallel with the founding of the United Nations, Roger Baldwin, as executive director of the American Civil Liberties Union, was slowly but surely broadening his interests to include international civil liberties and human rights. He retired as the executive director of the ACLU in 1950, in fact, to officially expand the ACLU's reach in international work. That required Baldwin to take trips to the United Nations headquarters, then to Lake Success in New York, as well as going to conferences at home and abroad. He continued to work at the ACLU office on international-connected subjects. As the ACLU's international mentor, in the summer of 1950 he made a six-month fact-finding tour of the world promoting international human rights. He this time "engaged in his new crusade to take civil liberties on to the international stage."[3]

—W. K.

NOTES

1. The twenty-six signatories were the United States of America, the United Kingdom of Great Britain and Northern Ireland, the Union of Soviet Socialist Republics, China, Australia, Belgium, Canada, Costa Rica, Cuba, Czechoslovakia, Dominican Republic, El Salvador, Greece, Guatemala, Haiti, Honduras, India, Luxembourg, Netherlands, New Zealand, Nicaragua, Norway, Panama, Poland, South Africa, Yugoslavia.

2. The founding members of the UN included in the charter their goal of "promoting and encouraging respect for human rights and for fundamental freedoms for all without distinction as to race, sex, language or religion."

3. Robert C. Cottrell, *Roger Nash Baldwin and the American Civil Liberties Union* (New York: Columbia University Press, 2000), 331.

CHAPTER 11

A WORLD UNITED BY
THE RULE OF LAW

*We must abandon, as we have I think in part, the concept that
those who are not with us are against us.*
                                        —Roger N. Baldwin, 1960

Author's Note: Roger Baldwin's emergence as a player on the world stage at
the United Nations started just before his retirement as ACLU executive
director in 1950 and continued until his death in 1981. Having founded
the International League for the Rights of Man in 1942 (later changed to the
International League for Human Rights) and, parallel with the founding of
the United Nations in 1945, Baldwin slowly broadened his interests to
include international civil liberties and human rights. He officially extended
the ACLU's reach in international work, requiring him to travel to United
Nations headquarters, then to Lake Success in New York as well as to
conferences at home and abroad. He spent virtually all of his time "engaged
in his new crusade: to take civil liberties onto the international stage."[1]

One of the people he most admired at the UN was Eleanor Roosevelt.[2]
Baldwin wrote: "I didn't come to know her at all well—to know her mind
and her activities and her purposes—until she became a member of the first
Human Rights Commission at the United Nations, the only commission
authorized by the charter. She became chairman of the commission in those
critical years when they developed a program that resulted in the Universal
Declaration of Human Rights in 1948, which was the basis for everything the
United Nations has done since." Baldwin immersed himself into activities
on the international stage. He recalls with great satisfaction two memorable
assignments as a consultant to the U.S. State Department when he was
asked to set up civil liberties programs in post–World War II Japan by Gen.

Douglas A. MacArthur and in Germany by Gen. Lucius B. Clay. Below, a compendium of his views in the international arena.

—W. K.

——•——

In Baldwin's Words

HUMAN RIGHTS: WORLD DECLARATION AND AMERICAN PRACTICE (1950)

For the first time in history most of the nations of the world have united on a declaration of what the rights of all men and women should be. This Universal Declaration of Human Rights was agreed upon by the 1948 General Assembly of the United Nations. Though made up of only thirty brief paragraphs, the Declaration was the result of three years of earnest debate by the Commission on Human Rights, the only specialized agency named in the UN Charter. The Charter alluded to these rights in general terms. The Declaration spelled them out.

The Declaration is not law. No provision is made for its enforcement. It is simply a statement of moral political principle on which legally binding agreements between the nations may be based. As an outline of goals it clearly reaches far beyond what most countries, even the most democratic, actually achieve in law or practice. But all the nations recognized the goals as desirable and possible for ultimate adoption. They cover not only the traditional political and civil liberties on which political democracies rely for progress, but also the newer economic and social rights which have not yet been embodied in the constitutional guarantees of most democracies.

Such a far-sighted document is, of course, dismissed by skeptics as just another well-meaning piece of idealism. It is regarded by them as a mere paper affair to be forgotten or ignored, like the international pledges against the resort to war as an instrument of national policy or the pious demands of international economic congresses for a larger amount of free trade.

It might be so dismissed if it stood alone. But it must be viewed side by side with a whole series of efforts by the United Nations to promote human rights. The Charter itself, unlike that of the old League of Nations, is clearly committed to universal rights as one of the guarantees of peace. The Charter's preamble states that object; the Economic and Social Council is charged with developing it. The Trusteeship Council applies those guarantees to trusted territories and non-self-governing peoples. The Commission on Human Rights, specified as the agency to work out the practical measures, is divided into subcommissions on discrimination and freedom of international communication. Never before has an international body engaged in such searching tasks to find agreement among the nations on the complex problems of human rights. (Public Affairs Pamphlet No. 167, Public Affairs Committee, New York, N.Y., first edition, 1950.)

CIVIL LIBERTIES IN GERMANY (1950–53)

I nourished the idea of a strong German civil liberties agency, and was delighted when I received an invitation from the State Department to serve as a consultant. I was prepared to do whatever was useful to the scheme of setting up the new national [civil rights] agency. Obviously the most useful was to arouse local groups to action, and I was at once invited to make a schedule to cover all West Germany. Not a single big city was missed. In each city a group had been organized; in each I outlined the plans based on the conference, and the need for a national agency and thereby German participation in the international work of the League for the Rights of Man. I was impressed with the interest shown, but I was not impressed with the chances for volunteer leadership.

It was steep uphill going. You could feel the rise of nationalism and conservatism, and the cockiness of Germans who now knew how essential they were to Western defense. Not one of my liberal friends supported the idea of a militarized Germany in any form. They had enough. From High Commissioner John J. McCloy down I found what struck me as distrust of the Germans and a naïve confidence in American advice and supervision. I urged withdrawing from the bottom up, beginning with the American county agents and gradually leaving controls only at the top, the Allied Commission. Their view was precisely the opposite: relax at the top, but keep an eye on the Germans down at the lowest levels.

But I was persistent in what was doubtless an impossible and perhaps romantic project—to get a sense of national unity in West Germany based on democratic activity strong enough to offset what was apparently developing in the East, so that if and when unification of Germany became a practical proposal, the East would be faced with a network of agencies so strong that Communism would not have a chance. To do so, the Germans would obviously have to be freed from the minute supervision that the Allies were still imposing despite their professions.

I was asked for any letters I might have, to show approval by high officials of my previous activities in Japan and Germany. Fortunately for the Department and me, I had flattering letters from General MacArthur[3] and Clay, written on the occasion of my retirement in early 1950 from the directorship of the Civil Liberties Union and included in the usual volume of testimonials presented on such an occasion. I sent Photostats.

With Germany still divided, still not sovereign, still living under artificial life, it is a wonder that so much has been apparently changed. A working democracy means citizenship participation at all levels of society, from the village to the national parliament, a fact still not sufficiently recognized by both leaders and the masses in Germany. Very few Germans see that this knowledge and feeling of being a citizen might lead to something more comprehensive and uniting than party politics. I look with hope and trust to the younger generation for it does not remember the fat years to which the older people want to return. (Columbia University, Oral History Research Office, draft, chapter XII, unpublished biography, Germany, 1950–53, pp. 592–613.)

UNDERDEVELOPED COUNTRIES
AND DEMOCRACY (1957)

When we consider the area of special concern at the United Nations—the so-called "underdeveloped" countries, which are either those under colonial rule or newly liberated—the fact is indisputable that many are as yet unprepared for the self-government on which democracy rests. But this fact does not concede the claims of European colonial powers for indefinite postponement of self-government, nor their refusal even to entertain proposals for target dates on the road toward it. Obviously a point will be reached in the development of any backward long-dependent people when a decision should be made concerning their capacity for self-government and democracy. The two are in fact synonymous; nobody anticipates a judgment on self-government and dictatorship. Since democracy is learned only by long experience, a decision should not wait until all its elements are satisfied; the world can fairly act on reasonable prospects.

The progress toward the goal is today so rapid, even in the most backward African tribal regions, that it would not be too great a speculation to figure that within twenty-five years all the peoples of Africa will be prepared to govern themselves democratically. The European powers will not, of course, concede any such timetable, but the evolutionary changes of the last decade indicate the pressures to that goal. (Roger N. Baldwin, "Can They Rule Themselves?" *The Spark*, a publication of the American Foundation for Political Education: A Non-Partisan and Non-Profit Organization for Adult Education, November, vol. 1, no. 3, 1957.)

PROSPECTS FOR A BETTER FOREIGN POLICY (1960)

I appreciate that foreign policy is a subject about which no personal influence can be exerted. But on the conduct of foreign policy depends the peace and security of our country and of the world. Feeling incapable to exert personal influence, our tendency is to trust the government, particularly the president and secretary of state, charged with the conduct of foreign affairs and whose judgments we are reluctant to question in critical times for fear of disrupting national unity. The doctrine that politics stops at the water's edge and a patriotic concept of my country right or wrong reduces the area of criticism in which foreign policy can be controversially discussed. But there is no time more challenging than the present where great decisions lie ahead in conflict threatening the very survival of the human race.

I hope that if I suggest that the greatest change ever in history is the conviction now among all statesmen of all peoples that war as an institution is no longer thinkable. In the midst of the greatest arms race in history the dangers are apparent, but no country will risk starting a suicidal catastrophe. The world is unable to make war and it appears equally unable to make peace. The very success of American power in terms of both our economy and democratic performance at home have made us appear to the world a self-righteous people proud of our American way of life, which in our view others would profit by following. It is not only self-righteous but a sort of double-entry standard of morality from which we suffer. What is right for us is wrong for others.

In the United Nations, American policy reflects, of course, its outside commitments to its allies in NATO and other military alliances. Unhappily the United Nations is the scene of constant and bitter Cold War debates. The United States has emphasized the aggressions and colonialism of the Soviet Union in Hungary, Tibet, Korea, and elsewhere. The Soviet Union attacks the United States and the Western alliance on their support of colonialism and racism. I wish that the American position had been clearer on issues to which we are committed in principle, namely the freedom of all peoples from foreign rule and the equality of all races.

In the field of human rights in which I work, I regret to say that the United States has been completely isolated from the efforts of the United Nations to create workable world law by the opposition in the Senate to any treaty which would either give the world court the opportunity to pass upon American practices or which would invade the rights of the states. We have adopted some years ago an amendment to our adherence to the world court which hamstrings its jurisdiction by reserving our domestic jurisdiction. We, not the court, is the judge of that. This reservation should be repealed.

It is of course a truism that foreign policy is determined by pressures at home. The president, who is in charge of foreign policy, is undoubtedly in advance of American opinion so little concerned with foreign affairs and in many respects so prejudiced and chauvinistic. The support of the United Nations throughout the country is thin. I wonder sometimes whether we would still remain a member if Red China is admitted. Congress has almost expressed itself to that effect. International affairs may be an issue in a political campaign but generally speaking the attitude of Congress on all these issues cuts across partisan lines. On the whole the press supports the conduct of foreign policy whatever a secretary of state or a president may do. National unity must be preserved, especially in times of crisis despite the obvious fact that the debate, criticism and controversy should be applied equally to the far more dangerous area of foreign policy than of domestic politics. The national temper is so powerful and a country so rich tends to emphasize the supremacy of the United States. We must be first and first in everything. We must win against the Soviet Union. International affairs are a game in which somebody must always win and somebody lose. My country right or wrong is not yet rejected as an attitude inconsistent with internationalism.

There is little understanding in American public opinion of the attitudes of the United States in most of the world. Our image, as the advertising men call it, is not the image we have of ourselves. There is a very widespread anti-Americanism varying in different countries. Among the darker peoples our racism belies our professions of democracy. *Too often American generosity, even where it is completely disinterested, is resented as the benefactions of a rich Uncle Sam who is not loved any more than other rich uncles among poor relatives* (italics author's). Help is especially resented when it comes with the implication that the American way of life is superior and that American standards are the goal to which all people should aspire. Material comfort, two cars in every garage in a nation of gadgets, is not what people are looking for in countries where they do not even have iron plows, a water supply, decent roads, hospitals or a school under a roof.

What are the prospects for a better foreign policy? The next president of the United States must understand that if that policy is to be better that some fundamental preconceptions must be changed. *I would say that the most important of them is the recognition that our major enemy is not Communism, but war* (italics author's). I would add that we must not look upon the world in terms of Russian vice and American virtue. We should abandon the notion that there is to be a victory over Communism except in a sense that we prove democracy is superior to it. That we can do. Instead of standing up to the Russians, we should, as someone has suggested, sit down with them. Negotiation is the only road to peace. We must abandon the idea that all negotiation is appeasement. There need be no victor or vanquished in a common effort to save mankind from the catastrophe of war and to create a world order through a strengthened and expanded United Nations with an international police force alone the repository of military power.

We must abandon, as we have I think in part, the concept that those who are not with us are against us (italics author's). Our role in developing a world community must recognize that the ultimate arbitrator is to be law, not force. We have the obligation as the [Eisenhower] administration has already made clear to play our role in the administration of international justice through the world court by abandoning any reservations that give the United States a privileged position.

> *Our role in developing a world community must recognize that the ultimate arbitrator is to be law, not force.*

The natural, almost professional, optimism which has sustained me through the turbulent years prompts me to suggest that we will not fail our democratic traditions nor our high ideals or an ordered world in which we, with other nations, will be willing to sacrifice a degree of our sovereign independence for the welfare of all. Every opinion poll on that issue has testified to the internationalism of the American people. We are occasionally diverted by our fears, our hostilities and sometimes our chauvinism but I venture the hope is not unjustified by the evidence that the dominant good sense of the American people will vindicate our faith in our American democracy sustained by the very diversities of our national life in the universal achievement of freedom, equality and security for all men and women everywhere. Only in an ordered world through the international community now represented in the United Nations can we move toward a goal so long dreamed of, so little realized and yet so insistently imperative to meet the colossal dangers of the atomic age in which only security of all guarantees the security of each. (Roger Nash Baldwin Papers, Box 23, Folder 17, "Prospects for a Better Foreign Policy," speech in St. Louis, October 1960, Seeley G. Mudd Manuscript Library, Princeton, N.J.)

HUMAN RIGHTS IN THE MIDDLE EAST (1960)

A few weeks in Israel and the neighboring Arab states cannot qualify even an old hand like myself for always balanced judgments of the shifting complexes of power politics in terms of human rights. But they at least can reflect the judgments of the scores of officials and heads of private agencies whom our party of seventeen Americans interviewed in a tour under the auspices of the American Christian Palestine Committee.

The major conclusion to which I came—and I find it shared by many competent observers—is that progress toward Israel-Arab peace and toward democratic liberties in Arab lands depends on the great powers, England, France, and the United States, and the USA most of all. Israel has her own independence and is anxious to make peace. The spokesmen for the Arab states, bitter as they are against Israel and hostile to any discussion of peace, are even more hostile to England for its treatment of Egypt, to France for its tough imperialist repression in North Africa, and to the United States for backing them up.

Although the plight of the three-quarters of a million Arab refugees and the unhappy Arab minority in Israel obviously contribute to the bitterness, the evidence indicates that even if those problems were solved, peace would not be made so long as the Arab states suffer under what they conceive to be foreign domination. It is difficult unless you hear it on the spot to sense the depth and violence of this nation-alism, not confined, as is often stated, to the ruling oligarchies to divert attention from the poverty and degradation of the masses. Even the man in the street will tell you: "We have two masters, a foreign and our own. We must get rid of the foreigner before we can fight our own."

I speak of Arab aspiration because their satisfaction is the key to any development toward democracy of these feudal Moslem states, and therefore toward a recognition of Israel as a neighbor. Israel is already a democratic state in the best of the Western principles. Equality for the Arabs as citizens will take time, and the [Israeli] government is obviously sensitive to the criticism that Jews cannot defend before world opinion discrimination in Israel which Jews have suffered in other lands. (Roger Nash Baldwin Papers, Box 23, Folder 18, "Human Rights in the Middle East," Roger N. Baldwin, chairman of the International League for the Rights of Man, a United Nations consultant agency, 1960, Seeley G. Mudd Manuscript Library, Princeton, N.J.)

Bringing Civil Liberties To Post–World War II Japan (1974)

The movement I was asked to help organize—which was the basis of my invitation to go to Japan [by the U.S. State Department]—resulted at the time in the formation of the Japanese Civil Liberties Union. It was inspired primarily by leaders in the Federation of Bar Associations, with whom I had a number of meetings on the details of organization, based upon American experience. The suggestion was also made that the government itself should take responsibility for the protection of citizens' rights under the Constitution. The then–attorney general, a Mr. Suzuki, attended our meetings and seemed to be greatly impressed with the need for a governmental role. This developed later in directions that I hardly anticipated—not, I think, under any prodding or prompting by the Occupation, although the Occupation was responsible for getting out through the Japanese several million copies of a one-page statement of the principles of citizens' rights, and this was intended to promote democratic concepts and also intended, of course, to offset Communist ideas.

Later—and this was some time after I returned—I learned that the Japanese government had established in the attorney general's office a division of civil rights to protect the citizens who put in a complaint, and that all the prefectural governments in the Prosecutor's Office had also established a section in which complaints were considered and sifted and inquired into and action was taken when violations were reported. In addition, Japan adopted a unique system of appointing civilian civil liberties commissioners. I believe there are some six thousand of them in Japan, citizens not paid but appointed in each town, each village, even—I think others got down pretty far into the countryside—citizens whose responsibility it is to listen to their fellow citizens who have complaints about their civil rights, and to report them to authorities . . . I got reports that on the whole it was working pretty well.

I would think, of all the countries I've seen in the years since I was in Japan in 1947, that the Japanese probably have the most thoroughgoing system (as they usually do, when they take hold of an idea) of any country in the world. Of course, the Occupation, from the very beginning, followed the American example. Generally speaking, I think almost all of the high officials in the Occupation, beginning with General MacArthur, thought that whatever was good in the United States and worked well over here ought to work well in Japan. That was one of the erroneous assumptions, but it's a common American assumption everywhere and has some justification, if you believe that a basic democracy works in one place as well as it will in another, because it's inherently good, and without regard to tradition and attitudes. (Columbia University, Oral History Research Office, "A Conversation with Roger Baldwin with Alan F. Westin," editor, *Civil Liberties Review*, and professor of Public Law, Columbia University, December 18, 1974, pp. 68–116.)

STATUS OF DEMOCRACY IN THE WORLD (1974)
IN INTERVIEW WITH CIVIL LIBERTIES REVIEW

Q. If you take the number of countries in the world that would be called democratic or parliamentary and you look at those that could be called one-party states and dictatorial states, the numbers are running against Wilsonian optimism.

A. I think the reason for that is this: that at this particular time, when nationalism is so strong, the sense of security by a state is number one. Nothing can take its place. And so all these states that are fearful, either of a war or fearful of interference by other states, tighten up their controls and make themselves one-party states or police states or military states, whatever they may be. Communist states, feudal states. And democracy suffers. If the fear of war and the fear of interference, domination, as in the case of the African states, is removed, I think that then the character of these governments will change. It has to change. I don't think people have those governments by preference. They don't have them as a response to any popular need or claim. They have them out of the necessity of security.

Q. A lot of the writing on the history of liberty has tried to suggest that its experience with opposition and freedom of expression and parliamentary institutions is that it's necessary to teach people how to live within the rules of a democratic system. Do you see a problem there?

A. Of course, there's a problem there. Surely. Even in our democracy, where we're supposed to be trained by long experience going back to our British origins, we have a very difficult time trying to create a functional democracy. Less than two-thirds of our people vote at all in the national elections, maybe even fewer in local elections. The nonparticipating segment of our population in all respects is very large in taking any interest in public affairs. Even reading newspapers that deal with them, perhaps getting almost all of their news by television and radio, and not paying much attention to that. I mean, we have the same problem. But I don't think that self-government, freedom and equality and even justice, which is more difficult, I don't think those are instincts that require much training.

Q. It is clear that since you left the ACLU, your effort has been focused in the world community. There's no handle that you and others have been able to get on human rights on the international scale that matches the handle that you developed in the United States.

A. Well, of course, for this reason: that we have no law. We have no world law on human rights. We have no enforceable agency like a court. We have nothing but moral influence. We have a forum in the United Nations. We have a collection of principles that people agree upon, but it's obviously just the initial stages of the creation of world law that will give us an analogous situation in the world to what we have in the United States. They've already got it in Europe with a court of human rights and a convention. They're trying to do it in Latin America. It's not the right time. Mark Twain said once that few things in history happen at the right time, and certainly it's true that this attempt to create a world order in the face of the Cold War and arms race and colonial revolution, it's quite out of key. (Columbia University, Oral History Research Office, "A Conversation with Roger Baldwin with Alan F. Westin," editor, *Civil Liberties Review*, and professor of Public Law, Columbia University, December 18, 1974, pp. 8–94.)

THE INTERNATIONAL LEAGUE FOR
THE RIGHTS OF MAN (1976)

The League with which I have worked since its French founders started it in New York in exile in the 1940s is an association of affiliated national agencies all over the world, neither numerous nor influential but devoted to principle, with U.S. contributing members supporting a tiny budget, and volunteers doing most of the work. I put in my time with conviction that our role was important to the UN's efforts, a view shared by only a few in the UN. The human rights agencies were a handful among them, the most influential the religious—Jewish, Catholic and Protestant. I got along with my assorted colleagues without trying to play leader of lobbying them to share our views.

Much of the sense of participation in these late years has come from travel around the world, beginning with Japan and Germany under occupation in the late 1940s and continuing right up to the present. *I felt for the first time at home in all the world* [italics author's]; I had visited every country I could where I had a purpose—a round-the-world trip, arranged in part by the UN for me in 1959, trips to Africa, the Near East, Latin America, Japan again—quite enough to see firsthand the struggles for freedom and equality and even more, the commitment to international goals.

I have survived intact all the discouragements and frustrations as the world has over these years retreated from the goals of the UN to the power struggles of the Cold War, the colonial revolution and the arms race. It has been a bad time for optimists, but I have held out. Behind the discouragements and retreats stands the steady growth of internationalism in cooperation, trade, credits, monetary controls, communications—indeed, a host of agencies, public and private, that for the first time in history begin to tie the world's peoples together. Never before has such a network existed because not until the last quarter century has communication by radio, air and telephone promoted such instant cooperation. (The Roger Nash Baldwin Papers, Box 25, Folder 2, International League for the Rights of Man, Seeley G. Mudd Manuscript Library, Princeton, N.J., March 1976.)

Notes

1. Robert C. Cottrell, *Roger Nash Baldwin and the American Civil Liberties Union* (New York: Columbia University Press, 2000), p. 331.

2. Author's Note: As a representative of the International League for the Rights of Man, Roger N. Baldwin served as a consultant to the United Nations in the preparation of the Universal Declaration of Human Rights and worked closely with Eleanor Roosevelt. (Columbia University, Oral History Research Office, "A Conversation with Roger Baldwin at Columbia University, with Thomas F. Hogan," April 11, 1963, pp. 96–101.)

3. General MacArthur sent the following letter, dated December 30, 1949, to Baldwin: "Roger Baldwin's crusade for civil liberties has had a profound and beneficial influence on the course of American progress. With countless individuals finding protection in the nobility of the cause he has long espoused, he stands out as one of the architects of our cherished American way of life." Baldwin wrote in a memorandum reacting to this letter: "The general's handwritten letter was in response to a request for a statement to be included in the book of letters presented to me upon my retirement as executive director of the Union in 1950. The letter, in the general's best hyperbole, has not hurt me, even among liberals."

COMMENTARY
A Very Important Force
An Interview with Leo Nevas, Former President, International League for Human Rights

---

Q. When did you first meet Roger Baldwin?

A. When I joined the board of the League[1], I was a non-governmental organization (NGO) representative at the UN for the World Peace Through Law group. I was chairman of the Human Rights Committee of that organization. I met Baldwin at the UN.

Q. How would you describe him, having worked with and having dealings with him?

A. He was a beautiful man. I don't remember that there was ever an issue I disagreed with him on. I just had a lot of admiration for his devotion to human rights and what he had done in starting the International League for the Rights of Man. I worked with him on several projects and at that time, at the beginning, human rights in Russia and in South Africa were the two subjects of concern. We at the League at the time were devoting a lot of attention to those two places. He was a guide to all of us—he was a person who had a good grasp of the subject and he also had a very balanced view about what he said and what he wrote. He understood we weren't going to be able to go into Africa to protect the human rights of everybody in, say Uganda. He was just a wonderful human being.

Q. What is it that you admired about his way of working?

A. He was a very persuasive individual, aside from his own personality, he had such credibility among everyone he dealt with that he was a very important force in the field by virtue of his own integrity, his beliefs—he wasn't a guy who went overboard, either—he had a really very balanced view of the situation.

Q. How did Roger Baldwin conduct meetings and one-on-one encounters?

A. I knew him for maybe ten or fifteen years. I have known many people in the human rights field and so many of them are so idealistic and unrealistic about what is doable and what is not doable. It's very frustrating. The fact about Roger was—I attended many meetings with him—I had never seen him take an extremist position on anything. His views were all thought out. They went to the heart of the situation. And weren't diverted by an incident here or an incident there. The incidents were symptomatic of what was underlying the problems. He was just a fantastic guy. No discussions that I can recall ever became heated discussions when he was around. He always had the knack of stepping in somewhere along the line, putting things in perspective, and getting agreement. He would have been a good negotiator.

Q. He was once asked why he wanted to be secretary at his meetings in addition to other roles, and he replied, "Well, if I take the notes, whatever I was fighting for in the meeting would come out on top. People don't remember everything."

A. That's right. I have been secretary of many organizations and I know how true that is. Let me say this, I had such admiration for this guy, if he had any faults, I never paid any attention to them.

Q. Isn't it ironic that with his background as a pacifist and fighter for peace that he was called by General Douglas MacArthur to Japan and General Lucius Clay to Germany to set up civil liberties agencies after World War II?

A. Yes, indeed. But I can't picture him with MacArthur.

Q. He did not talk about himself much, did he?

A. No he didn't. On this one TV program I was on with him, it was hard to get him to talk about himself and his formation of the civil liberties union and what he went through on that. He was such a solid person you didn't picture him as way off in left field. He may have been left but he wasn't in left field.

Q. I want to read you a quote from what he wrote in the 1970s and ask for comment:

> I am convinced democracy is the best form of government because it is the least evil. Some forms of it are working well; I think, in local governments fairly well, in some aspect of the United Nations, for example, where all the states are equal whether they are little or big, weak or powerful. That's a form of democracy where each one has a single vote and while their recommendations and decisions don't carry great weight, nevertheless it's a form of democracy and that's the only kind you could have that would suit the needs of all nations; democracy works in some nations and it doesn't work in others. In terms of individual liberties and human rights, the greatest struggle is still going on. I hate to use the word for world order, but it's something like that. It's a search and I suppose in all countries, to try and relate themselves to the rest of the world. I think every people, tied together in one sector of their lives or another forum, can universalize their experiences.

Q. In light of this statement, what do you think Roger Baldwin would have to say about the world situation now?

A. I think he would be heartbroken to see what's happened in the Human Rights Commission at the UN. For ten or fifteen years I used to attend full sessions of the Human Rights Committee of the UN at Geneva for the full six weeks of those sessions, and they broke my heart. First, they were a collection of incompetents. The state of knowledge of these human rights people was zero, in some instances. I tell the story of a very lovely and nice man from Nigeria who was a member of the Human Rights Commission. We would go to lunch frequently. Some issue was coming up and he wanted to talk about it. He had been a high school principal in Nigeria. He had never read the Universal Declaration of Human Rights until he got on the plane to Geneva. And he used to come to me with the agenda and talk about the subject. He was a gentleman.

Roger would have been heartbroken. Recently it's gotten even worse. It's a disgrace to call it a Human Rights Commission. It's one of the things that the UN, unfortunately, is trying to talk about reforming. To reform it they would have to reduce it in size, they would have to eliminate Libya and Syria, and so on. Libya was chair of the commission four years ago. I think he would be tremendously upset with what's happened on the UN Commission on Human Rights. I am a member of the United Nations Association. They just can't sit back and say the UN is a good thing and we have to support it. When it does a lousy job—like with the Human Rights Commission—if they want any credibility, they have to come out and talk about it. There are certain areas of the UN that are a disgrace to the organization.

Q. In light of Baldwin's hope for democracy around the world, what do you think he would have to say about our current policy of proactively trying to spread democracy throughout the world—in the Middle East and beyond?

A. That's interesting. I think, in general, he would be supportive of the idea, but I would think that he also would be critical of the attempt to force democracy in those places. And, unfortunately, I am afraid it's going to fail in many places. He would think of it as a good concept, the right concept, but I think he would be afraid of the fact that it was being imposed on other nations and that it was not a matter of their choice.

Q. What about the United States' unilateral actions, like attacking Iraq?

A. He definitely would not have been sympathetic to that. That was not his concept of what the world was like or should be. And he would have been in favor of the United States taking strong positions on matters of principle but taking these positions in accord with other similar countries, with the Western bloc at least. Frankly, he was certainly a person of peace, and he believed that regardless of who the other countries were, if they sought peace, they deserved to be treated as equals in society. If they are unequal in some financial or other ways, that could have happened to us, too. But he was as broad-minded a person I think I have ever known.

Q. If Roger Baldwin was to come back today and attend a meeting at the UN, what do you think he would say?

A. He would be disappointed in what's happened and what has not happened. He would be supportive of the environmental work, a certain amount of relief—food, medical, and health. Politically, he would be very disappointed. In human rights, they've made no progress.

I think there was more hope for human rights then when he was around than there is now.

Q. What do you think he would say about Guantánamo and Americans torturing people in Iraq?

A. Unbelievable. A judge just ordered the release of one of the individuals. I've heard comments on TV and in the media, "They are releasing a terrorist." They don't comprehend that he's been held now for three years and they haven't charged him or brought him to trial. Is that what we stand for? There is no excuse. People don't speak out because they have been cowed by the last election. I think that most of the people are supportive of what Bush is doing. Baldwin would have spoken out. There is no question about it. He would not have sat quietly by. It's so obvious to me that he would speak out.

Q. How effective was he as head of the International League for the Rights of Man?

A. At that time, the NGOs were not accorded very much of a stature at the UN. They were tolerated. Roger Baldwin was more than tolerated. Roger Baldwin talked not only as the voice of the International League, but also the voice of Roger Baldwin. Anybody who knew anything about what was happening—and many of them didn't—knew he was an outstanding person and he was someone you listened to. Among the important people at the UN, the officers and the NGOs, he was at the top.

Q. He was an internationalist before it became popular?

A. Yes. I recall specifically that it was only a matter of months before he and I were on close terms. I became a great admirer of his. He certainly was a people's man. We talked regularly, not about social matters, but he would call me on some project.

Q. Baldwin had a way of bringing people together.

A. Well, you know we had all kinds of people on our board, and they were some of the émigrés from Europe and from other countries, and they all had different views of human rights. To them it was a very specific thing that was a violation. He was great at putting together an issue or a statement in terms that satisfied these people, not by weakening it, but by stressing a position and making it all-encompassing, He had the knack of doing that. He was a peacemaker.

Q. What do you think Roger Baldwin would say today of the USA Patriot Act, which some say infringes on individual civil liberties?

A. He would have spoken out very strongly against it. He would not tolerate it. I think we went from a situation that was terribly lax—they were not enforcing the rudimentary laws that should have been, and now they are certainly impinging on civil liberties.

Q. In 1974, Baldwin wrote:

> President Kennedy once remarked at the United Nations that we have the power to make this era the greatest in history or the last. We assume it won't be the last, but it may be the right time to think of our generation as the beginning of one of the greatest; if, in fact, war and empire no longer threaten, the road is open for the first time in history to move forward to peace, order, and law.

Do you feel Baldwin would believe the road is still open to peace, order, and law?

A. Yes. The UN has the power to make the world free of massacres and genocide. I think that we have that power again now—another chance. And the UN, to help make this happen, has got to reform itself so that it is an operative world agency. The frivolous stuff that goes on, the back-scratching and the like, is horrible. In the General Assembly we could work for four weeks and accomplish anything that's worthwhile. I think it is possible now to have peace, but I don't know whether it's going to happen. What I do hope is they start making some progress.

Q. You have been around a while—you are ninety-three years old—and you met a lot of important people over the world. Do you think Baldwin ranks among the top?

A. It's hard to measure him and his accomplishments because they were not done in the limelight. He was a figure who was not universally accepted as a leader because he was telling people things they did not necessarily want to hear. So it's hard to compare him with others.

Q. How would you assess his role in American history and, indeed, in world history?

A. Well, the creation of the American Civil Liberties Union in 1920 in itself is a major accomplishment. And taking it through the years, there is no question he provided in the public debate and discussion a sense of steadiness, a sense of balance that was extremely important.

————

Leo Nevas, a former President of the International League for Human Rights who worked alongside Roger Baldwin, is a lawyer who has been active in numerous international organizations, including the United Nations Association.

NOTE

1. Interview with the author, March 6, 2005.

CHAPTER 12

FAMILY REFLECTIONS

About Roger Baldwin

CARL R. BALDWIN

It is a good time for all of us to follow Roger Baldwin and be peace-loving civil liberties citizens.

—Carl R. Baldwin, 2004

Growing up, it was rather confusing having famous parental, and even grandparental, figures to reckon with. My grandfather on my genetic father's side was Walter Rauschenbusch, the author in 1907 of *Christianity and the Social Crisis*, and the chief architect of the progressive or radical religious movement called the Social Gospel. Although Walter died long before my birth, I could read about him while growing up (my mother kept his biography), and I eventually learned that he was, and still is, as celebrated in his sphere as is Roger Baldwin in his.

My mother was Evelyn Preston, and my father was Stephen Rauschenbusch, who was Walter's eldest son. In spite of his father's hopes and expectations, Steve steered clear of religion and entered the progressive politics of the 1930s. By the time I was five or six, Evelyn and Steve had separated and then divorced. Evelyn and Roger, who had met some years earlier, were married in a private ceremony by Dorothy Kenyon, Evelyn's close friend and one of the few women who in that early era were admitted to the New York State Bar. Dorothy Kenyon's distinguished legal career included a position as a family court judge, and a tussle with Sen. Joe McCarthy in the early fifties that, by many accounts, left the senator, not Kenyon, in retreat.

It was around this time, the mid-thirties, that my older brother Roger invented the name "Bunkle" as a nickname for Roger Baldwin. Whatever the origin or original meaning of the nickname was, it caught on, and was soon used by family and, indeed, by many friends.

As a boy, my recollections of my stepfather were not oriented to New York City and his civil liberties work, but to the family's week-end place, called Dellbrook Farm, or Dellbrook for short, in Mahwah, New Jersey. Evelyn had the money and good sense to buy that property, and it was heaven for Bunkle, because it was on the Ramapo River. That lovely river meandered through Dellbrook and enabled Bunkle to indulge one of his great loves: canoeing. To have Bunkle in the stern of the canoe, expertly guiding it through perilous rocks and rapids, was an experience that a boy cannot forget.

Equally impressive was Bunkle's ability to know and name all the trees and plants on the property, and its many birds. Somewhat more intimidating was his knowledge of, and evident respect for, the snakes on the property, which were said to include poisonous copperheads and rattlesnakes.

Every winter a pond on Dellbrook would freeze, and family skating and hockey-playing between the brothers was something we all loved. When we tired of the beginners' slopes on Dellbrook, we also hiked to nearby properties to go skiing on somebody else's land. Had the curious property owner shown up, I was sure that Bunkle could have charmed him into giving consent to the trespass.

Once or twice each winter the family would go to Bear Mountain for skiing, and that wonderful hot chocolate offered by the Bear Mountain Inn. The family once decided to explore westward, stopping at a small facility on Greenwood Lake, New York, for ice skating. We were greeted with a huge sign that said "Christians Welcome." Evelyn and Roger drew the right conclusion: This was homegrown anti-Semitism. They angrily made their disapproval known to the owner, and the family left in a hurry. As a boy, I thus learned that human rights were more vital than a winter sport.

There was also the summer country place on Martha's Vineyard, called Windy Gates. Bunkle somehow managed to attend to civil liberties emergencies in New York City and also to these country pursuits, I don't know how. On the Vineyard I remember seeing a lot of a couple who may have been the closest friends of Evelyn and Roger: Alec and Helen Meiklejohn. Alec was a philosopher, college president, and First Amendment theoretician and advocate. I recall Alec saying one evening at dinner about Baldwin: "This man is doing the most important work being done in America right now." I wonder if that was during the summer after the ACLU took on the cause of the internment of the Japanese-Americans, a cause that other civil rights groups shied away from. After all, we were at war! (Sound familiar?)

Anyone who has ever heard Roger Baldwin give a public speech will recall that he was a consummate actor, a sort of Burt Lancaster or Laurence Olivier of civil liberties. This skill was shown one weekend at Dellbrook, probably in 1946, as the family got ready to see Olivier's interpretation of Shakespeare's *Henry V*. I should first mention parenthetically that Evelyn and Roger were generally indifferent to popular art and the movies. To be fair, I gratefully recall that we were taken to *The Wizard of Oz*, *Pinocchio*, and *Fantasia*. I remember, however, being hustled out of movies that were deemed too sultry, ironically an apparent violation of my youthful civil liberties. But Shakespeare and Olivier were okay. In reading the play aloud, Bunkle assumed every role, and I remember his portrayal of the war-hungry Archbishop of Canterbury as especially gripping. I continue to love the movie to this day, along with the memory of Bunkle's great Dellbrook performance for the family.

Fast forward about two decades. It was April 1965 and college campuses were beginning to speak out on the war in Vietnam. I was teaching art history at Hunter College in New York City. A number of us decided to put together a "Workshop on Vietnam" that would express opposing views on the issue. As my contribution to the workshop, I managed to sign up Roger Baldwin, the civil libertarian, and Norman Thomas, the democratic socialist and 1932 presidential candidate, as speakers. Baldwin and Thomas were marvelous, and I relish the memory of the event. Following the workshop, my wife Mary Ellen and I, and our two children, Steve and Kathleen, were regular participants in antiwar demonstrations, including several huge ones in our nation's capital.

Today, under Bush and Ashcroft, civil liberties and human rights are once again imperiled. Bunkle would be pleased to see that the ACLU is going strong under the leadership of Anthony Romero. Baldwin got the ball rolling back in 1920, just after "the Great War." At this writing, we now have a president who boasts of being "a war president." It is a good time for all of us to follow Roger Baldwin and be peaceloving civil liberties citizens.

AFTERWORD

Roger Baldwin: A Patrician Heretic

ANTHONY LEWIS

When an American gets into trouble for disagreeing with the government—by making a radical speech, leading a protest—we take it for granted that the American Civil Liberties Union will come to his or her defense.[1] That is our system: the especially American way in which a private organization protects the individual's right to disagree with authority.

But it was not always so. When the United States entered World War I in 1917, dissenters fell victim to the official rallying of patriotic fervor. The Espionage Act of 1917 was used to punish criticism. Eugene Debs, the great socialist leader, was convicted and sentenced to ten years in prison for expressing sympathy with men who were in jail for counseling others who tried to avoid the draft. Men who threw leaflets from the tops of buildings in New York deploring President Woodrow Wilson's dispatch of American troops to Russia after the Bolshevik revolution drew twenty-year sentences.

Out of such incidents came the American Civil Liberties Union, created first as the National Civil Liberties Bureau of the American Union Against Militarism in 1917, with the purpose of defending critics of the war. It was reborn as the ACLU, with a broader charter, in 1920. It was primarily the work of Roger Baldwin.

From 1917 to 1981, Roger Baldwin battled for freedom—freedom, in the phrase of Justice Oliver Wendell Holmes Jr., "for the thought we hate." Baldwin was a remarkable combination of patrician heretic, a pacifist who fought for the right to be different. He directed the Civil Liberties Union until his formal retirement at age sixty-six in 1950. But retirement did not stop his involvement with the ACLU, or a dozen other organizations, including the United Nations. Nor did it stop his lifelong avocations, canoeing and bird-watching.

I interviewed Baldwin on his farm in New Jersey in June 1981. He was ninety-seven—he died two months later—but he was as sharp as ever that day. Which is to say, more articulate than most of us can ever hope to be. He left us a happy legacy of writings; many are contained in this book, compiled by his friend, journalist Woody Klein. They cover a broad spectrum of Roger Baldwin's views, many relevant in today's continuing fight for civil liberties.

What struck me about the conversation I had with him in 1981 was how optimistic Roger was. He had seen the worst of human intolerance and cruelty: the excesses of World War I, the Nazis, the American Red scare in the McCarthy years. He had no illusions about the perfection of mankind. But he radiated confidence that our better selves would triumph. The patrician side of him showed once or twice, as when he referred to President Franklin D. Roosevelt as "Frank"—a memory of a shared boyhood perhaps. But there was nothing condescending in that; it conveyed a belief that we were all the same when it came to our rights.

Baldwin's determination and optimism seem to me even more important today than they were in 1981. The freedom of speech for which he battled is largely accepted now, by conservatives as well as liberals; the dissents of Holmes and Brandeis have become the law. But fear of terrorism since the attacks of September 11, 2001, has led to dangerous new forms of repression. A president and his attorney general have claimed the right to imprison any American citizen, on suspicion of terrorist connections, without trial and without access to counsel. The president has unilaterally renounced adherence to the Geneva Convention protecting the rights of those captured in war. Lawyers in the United States government have asserted that the president can authorize his agents to torture suspects despite a law and treaty forbidding torture.

The voice of Roger Baldwin, and his beliefs, call out to us as strongly as ever today. Following, the Q&A with Baldwin.

Q. Over your long lifetime, I suppose, you've witnessed the fading of that Spenserian notion that every day in every way we're getting better and better. Is it still possible to be optimistic near the end of this terrible century?

A. For the first thirty years of my life, I felt the kind of optimism you describe. I believed in the perfectibility of mankind and in the perfectibility of its institutions; World War I destroyed that. It has been a terrible century, but things are immensely better for this country and the world today than they were at my birth. No comparison. For one basic reason: The world is now conscious of being one. When I was born we were not aware of anything beyond our own borders. Now we have a multitude of international institutions that serve all the countries of the world, from the World Bank and the International Monetary Fund to the agencies of the United Nations. You can't get on an airplane without getting permission from the international authority that governs all air traffic. All television and radio wavelengths are prescribed by another international authority. Therefore, having created the basis of a united world, we now have the possibility of getting a civilized one.

Q. At the same time, ever-growing arsenals of nuclear weapons threaten the destruction of human life. Are you confident that they will never again be used in war?
A. If they are, it's the end of us. We haven't even started to control nuclear weapons yet. The arms race gets more and more desperate. George Kennan [a former United States Foreign Service official and foreign policy planner in the 1950s, who is considered to have been the "architect" of the Cold War] says let's get together and decide to get rid of half of the stuff. It's good counsel, but we're not doing it. It will take someone with high moral authority to break the impasse. Alas, I don't see any leader on either side who is capable of it.

Q. And despite this you are still an optimist?
A. Well, there is a great basis for optimism in the fact that communications now give us almost instant knowledge of what goes on everywhere in the world.

Q. You mean, people should be more aware of their common humanity?
A. Yes, and their common dangers. You've got to assume that the human race's instinct for survival is greater than its instinct for death. Another hopeful phenomenon in this area is that nationalism has proven to be stronger than ideology. China's hostility to the Soviet Union, for example, helps guarantee our security. The power of nationalist feeling is a very fortunate thing for the future.

Q. Is that a change in your thinking? Weren't you at one time a one-worlder?
A. Yes, I was. I didn't appreciate that nationalism was the essential ingredient of internationalism until the emergence of the Third World after World War II. Then I realized that the littlest country was never going to surrender any of its powers to an international body unless it

felt secure as a sovereign state. And the United Nations has taken the right course by recognizing even insignificant little islands as states with an equal vote.

Q. You have not always felt the way you do now about the Soviet Union. When you visited that country in the late twenties, you took a more generous view of the effects of the Revolution, didn't you?

A. Yes, I did. I didn't become disillusioned until the first revelations of the Stalin years and the signing of the Nazi-Soviet Pact. I still had hopes then that the Russians would not tolerate dictatorship—at least for very long. I don't think any event in my life troubled me more than when they found common cause against the Western Allies.

Q. Do you foresee the Soviet Union becoming a major democratic society in the next ten or twenty years?

A. It all depends—not on how the Communist society develops, but in how much confidence we put in international institutions. If these grow, and if the Communist countries go along, there will be a softening of all tyrannical regimes. At the same time, we have got to learn to live with Communists. One of the great errors of United States foreign policy, in my opinion, is to look on the Soviet Union as the source of all evil. People are going to revolt against tyranny whether they get Soviet help or not. The Soviets don't cause it. It's there. They just go fishing.

Q. Some people in the United States feel that by protesting against injustice in the Soviet Union, or in Argentina or in the Philippines, we display a kind of moral arrogance. Do you agree?

A. There is a great deal of self-righteousness about the United States. We inherited it. The English are self-righteous, too. We've never hesitated to point the finger. But there is a good case for the moral superiority of the United States. I don't believe that we're superior to others as people, but on the whole our institutions are better. No other country with so many people of different origins has done as well as the United States. Our democracy is not a model for the world, but I think it is a great *example* [italics Baldwin's]. I marvel sometimes that we preserve it, but we do.

Q. To which institutions do your think the United States owes its survival as a democracy?

A. The great evil, as all history has shown, is the concentration of power in a few hands. The division of power within the federal government and among the states, and the fact that we have strong local self-government and the welfare state above the local divisions of our society—these all guarantee that we continue to get along, never mind how intense the strain is. In the middle of a war, with some exceptions, we have managed to preserve our democratic institutions.

Q. *When you talk about the distribution of power, you are sounding the central theme of the United States Constitution. Do you think that the Constitution, an eighteenth-century document, is still meaningful for us?*

A. People will always be jealous of their power. States are jealous of their power and localities are jealous of their power.

Q. *And, of course, the various branches of the federal government are jealous of their power.*

A. Exactly. And I think that the saving institution in the long run has been the United States Supreme Court. I've often had occasion to deplore its decisions over the years, but I have a higher regard for it now than when I was young. Of course, I was raised on the dissents of Brandeis and Holmes, and now the attitude of those men toward the law is the prevailing opinion in the Supreme Court.

Q. *This is surely one of the curiosities of our history. In 1941, Justice Jackson described the Supreme Court as an inherently conservative influence in this country. How is it that it has become a libertarian influence?*

A. I think it had a lot to do with the rise of the belief that the disadvantaged are the responsibility of the whole community, and with the great shift of power to the federal government in Franklin Roosevelt's New Deal.

Q. *In 1954, when the Court voted against the separate and equal treatment of blacks, was the Court similarly responding to public feeling, to a general uneasiness about segregation?*

A. That unanimous decision, an extraordinary feat for the Court at any time, was largely due to the persuasive powers of an extraordinary chief justice, Earl Warren. But yes, the feeling of guilt about slavery and race relations was so strong that when they were faced squarely with the issue of separate and equal, the justices had to come down for equality.

Q. *In 1950, four years before that decision, when you retired as director of the American Civil Liberties Union, you described "inequality in law and oppor-*

tunity based on race and national origin" as "our greatest national failure."
With all the things that are wrong in this country, we have made progress there,
haven't we?

A. In law we have. There are a few "white" and "colored" signs in
the United States. There is no segregation on public carriers. There is
even preference in employment. We have this affirmative action program, which recognizes our sins and tries to make amends. But there is
still segregation in social life, in employment and largely in education.
Ours is still basically a racist society.

Q. Is there reason to hope that this will change?
A. Yes, but it's the most difficult of all changes because it runs
contrary to people's tribal instincts. People naturally flock with their
own kinds. For that reason, I think that the struggle for equality is even
more difficult than the struggle for freedom.

Q. There are those who believe that we are entering a period like the Palmer
raids of the 1920s or the McCarthy hearings of the 1950s, when free speech and
other civil liberties were repressed. Are our civil liberties secure?
A. Liberty in any country depends upon the kind of resistance that is
put up to abusive authority. When the American Civil Liberties Union
defended the Nazis in Skokie, Illinois, in 1977 and 1978, we discovered
how much support there is today for the idea of defending your enemies
as well as your friends. Everybody wants to be able to express themselves. That's a natural right, not a constitutional right. A very wise man,
Benjamin Franklin, once said that granted, abuses of free speech should
be suppressed, but to whom dare you entrust the power to do so? We
have been extremely careful not to entrust that power to anybody but
the Supreme Court, and the Supreme Court has on the whole proved to
be a pretty good First Amendment court. Fortunately, we have enough
people in the United States who are willing to exercise their right to
protest. It's hard to see a return to an era of fear and suppression.

Q. You're optimistic even though Edwin Meese, counselor to the president of
the United States, has said that the American Civil Liberties Union is part of a
"criminal lobby"?
A. Yes, that man was very stupid. The logic of his position was that
if you defend criminals, you must be a partner. No, civil rights are
not among this administration's top priorities. But I do think that
the damage they can do—and they've done some already—will be
minimal.

Q. You don't see them dismantling the social programs that have been legislated over the last thirty years?

A. How Reagan's new order will be reconciled with the New Deal, I don't know. But we aren't at the end of it yet. I think most of the welfare state will be preserved. But it's hard to deal with social problems in a sensible way with all this pressure for more and more armaments and the fear of war that it creates.

Q. In recent years we have seen a religious revival that has gradually extended itself into politics, as shown by the rise of the Moral Majority and similar groups. Is the Constitution, with its separation of church and state, adequate to prevent religious and social strife from developing?

A. It doesn't prevent conflicts. All the Constitution does is separate them, not prevent them. The Moral Majority owes much of its power to the airwaves, where it can appeal to people's prejudices and impose certain biblical moral concepts based not on the words of Jesus but on the sense of sin. These people represent an offshoot of Christian morals. They believe in the old evangelical notion that salvation is achieved through repentance. Not only that, you've got to carry your repentance into law. You've got to insist that abortion is murder.

Q. Do you see no danger then, in the purging of libraries and the return of prayer in schools?

A. Of course I see a danger there, but I have confidence that the imposition of moral standards by a minority just won't work, at least for very long. There are too many competing influences in our society. The people who want to stop us from reading something are up against the people who want to read. I don't think that freedom, once established as it has been in this country, can be eclipsed by minority movements.

Q. The American Civil Liberties Union has done a great deal to raise the consciousness of Americans in general, and judges in particular, to the value of liberty. Given your confident attitude toward the security of the nation's civil liberties, do you feel that the Union still has a role to play?

A. Well, now as then, people get themselves into trouble by expressing radical and nonconformist views. We still rely largely on volunteer lawyers to defend them. But the ramifications of the concept of freedom have become more widespread—the rights of prisoners, the rights of children, the rights of women, the abortion cases, the homosexual cases, you name 'em. Fifty years ago we never contemplated having such a wide range of clients.

Q. Do you feel that there are fewer people toiling for the public good these days?

A. No. We have enough people who aren't entirely consumed by getting a living by greedy ambitions. We're a nation of joiners—we like to get up and express ourselves.

Q. You believe in pluralism, then?

A. Yes, I think that the strength of our country is in private organizations and not in government. People in government are restricted, whereas people in the private sector can assert their purposes without fear of adverse reaction. There are thousands and thousands of private organizations all over the country—men's clubs, women's clubs, trade unions, chambers of commerce. No other country, even the most democratic, has such width and depth of private organizations bringing their influence to bear on government.

Q. What are the great unsolved problems that the world faces?

A. I have my own list of problems and they all happen to begin with P—peace, population, poverty, and pollution—and I put them in that order of importance.

Q. Six years ago, in an interview with Thomas Lee for Harvard *magazine, you said that most people believe in the future, "desperate as they are." After six years of economic and political stress, do you still feel the same way?*

A. Yes, I do. People don't express these things clearly and openly. But they live then. People live hope, they don't talk about it. The mere fact that they don't commit suicide is enough to express it.

Q. And yourself?

A. I am one of those people who looks more hopefully upon the world than the evidence warrants.

Q. What is it that you are choosing to overlook?

A. Mark Twain called it the general cussedness of mankind.

Q. So you admit that it exists?

A. That it exists and that it can be overcome.

NOTES

1. Editor's Note: This previously unpublished interview by Anthony Lewis with Roger N. Baldwin took place only two months before Baldwin died in August 1981. Lewis, a former Pulitzer Prize–winning columnist for the *New York Times* and an authority on equal justice and the courts, provided it exclusively for this book. In 2001, Lewis was awarded the Presidential Citizens Medal, and in 2003 he was the recipient of the Roger N. Baldwin Medal of Liberty Award for his outstanding writing on civil liberties.

APPENDIX

Amendments to the U.S. Constitution

(The Bill of Rights consists of Amendments I–X)

AMENDMENT I

(December 15, 1791)
Congress shall make no law respecting an establishment of religion, or prohibiting the free exercise thereof; or abridging the freedom of speech, or of the press; or the right of the people peaceably to assemble, and to petition the government for a redress of grievances.

AMENDMENT II

(December 15, 1791)
A well regulated militia, being necessary to the security of a free state, the right of the people to keep and bear arms shall not be infringed.

AMENDMENT III

(December 15, 1791)
No soldier shall, in time of peace, be quartered in any house without the consent of the owner, nor in time of war, but in a manner to be prescribed by law.

AMENDMENT IV

(December 15, 1791)
The right of the people to be secure in their persons, houses, papers,

and effects, against unreasonable searches and seizures, shall not be violated, and no warrants shall issue, but upon probable cause, supported by oath or affirmation, and particularly describing the place to be searched, and the persons or things to be seized.

AMENDMENT V

(December 15, 1791)

No person shall be held to answer for a capital, or otherwise infamous crime, unless on a presentment or indictment of a grand jury, except in cases arising in the land or naval forces, or in the militia, when in actual service in time of war or public danger; nor shall any person be subject for the same offense to be twice put in jeopardy of life or limb; nor shall be compelled in any criminal case to be a witness against himself, nor be deprived of life, liberty, or property, without due process of law; nor shall private property be taken for public use without just compensation.

AMENDMENT VI

(December 15, 1791)

In all criminal prosecutions, the accused shall enjoy the right to a speedy and public trial, by an impartial jury of the state and district wherein the crime shall have been committed, which district shall have been previously ascertained by law, and to be informed of the nature and cause of the accusation; to be confronted with the witnesses against him; to have compulsory process for obtaining witnesses in his favor, and to have the assistance of counsel for his defense.

AMENDMENT VII

(December 15, 1791)

In suits at common law, where the value in controversy shall exceed twenty dollars, the right of trial by jury shall be preserved, and no fact tried by a jury, shall be otherwise reexamined in any court of the United States, than according to the rules of the common law.

Amendment VIII

(December 15, 1791)
Excessive bail shall not be required, nor excessive fines imposed, nor cruel and unusual punishments inflicted.

Amendment IX

(December 15, 1791)
The enumeration in the Constitution, of certain rights, shall not be construed to deny or disparage others retained by the people.

Amendment X

(December 15, 1791)
The powers not delegated to the United States by the Constitution, nor prohibited by it to the states, are reserved to the states respectively, or to the people.

Amendment XI

(February 7, 1795)
The judicial power of the United States shall not be construed to extend to any suit in law or equity, commenced or prosecuted against one of the United States by Citizens of another State, or by Citizens or Subjects of any Foreign State.

Amendment XII

(June 15, 1804)
The electors shall meet in their respective states and vote by ballot for President and Vice-President, one of whom, at least, shall not be an inhabitant of the same state with themselves; they shall name in their ballots the person voted for as President, and in distinct ballots the person voted for as Vice-President, and they shall make distinct lists of all persons voted for as President, and of all persons voted for as

Vice-President, and of the number of votes for each, which lists they shall sign and certify, and transmit sealed to the seat of the government of the United States, directed to the President of the Senate;—The President of the Senate shall, in the presence of the Senate and House of Representatives, open all the certificates and the votes shall then be counted;—the person having the greatest number of votes for President, shall be the President, if such number be a majority of the whole number of electors appointed; and if no person have such majority, then from the persons having the highest numbers not exceeding three on the list of those voted for as President, the House of Representatives shall choose immediately, by ballot, the President. But in choosing the President, the votes shall be taken by states, the representation from each state having one vote; a quorum for this purpose shall consist of a member or members from two-thirds of the states, and a majority of all the states shall be necessary to a choice. And if the House of Representatives shall not choose a President whenever the right of choice shall devolve upon them, before the fourth day of March next following, then the Vice-President shall act as President, as in the case of the death or other constitutional disability of the President. The person having the greatest number of votes as Vice-President, shall be the Vice-President, if such number be a majority of the whole number of electors appointed, and if no person have a majority, then from the two highest numbers on the list, the Senate shall choose the Vice-President; a quorum for the purpose shall consist of two-thirds of the whole number of Senators, and a majority of the whole number shall be necessary to a choice. But no person constitutionally ineligible to the office of President shall be eligible to that of Vice-President of the United States.

Amendment XIII

(December 6, 1865)

Section 1. Neither slavery nor involuntary servitude, except as a punishment for crime whereof the party shall have been duly convicted, shall exist within the United States, or any place subject to their jurisdiction.

Section 2. Congress shall have power to enforce this article by appropriate legislation.

Amendment XIV

(July 9, 1868)

Section 1. All persons born or naturalized in the United States, and subject to the jurisdiction thereof, are citizens of the United States and of the state wherein they reside. No state shall make or enforce any law which shall abridge the privileges or immunities of citizens of the United States; nor shall any state deprive any person of life, liberty, or property, without due process of law; nor deny to any person within its jurisdiction the equal protection of the laws.

Section 2. Representatives shall be apportioned among the several states according to their respective numbers, counting the whole number of persons in each state, excluding Indians not taxed. But when the right to vote at any election for the choice of electors for President and Vice President of the United States, Representatives in Congress, the executive and judicial officers of a state, or the members of the legislature thereof, is denied to any of the male inhabitants of such state, being twenty-one years of age, and citizens of the United States, or in any way abridged, except for participation in rebellion, or other crime, the basis of representation therein shall be reduced in the proportion which the number of such male citizens shall bear to the whole number of male citizens twenty-one years of age in such state.

Section 3. No person shall be a Senator or Representative in Congress, or elector of President and Vice President, or hold any office, civil or military, under the United States, or under any state, who, having previously taken an oath, as a member of Congress, or as an officer of the United States, or as a member of any state legislature, or as an executive or judicial officer of any state, to support the Constitution of the United States, shall have engaged in insurrection or rebellion against the same, or given aid or comfort to the enemies thereof. But Congress may by a vote of two-thirds of each House, remove such disability.

Section 4. The validity of the public debt of the United States, authorized by law, including debts incurred for payment of pensions and bounties for services in suppressing insurrection or rebellion, shall not be questioned. But neither the United States nor any state shall assume or pay any debt or obligation incurred in aid of insurrection or rebellion against the United States, or any claim for the loss or emancipation of any slave; but all such debts, obligations, and claims shall be held illegal and void.

Section 5. The Congress shall have power to enforce, by appropriate legislation, the provisions of this article.

AMENDMENT XV

(February 3, 1870)
Section 1. The right of citizens of the United States to vote shall not be denied or abridged by the United States or by any state on account of race, color, or previous condition of servitude.
Section 2. The Congress shall have power to enforce this article by appropriate legislation.

AMENDMENT XVI

(February 3, 1913)
The Congress shall have power to lay and collect taxes on incomes, from whatever source derived, without apportionment among the several states, and without regard to any census of enumeration.

AMENDMENT XVII

(April 8, 1913)
The Senate of the United States shall be composed of two Senators from each state, elected by the people thereof, for six years; and each Senator shall have one vote. The electors in each state shall have the qualifications requisite for electors of the most numerous branch of the state legislatures.
When vacancies happen in the representation of any state in the Senate, the executive authority of such state shall issue writs of election to fill such vacancies: Provided that the legislature of any state may empower the executive thereof to make temporary appointments until the people fill the vacancies by election as the legislature may direct.
This amendment shall not be so construed as to affect the election or term of any Senator chosen before it becomes valid as part of the Constitution.

AMENDMENT XVIII

(January 16, 1919)
Section 1. After one year from the ratification of this article the manufacture, sale, or transportation of intoxicating liquors within, the importation thereof into, or the exportation thereof from the United

States and all territory subject to the jurisdiction thereof for beverage purposes is hereby prohibited.

Section 2. The Congress and the several states shall have concurrent power to enforce this article by appropriate legislation.

Section 3. This article shall be inoperative unless it shall have been ratified as an amendment to the Constitution by the legislatures of the several states, as provided in the Constitution, within seven years from the date of the submission hereof to the states by the Congress.

AMENDMENT XIX

(August 18, 1920)

The right of citizens of the United States to vote shall not be denied or abridged by the United States or by any state on account of sex.

Congress shall have power to enforce this article by appropriate legislation.

AMENDMENT XX

(January 23, 1933)

Section 1. The terms of the President and Vice President shall end at noon on the 20th day of January, and the terms of Senators and Representatives at noon on the 3d day of January, of the years in which such terms would have ended if this article had not been ratified; and the terms of their successors shall then begin.

Section 2. The Congress shall assemble at least once in every year, and such meeting shall begin at noon on the 3d day of January, unless they shall by law appoint a different day.

Section 3. If, at the time fixed for the beginning of the term of the President, the President elect shall have died, the Vice President elect shall become President. If a President shall not have been chosen before the time fixed for the beginning of his term, or if the President elect shall have failed to qualify, then the Vice President elect shall act as President until a President shall have qualified; and the Congress may by law provide for the case wherein neither a President elect nor a Vice President elect shall have qualified, declaring who shall then act as President, or the manner in which one who is to act shall be selected, and such person shall act accordingly until a President or Vice President shall have qualified.

Section 4. The Congress may by law provide for the case of the death of any of the persons from whom the House of Representatives may choose a President whenever the right of choice shall have devolved upon them, and for the case of the death of any of the persons from whom the Senate may choose a Vice President whenever the right of choice shall have devolved upon them.

Section 5. Sections 1 and 2 shall take effect on the 15th day of October following the ratification of this article.

Section 6. This article shall be inoperative unless it shall have been ratified as an amendment to the Constitution by the legislatures of three-fourths of the several states within seven years from the date of its submission.

AMENDMENT XXI

(December 5, 1933)

Section 1. The eighteenth article of amendment to the Constitution of the United States is hereby repealed.

Section 2. The transportation or importation into any state, territory, or possession of the United States for delivery or use therein of intoxicating liquors, in violation of the laws thereof, is hereby prohibited.

Section 3. This article shall be inoperative unless it shall have been ratified as an amendment to the Constitution by conventions in the several states, as provided in the Constitution, within seven years from the date of the submission hereof to the states by the Congress.

AMENDMENT XXII

(February 27, 1951)

Section 1. No person shall be elected to the office of the President more than twice, and no person who has held the office of President, or acted as President, for more than two years of a term to which some other person was elected President shall be elected to the office of the President more than once. But this article shall not apply to any person holding the office of President when this article was proposed by the Congress, and shall not prevent any person who may be holding the office of President, or acting as President, during the term within which this article becomes operative from holding the office of President or acting as President during the remainder of such term.

Section 2. This article shall be inoperative unless it shall have been ratified as an amendment to the Constitution by the legislatures of three-fourths of the several states within seven years from the date of its submission to the states by the Congress.

AMENDMENT XXIII

(March 29, 1961)
Section 1. The District constituting the seat of government of the United States shall appoint in such manner as the Congress may direct: A number of electors of President and Vice President equal to the whole number of Senators and Representatives in Congress to which the District would be entitled if it were a state, but in no event more than the least populous state; they shall be in addition to those appointed by the states, but they shall be considered, for the purposes of the election of President and Vice President, to be electors appointed by a state; and they shall meet in the District and perform such duties as provided by the twelfth article of amendment.
Section 2. The Congress shall have power to enforce this article by appropriate legislation.

AMENDMENT XXIV

(January 23, 1964)
Section 1. The right of citizens of the United States to vote in any primary or other election for President or Vice President, for electors for President or Vice President, or for Senator or Representative in Congress, shall not be denied or abridged by the United States or any state by reason of failure to pay any poll tax or other tax.
Section 2. The Congress shall have power to enforce this article by appropriate legislation.

AMENDMENT XXV

(February 23, 1967)
Section 1. In case of the removal of the President from office or of his death or resignation, the Vice President shall become President.
Section 2. Whenever there is a vacancy in the office of the Vice Pres-

ident, the President shall nominate a Vice President who shall take office upon confirmation by a majority vote of both Houses of Congress.

Section 3. Whenever the President transmits to the President pro tempore of the Senate and the Speaker of the House of Representatives his written declaration that he is unable to discharge the powers and duties of his office, and until he transmits to them a written declaration to the contrary, such powers and duties shall be discharged by the Vice President as Acting President.

Section 4. Whenever the Vice President and a majority of either the principal officers of the executive departments or of such other body as Congress may by law provide, transmit to the President pro tempore of the Senate and the Speaker of the House of Representatives their written declaration that the President is unable to discharge the powers and duties of his office, the Vice President shall immediately assume the powers and duties of the office as Acting President.

Thereafter, when the President transmits to the President pro tempore of the Senate and the Speaker of the House of Representatives his written declaration that no inability exists, he shall resume the powers and duties of his office unless the Vice President and a majority of either the principal officers of the executive department or of such other body as Congress may by law provide, transmit within four days to the President pro tempore of the Senate and the Speaker of the House of Representatives their written declaration that the President is unable to discharge the powers and duties of his office. Thereupon Congress shall decide the issue, assembling within forty-eight hours for that purpose if not in session. If the Congress, within twenty-one days after receipt of the latter written declaration, or, if Congress is not in session, within twenty-one days after Congress is required to assemble, determines by two-thirds vote of both Houses that the President is unable to discharge the powers and duties of his office, the Vice President shall continue to discharge the same as Acting President; otherwise, the President shall resume the powers and duties of his office.

Amendment XXVI

(July 1, 1971)

Section 1. The right of citizens of the United States, who are 18 years of age or older, to vote, shall not be denied or abridged by the United States or any state on account of age.

Section 2. The Congress shall have the power to enforce this article by appropriate legislation.

AMENDMENT XXVII

(1992)
No law varying the compensation for the services of the Senators and Representatives shall take effect until an election of Representatives shall have intervened.

———————

Source: Byron Preis and David Osterlund, eds., *The Constitution of the United States: The Bicentennial Keepsake Edition* (New York: Bantam Books, 1987), pp. 51–83.

Selected Bibliography

Abaya, Hernando Jr. *The CLU Story: 50 Years of Struggle for Civil Liberties.* Quezon: New Day Publishers, 1987.

Abraham, Henry J. *Freedom and the Court: Civil Rights and Liberties in the United States.* London: Oxford University Press, 1967.

ACLU Annual Report, 1953. "The American Civil Liberties Union Sticks Out Its Tongue." *Law and Labor,* January 1931.

ACLU Annual Report, 1949. *In the Shadow of Fear.*

ACLU, 1953. *"We Hold These Truths . . .": Freedom, Justice, Equality; Report on Civil Liberties.*

Amory, Cleveland. *The Proper Bostonians.* New York: Dutton, 1947.

Arsenault, Raymond. *Crucible of Liberty: 200 Years of the Bill of Rights.* New York: Free Press, 1991.

Auerbach, Jerold S. *Labor and Liberty: The La Follette Committee and the New Deal.* Indianapolis: Bobbs-Merrill, 1966.

Baldwin, Roger N. "Conservatives and Liberals Unite to Conserve Liberty and Security," in Goldberg, Danny; Goldberg, Victor; and Greenwood, Robert, eds. *It's a Free Country: Personal Freedom in America after September 11.* New York: RDV Books, 2002.

———. "As the Executive Director:" In Alan Reitman, ed., *Pulse of Freedom: American Liberties, 1920–1970.* New York: New American Library, 1976.

———. "Recollections of a Life in Civil Liberties-II: Russia, Communism, and United Fronts, 1920–1940." *Civil Liberties Review* 2 (fall 1975): 10–40.

———. "Recollections of a Life in Civil Liberties-I." *Civil Liberties Review* 1 (spring 1975): 39–63.

———. "The Prospects for Freedom," Felix Adler Lecture, American Ethical Union. New York, 1952.

———. "Communist Conspirators and the Bill of Rights." *Progressive* April 5, 1949.

———. "American Liberties, 1947–1948." *Art and Action: Tenth Anniversary Issue.* New York: Twice a Year Press, 1948.

———. "Reds and Rights." *Progressive.* June 4, 1948.

———. "Of All the Literature on Gandhi." *Voice of India,* June 1946.

———. "The Japanese Americans in Wartime." *American Mercury,* December 1944.

———. "Japanese Americans and the Law." *Asia* 42. September 1942.

———. "Roger Baldwin Reviews the Japanese Evacuation Case." *Open Forum* 19. August 15, 1942.

———. "Conscientious Objectors." *Nation.* October 12, 1941.

———. "Conscience Under the Draft." *Nation.* August 9, 1941.

———. "Civil Liberties Comprise." *Social Work Year Book* 5. 1939.

———. "Baldwin Accuses Hague of Tyranny." *The New York Times.* December 16, 1937.

———. "Freedom in the U.S.A. and the U.S.S.R." *Soviet Russia Today.* September 1934.

———. "Free Speech for Nazis?" *World Tomorrow.* November 16, 1933.

———. "The Myth of Law and Order," Schmalhausen, Samuel D., ed., *Behold America!* New York: Farrar & Rinehart, 1931.

———. "While California's Governor Deliberates." *Unity.* August 12, 1929.

———. *Liberty Under the Soviets.* New York: Vanguard, 1928.

———. "Where Are the Prewar Radicals?" *Survey* 55. February 1, 1926.

———. Introduction, Alexander Berkman, ed. *Letters from Russian Prisons,* Westport, CT: Hyperion Press, 1925.

———. "The Immorality of Social Work." *World Tomorrow* 5. February 1922: 44–45.

———. "How Shall We Escape Private Property?" *World Tomorrow.* April 1922: 109–10.

———. "Freedom of Opinion." *Socialist Review* 9. August 1920.

———. *The Truth About the I. W W.* New York: National Civil Liberties Bureau. 1918.

———. "Social Work and Radical Economic Movements." *Proceedings of the National Conference of Social Work* 45. 1918.

———. "An Industrial Program after the War." *Proceedings of the National Conference of Social Work* 45. 1918.

———. "Conscience at the Bar." *Survey* 41. November 1918.

———. "The Use of Municipal Ownership to Abolish Trans-Mississippi Freight and Passenger Tolls." *National Municipal Review.* July 4, 1915.

———. "St. Louis' Successful Fight for a Modern Charter." *National Municipal Review.* October 3, 1914.

———. "The St. Louis Pageant and Masque: Its Civic Meaning." *Survey* 32. April 11, 1914: 52–53.

——— and Hamilton Fish Jr. *Should Alien Communists Be Deported for Their Opinions?* New York: ACLU, 1934.

——— and Alan Westin. "The ACLU and the FBI: 'They Never Stopped Watching Us.'" *Civil Liberties Review* 4 (November–December 1977): 17–25.

Bosworth, Allan R. *America's Concentration Camps.* New York: W. W. Norton, 1967.

Bovard, James. *Terrorism and Tyranny, Trampling Freedom, Justice, and Peace to Rid the World of Evil.* Palgrave, Macmillan, 2003.

————. *Lost Rights: The Destruction of American Liberty.* New York: St. Martin's Griffin, 1994.

Brant, Irving. *The Bill of Rights.* New York: Bobbs-Merrill, 1965.

Brill, Steven. *After: How America Confronted the September 12 Era.* Simon & Schuster, 2003.

Burns, James MacGregor, and Stewart Burns. *A People's Charter: The Pursuit of Rights in America.* New York: Alfred A. Knopf, 1991.

Chafee, Zechariah Jr. "Thirty-Five Years with Freedom of Speech." New York: Roger Baldwin Civil Liberties Foundation, 1952.

Chin, Steven A., Alex Haley, general ed. *When Justice Failed: The Fred Korematsu Story.* Austin: Raintree Steck-Vaughn Publishers, 1993.

Church, Robert L. *Education in the United States: An Interpretive History.* London: Free Press, Macmillan, 1976.

Coetzee, J. M. *Giving Offense: Essays on Censorship.* University of Chicago Press, 1996.

Cogan, Neil H., ed. *The Complete Bill of Rights: The Drafts, Debaters, Sources, and Origins.* David Lindsay Adams and Theresa Lynn Harvey, editorial assistants. New York: Oxford University Press, 1997.

Conley, Patrick T., and John Kaminski. *The Bill of Rights and the States: The Colonial and Revolutionary Origins of American Liberties.* Madison, WI: Madison House, 1992.

Contemporary American Speeches: A Sourcebook of Speech Forms and Principles. Cowan, Paul, Nick Egelson, and Nat Hentoff. *State Secrets.* New York: Holt, Rinehart & Winston, 1974.

Crotty, William, ed. *The Politics of Terror: The Response To 9/11.* Boston: Northeastern University Press, 2004.

Curtis, Merle. "Subsidizing Radicalism: The American Fund for Public Service, 1921–1941." *Social Service Review* 33. September 1959.

Davis, Howard. *Human Rights and Civil Liberties.* United Kingdom: Willan Publishing, 2003.

Dempsey, James X., and David Cole. *Terrorism & the Constitution.* Washington, D.C.: First Amendment Foundation, 2002.

Dershowitz, Alan M. *Shouting Fire: Civil Liberties in a Turbulent Age.* Boston, New York, London: Little, Brown, 2002.

————. *Taking Liberties: A Decade of Hard Cases, Bad Laws, and Bum Raps.* New York: Contemporary Books, 1988.

————. *Why Terrorism Works: Understanding the Threat, Responding To the Challenge.* New Haven and London: Yale University Press, 2002.

Dodge, David. *Casualty of War: The Bush Administration's Assault on a Free Press.* Amherst, NY: Prometheus Books, 2004.

Domino, John C. *Civil Rights and Liberties: Toward the Twenty-First Century.* New York: HarperCollins.

Donkin, Richard. *Blood, Sweat & Tears: The Evolution of Work.* New York: Texere, 2001.

Donohue, William A. *Twilight of Liberty: The Legacy of the ACLU.* New Brunswick (U.S.A.) and London (U.K.): Transaction Publishers, 1993, pp. 5–17.

Dorsen, Norman, ed. *The Unpredictable Constitution*. New York and London: New York University Press, 2002.

———. "Roger N. Baldwin." *Harvard* magazine 84. January–February 1982.

——— and Stephen Gillers, eds. *None of Your Business: Government Secrecy in America*. New York: Penguin Books, 1975.

Drinnon, Richard. *Keeper of Connecticut Camps: Dillon S. Myer and American Racism*. Berkeley: University of California Press, 1987.

Ernst, Morris L. "Liberals and the Communist Trial." *New Republic* 120. January 31, 1949.

Fallon, Shannon Leigh. *The Bill of Rights: What It Is, What It Means, and How It's Been Misused*. Irvine, CA: Dickens Press, 1995.

Fisher, Louis. *Presidential War Power*. University Press of Kansas, 1995.

Fiss, Owen M. *The Irony of Free Speech*. Cambridge, MA: Harvard University Press, 1996.

Freedman, Russell. *In Defense of Liberty: The Story of America's Bill of Rights*. New York: Holiday House, 2003, pp. 3–20.

Freeman, Joseph. *An American Testament: A Narrative of Rebels and Romantics*. New York: Farrar & Rinehart, 1936.

Garbus, Martin. *Ready for the Defense*. New York: Farrar, Straus and Giroux, 1971.

Gardner, Virginia. "Roger Baldwin: What Are You Hiding?" *New Masses* 63. May 20, 1947.

Gerberg, Mort, and Jerome Agel. *Twelve Documents That Shaped the World*. New York: A Perigree Book, Putnam Publishing Group, 1992.

Glasser, Ira. *Visions of Liberty: The Bill of Rights for All Americans*. Arcade Publishing, 1991.

Gunther, John. *The Riddle of MacArthur: Japan, Korea, and the Far East*. New York: Harper & Brothers, 1950.

Halperin, Morton. "National Security and Civil Liberties." *Foreign Policy* (winter 1975–76): 125–60. Reprinted by the Center for National Security Studies (1976).

Halperin, Morton H., Jerry J. Berman, Robert L. Borosage, and Christine M. Marwick. *The Lawless State: The Crimes of the U.S. Intelligence Agencies*. New York: Penguin Books, 1976.

Hamilton, Alexander, John Jay, and James Madison. *The Federalist Papers*. Introduction by Clinton Rossiter. New York: A Mentor Book from New American Library of World Literature, 1961.

Hammond, Phillip E. *With Liberty for All: Freedom of Religion in the United States*. Louisville: Westminster John Knox Press, 1998.

Hardy, Henry, ed. *Freedom and Its Betrayal: Six Enemies of Human Liberty*. Princeton University Press, 2002.

Henkin, Louis, and John Lawrence, eds. *Human Rights: An Agenda for the Next Century*. Supported by a grant from the Ford Foundation to the American Society of International Law, Studies in Transnational Legal Policy, No. 26. The American Society of International Law, Washington, D.C., 1994.

Henretta, James A., David Brody, and Lynn Dumenil. *America: A Concise History.* Boston, New York: Bedford/St. Martin's, 2002, p. 683.

Hentoff, Nat. *Living the Bill of Rights: How to Be an Authentic American.* New York: HarperCollins, 1998.

Heumann, Milton, Thomas W. Church, and Ed Redlawsk. *Hate Speech on Campus: Cases, Case Studies, and Commentary.* Boston: Northeastern University Press, 1991.

Heyman, Philip. *Terrorism, Freedom, and Security: Winning without War.* Cambridge: MIT Press, 2003.

Hirschkop, Philip J. "The Rights of Prisoners." In Norman Dorsen, ed. *The Rights of Americans.* New York: Random House, 1971, pp. 451–68.

Huscroft, Grant, and Paul Rishworth, eds. *Litigating Rights: Perspectives from Domestic and International Law.* Oxford-Portland, OR: Hart Publishing, 2002.

Johnson, Paul. *A History of the American People.* New York: HarperCollins, 1997.

Kairys, David. "Roger Baldwin." *In These Times* 5. September 9, 1981: 15.

Kaminer, Wendy. *Free For All: Defending Liberty in America Today.* Boston: Beacon Press, 2002.

Kruger, Johan, and Brian Currin, eds. *Interpreting a Bill of Rights.* Juta & Co. Ltd., 1994.

LaPierre, Wayne. *Guns, Freedom, and Terrorism.* Nashville: WND Books, 2003.

Lee, Francis Graham. *Equal Protection, Rights, and Liberties and the Law.* Santa Barbara; Denver; Oxford, England: ABC-CLIO, 2003.

Levy, Leonard W. *Origins of the Bill of Rights.* New Haven and London: Yale University Press, 1999.

Linfield, Michael. *Freedom under Fire.* Boston: South End Press, 1990.

Long, Edward LeRoy Jr. *Facing Terrorism: Responding as Christians.* Louisville, London: Westminster John Knox Press, 2004.

Long, Robert, ed. *Rights To Privacy,* vol. 69, no. 3. H. W. Wilson Company, 1997.

Lowenthal, David. *Present Dangers: Rediscovering the First Amendment.* Dallas: Spence Publishing Company, 2002.

McElroy, Wendy. *Liberty for Women: Freedom and Feminism in the Twenty-First Century.* Chicago: Ivan R. Dee, 2002; published in association with the Independent Institute.

Meiklejohn, Alexander. *Political Freedom: The Control and Powers of the People.* New York: Harper & Brown, 1948.

Melanson, Philip H. *Secrecy Wars, National Security, Privacy, and the Public's Right to Know.* Washington, D.C.: Brassey's, 2001.

Mettger, Kathryn and Zak. *Justice Talking from NPR: Censoring the Web.* New York: New Press, 2001.

Meyssan, Thierry, *9/11: The Big Lie,* Carnot Publishing, London, 2002.

Michaels, C. William. *No Greater Threat: America after September 11 and the Rise of a National Security State.* New York: Algora Publishing, 2002.

Mileur, Jerome M., and Ronald Story. *"America's Wartime Presidents: Politics, National Security, and Civil Liberties,"* by Jerome M. Mileur and Ronald Story, 95–127, Chapter Three "Civil Liberties" in the *Politics of Terror, The U.S. Response to 9/11,* edited by William Crotty, Northeastern University Press, Boston, 2004.

Neier, Ayreh. *Taking Liberties: Four Decades in the Struggle for Rights.* New York: BBS Public Affairs; member of the Perseus Book Group, 2003.

New Republic. "The Baldwin Century." September 23, 1981, p. 6.

Norris, Pippa, Montague Kern, and Marion Just, eds. *Framing Terrorism: The News Media, the Government, and the Public.* New York and London: Routledge, 2003.

Novack, George. "Roger Baldwin/Fighter for Liberties. *The Militant* 45. September 11, 1981: 22.

Pikon, Roger, ed. *The Rule of Law in the Wake of Clinton.* Washington, D.C.: Cato Institute, 2000.

Reitman, Alan. *The Pulse of Freedom: American Liberties, 1920–1970s.* New York: W. W. Norton, 1975.

Roche, John P. "Remembering Roger Baldwin." *New Leader* 64. 1981: 14–15.

Samuels, Gertrude. "The Fight for Civil Liberties Never Stays Won." *New York Times Magazine.* June 19, 1966.

Schlesinger, Arthur M. *The Disuniting of America: Reflections on a Multicultural Society.* New York, London: W. W. Norton & Company, 1998.

Schwartz, Bernard, ed. *The Warren Court: A Retrospective.* New York: Oxford University Press, 1996.

———. *Constitutional Issues: Freedom of the Press.* New York: Facts On File, 1992.

———. *The Great Rights of Mankind: A History of the American Bill of Rights.* New York: Oxford University Press, 1977.

Shattuck, John H. F. "National Security a Decade after Watergate." *Democracy* 3. (winter 1983).

Strausser, Jeffrey; illustrated by Denise Gilgannon. *Painless American Government.* New York: Barron's Educational Series, 2004,

Striking A Balance: Hate Speech, Freedom of Expression, and Non-Discrimination. Sandra Coliver, Kevin Boyle, and Frances D'Souza, contributing editors. Article 19,International Centre against Censorship, Human Rights Centre, University of Essex, United Kingdom, 1992.

Strossen, Nadine. *Defending Pornography: Free Speech, Sex, and the Fight for Women's Rights.* New York: New York University Press, 2000.

Sunstein, Cass R. *The Second Bill of Rights: FDR's Unfinished Revolution and Why We Need It More Than Ever.* New York: Basic Books, a Member of the Perseus Books Group, 2004.

Symons, Ann K., and Sally Gardner Reed. *Speaking Out! Voices in Celebration of Intellectual Freedom.* Chicago and London: American Library Association, 1999.

Thoreau, Henry David. *Walden, and Civil Disobedience.* Boston: Houghton Mifflin, 2000.

Torr, James D. *Civil Liberties and the War on Terrorism.* New York: Lucent Books, Thomson-Gale, 2004.

Trinkl, J. "Baldwin of ACLU Dies." *The Guardian* 33. September 9, 1981.

Villard, Oswald Garrison. "On Being in Jail." *The Nation* 109. August 2, 1919.

Wall, Edmund, ed. *Theory: Philosophical and Political Perspectives,* Amherst, NY: Prometheus Books, 2001, 333–71.

About the Author and Contributors

Woody Klein, an award-winning author, journalist, and adjunct professor of journalism, has written about civil liberties, politics, and human rights for five decades. He is the author of *Towards Humanity and Freedom: The Writings of Kenneth B. Clark, Scholar of the* Brown v. Board of Education *Decision* (Praeger Publishing, 2004); *Westport, Connecticut: The Story of a New England Town's Rise to Prominence* (Greenwood Press, 2000); *Lindsay's Promise: The Dream That Failed* (Macmillan, 1973); and *Let in the Sun* (Macmillan, 1964). He has contributed numerous articles on civil liberties, to magazines and newspapers, including *The New York Times*. In addition, he served as editor of *Think* magazine, IBM's international employee publication, and as editor of the *Westport (CT) News*. He has been an Adjunct Professor of Journalism at New York University, the University of Bridgeport, Fairfield University, and Iona College, and taught a course in civil rights and civil liberties at the New School University.

Carl R. Baldwin taught art history for two decades at Hunter College and Herbert H. Lehman College (CUNY) before going to Columbia Law School. After a short stint with the New York City Law Department, he entered private practice as an immigration lawyer. He died in 2004 after a long illness.

Sen. Robert C. Byrd (D-WV) was first elected to the Senate in 1958 and has become known as the foremost expert on the United States Constitution in Congress. He has repeatedly spoken out on the war in Iraq and the USA Patriot Act to preserve the delicate balance between protecting civil liberties and maintaining national security.

Rev. William Sloane Coffin Jr. is a clergyman and a longtime peace activist. He served as Chaplain at Yale from 1958 until 1975, during which time he preached civil disobedience and played a prominent role in the "freedom rides" in the South, challenging segregation and the oppression of blacks. He also was one of the foremost leaders of the anti–Vietnam War peace movement in the 1960s and the movement against nuclear weapons. He later served as Senior Minister at the Riverside Church in New York City.

SEN. CHRISTOPHER J. DODD (D-CT) is a senior Democratic leader in the United States Senate. A respected legislator who works in a bipartisan fashion to enact meaningful legislation, he is a recent recipient of the Edmund S. Muskie Distinguished Public Service Award recognizing leadership in foreign policy. As a senior member of the Senate Foreign Relations Committee, he has worked for peace and democracy abroad.

NORMAN DORSEN is Counselor to the President of New York University and Stokes Professor of Law, NYU School of Law, where he has taught since 1961. He is codirector of the Arthur Garfield Hays Civil Liberties Program and was the founding director of NYU's Hauser Global Law School Program in 1994. In 2000, President Clinton awarded him the Eleanor Roosevelt Medal at the White House for exceptional service to human rights.

SEN. RUSSELL D. FEINGOLD (D-WI) is a leading voice for protecting privacy and personal freedoms. First elected to the Senate in 1992, he cast the Senate's lone vote against the USA Patriot Act. He has also brought critical attention to the need to combat terrorism without undermining the privacy and civil liberties of law-abiding Americans. He was a leader in passage of the campaign finance reform, known as the McCain-Feingold bill.

IRA GLASSER, the immediate predecessor of Anthony Romero as executive director of the American Civil Liberties Union, worked with Roger N. Baldwin for many years. He was known as a "First Amendment absolutist." He was equally committed to fighting discrimination based on race, gender, and sexual orientation and defending reproductive rights.

NAT HENTOFF, a nationally known award-winning journalist, is a longtime civil liberties commentator. His column is published weekly in the *Village Voice*, and a different column is syndicated by United Media and appears in 250 newspapers, including the *Washington Times*. His book *The War on the Bill of Rights and the Gathering Resistance* focuses on the increasing resistance in America to the incursions of government on the Bill of Rights in the post-9/11 era.

SEN. EDWARD M. KENNEDY (D-MA) has represented Massachusetts in the U.S. Senate since he was first elected in 1962. He has been reelected seven times, and he is now the second most senior member of the Senate. Kennedy is active on a wide range of other issues, including civil liberties and civil rights, homeland security, and national defense.

SEN. PATRICK J. LEAHY was elected as a Democrat to the U.S. Senate in 1974 and remains the only Democrat elected to this office from Vermont. Leahy is the Ranking Member of the Judiciary Committee and ranks seventh in seniority in the Senate. Active on human rights issues, Leahy wrote and enacted civilian war victims relief programs that are underway in Afghanistan and Iraq. Leahy added checks and balances to the USA Patriot Act bill to protect civil liberties and has crusaded for the protection of privacy rights.

ANTHONY LEWIS, columnist for *The New York Times* from 1969 to December 2001, has twice won the Pulitzer Prize. In 2001 he was awarded the Presidential Citizens Medal. Mr. Lewis was for fifteen years a Lecturer on Law at the Harvard Law School, teaching a course on the Constitution and the Press. He is the author of three books: *Gideon's Trumpet*, about a landmark Supreme Court case; *Portrait of a Decade*, about the great changes in American race relations; and *Make No Law: The Sullivan Case and the First Amendment.*

VICTOR NAVASKY, author of the award-winning *Naming of Names* (2003) and *A Matter of Opinion*, has served as editor and publisher of *The Nation*, and is now Delacorte Professor of Magazine Journalism at Columbia University's Graduate School of Journalism.

ARYEH NEIER is head of the Open Society Institute (OSI) and has been head of the Soros Foundations network since 1993. He spent twelve years as executive director of Human Rights Watch. Among his books are *War Crimes: Brutality, Genocide, Terror, and the Struggle for Justice*, and *Taking Liberties: Four Decades in the Struggle for Rights*. Neier has also contributed chapters to more than twenty-five books.

ANTHONY ROMERO is the sixth executive director of the ACLU. He is a graduate of Stanford University Law School and Princeton University's Woodrow Wilson School of Public Policy and International

Affairs. Romero is a member of the New York Bar Association and has sat on numerous nonprofit boards.

Arthur M. Schlesinger Jr., the author of sixteen books, is a renowned historian and social critic. He has twice won the Pulitzer Prize, in 1946 for *The Age of Jackson* and in 1966 for *A Thousand Days.* He is also the winner of the National Book Award for both *A Thousand Days* and *Robert Kennedy and His Times* (1979). In 1998 he received the Presidential Medal of Freedom.

John Shattuck, former executive director of the ACLU Washington office, is now Chief Executive Officer of the John F. Kennedy Foundation Library in Boston. A recipient of the Roger Baldwin Award in 1984 for his contribution to civil liberties, he was named in 1993 by President Clinton as Assistant Secretary of State for Democracy, Human Rights and Labor. He received an International Human Rights Award from the United Nations Association in 1998. From 1984 to 1993 he was vice president for government, community, and public affairs at Harvard University and lectured on civil liberties at the Harvard Law School and the Kennedy School of Government.

William J. Vanden Heuvel, an international lawyer and investment banker, served as president Jimmy Carter's U.S. Deputy Permanent Representative to the UN in New York and as Ambassador to the European office of the United Nations in Geneva. He is now Cochairman of the Franklin and Eleanor Roosevelt Institute, and a member of the Council on Foreign Relations. He was a member of the International League for the Rights of Man, working closely with Roger N. Baldwin.

Samuel Walker is Isaacson Professor of Criminal Justice at the University of Nebraska at Omaha since 1974. Walker is the author of eleven books on policing, criminal justice history and policy, and civil liberties, including *In Defense of American Liberties: A History of the ACLU* (Southern Illinois University Press, 1999).

Alan F. Westin is Professor Emeritus of Public Law and Government at Columbia University, where he taught for thirty-seven years, retiring in 1997. He is a former editor of the *Civil Liberties Review*, the monthly publication of the ACLU. He earned his LL.B. from Harvard Law School and his Ph.D. in political science from Harvard University. He is the author or editor of twenty-six books, including *The Anatomy of a Constitutional Law Case.*

Index

Notes are referenced by the letter *n* following the page number(s).